Battl
the Ea... End

*For Julia, Jacob
and Reuben*

Battle for
the East End
Jewish responses to fascism
in the 1930s

David Rosenberg

Five Leaves Publications
<u>www.fiveleaves.co.uk</u>

Battle for the East End:
Jewish responses to fascism in the 1930s
by David Rosenberg

Published in 2011
by Five Leaves Publications,
PO Box 8786, Nottingham NG1 9AW
www.fiveleaves.co.uk

ISBN: 978 1 907869 18 1

Five Leaves acknowledges support from the Barry
Amiel and Norman Melburn Trust for all our titles
related to Cable Street

Cover image and those on pages 206 and 209 courtesy
of the People's History Museum in Manchester

Five Leaves acknowledges
financial support from
Arts Council England

Five Leaves is represented by Turnaround
and distributed to the book trade by Central Books

Typesetting and design by
Four Sheets Design and Print

Printed in Great Britain

Contents

Preface

Five years ago I had a great privilege that, unfortunately, I will not be able to repeat. I spoke at a public meeting recalling and reflecting on an iconic event of the 1930s that took place in London's East End. That event has gone into history as the Battle of Cable Street, a dramatic street confrontation in which East Enders – Jewish and non-Jewish – and their supporters, dealt an immense blow to the political ambitions and credibility of Britain's pre-war fascist party, Sir Oswald Mosley's British Union of Fascists. What made the meeting such a privilege was that I was sharing the platform with one of the ordinary heroes of that day, Aubrey Morris, who helped build the barricades that prevented Mosley's fascists from invading the East End.

Aubrey was typically diffident about his role on that day. Living within a beleaguered community that feared the consequences of allowing the fascists to invade and intimidate, he claimed that he did what any young Jewish person in that time and place would have done. There were many like him and, sadly, so few still with us, Aubrey himself having died in 2009.

The Battle of Cable Street, on October 4th 1936, was a turning point within a much longer and complex narrative. It is a narrative I have been fascinated by since the mid-1970s when I first went with friends on an anti-fascist demonstration. We were protesting against the National Front, who were marching from Smithfield Market, on the edge of the City of London, to Trafalgar Square to spread their message of hate. I was probably a similar age to Aubrey when he went to Cable Street. My friends and I had an advantage though. We were the generation who knew that fascism could be defeated. Aubrey and his comrades did not know that yet. He was demonstrating in a period when fascism was triumphant abroad and threatening and menacing at home. We could look back into history for inspiration from his generation – the people who fought and ultimately won these battles. He and his activist friends could not.

Back in the mid-1970s I knew the bare bones of what had taken place in Britain in the 1930s. Discovering so much more about how and why fascism grew here, why it came to focus much of its attention on London's East End, and finding out who organised to stop it in its tracks, where and how that happened, has been an inspiring and pleasurable journey. On the way I was fortunate to have long conversations with others who had personal memories of the day, the period, and a pride in the way their generation contributed to altering the course of events. I am very grateful for those opportunities to talk at length, in particular, with Charlie Goodman, Mick Mindel and Issy Pushkin, all now deceased.

Many historians delving into these events have been fascinated, above all, by the role of Sir Oswald Mosley, the flamboyant leader of Britain's fascists. They have been engrossed by his personal history, his personality, the vision he created and communicated of "the Greater Britain", how he convinced others to share that vision and, literally, to fight for it, and ultimately how he and his movement failed in every way. Historians have dissected that failure, especially in terms of Mosley's personal weaknesses and those of his party, and the role of other political forces and economic factors. I will happily admit to being fascinated by the man as well, but I have long been more motivated to find out the story of the ordinary people who suffered the attentions of his movement's activities, but who changed reality by making a stand in several arenas, often in the face of criticism from those who thought they knew better. And this year, as we mark the 75th anniversary of the Battle of Cable Street, seems an appropriate time to reflect more closely on their role.

In comparison with the tremendous output of material on Mosley and his party, relatively little has been written which focuses directly on the community most directly in the firing line at that time, which examines their discussions and arguments, the fractious internal debates that occurred as they strove to find collective ways to counter the threats they faced and find allies to help them do so. I hope, therefore, that this study will contribute to the growing volume of people's histories of this period and on this subject.

In recent years my working life has branched out in ways I hadn't anticipated, as a result of which I spend more of my time in the area where my family lived in the 1930s – in the East End. I lead walks that attempt to recreate and convey the social and political history of the area. One of these walks is called "Anti-Fascist Footprints: a walk through the 1930s East End from Gardiners Corner to Cable Street". Every iconic moment has a back-story and on this walk I try to convey the back-story to the Battle of Cable Street, which I first examined in detail through an academic dissertation in the early 1980s. I have returned to that material with a renewed fascination but also having gained much from the insights of others who have explored this history since then. I have followed new lines of research and feel I can put many more pieces of the jigsaw in place. The individuals who have come on my walks, who have ranged from local primary school children to people in their 80s, have prompted me to carry out further fruitful research by their searching questions. They have also shared stories and family memories and I am extremely grateful to them for their contribution to this book.

There are a few other people to whom I am particularly grateful and without whom this book would not have been possible. I want to thank the staff of various archives who have been very helpful in providing access to material I have used: Sheffield University Library, which houses the Zaidman papers; the Modern Records Centre at Warwick

University; the People's History Museum, Manchester; the Working Class Movement Library, Salford; the Imperial War Museum; the London Metropolitan Archives; the Jewish Museum, London; Tower Hamlets Local History Library; Lambeth Palace Library; the Bishopsgate Institute Library and the British Newspaper Library.

I would like to thank Ross Bradshaw of Five Leaves Publications for his commitment to this study and to anti-fascism in general, and last but not at all least, I would like to thank Julia Bard for her personal support, encouragement and expert editing.

David Rosenberg
August 2011

Introduction

In May 1932, a Jewish community building in the northern English city of Leeds was vandalised and desecrated. Every room in Leeds Talmud Torah, including its synagogue, had been ransacked. The synagogue Ark had been forced open, a scroll of the law thrown to the ground, pictures destroyed and prayer books scattered. The attack shook and distressed the local community, but the *Jewish Chronicle* interpreted it as an "isolated and, indeed, unique event" which, it confidently assured its readers, "will be deplored by the vast majority of non-Jews".[1] Antisemitism might have been a feature of Germany or Eastern Europe but surely not of Britain. For generations, the newspaper added, Jews in Britain had experienced "only feeble and casual manifestations of Jew-hatred". Which is perhaps why the country's most prominent Jewish newspaper recounted instances of violent antisemitism in other European nations at this time with such a sense of incredulity as well as outrage. Three years later, though, in spite of the fact that incidents similar to the one in Leeds had been repeated in other major British cities, with attacks on Jewish property often accompanied by defamation and assaults upon Jewish people, the *Jewish Chronicle* nevertheless felt able to reassure its readers that: "Race hatred is a weed which fortunately it is difficult to plant in British soil."

This statement may have been comforting but it wasn't true. The facts on the ground pointed unmistakeably to a widespread and intensifying antisemitic campaign, pursued through a variety of channels, but mostly by a political party – the British Union of Fascists – formed in October 1932 by the flamboyant aristocratic politician, Sir Oswald Mosley. Nor was this statement consistent with the anxieties and awareness of a very real, danger expressed by increasing numbers of Jews, particularly in the areas of East London, Leeds, Lancashire and South Wales, where this campaign was most pronounced. Jews who suffered the attentions of Mosley's fascists knew only too well that there was nothing "feeble" or "casual" about the threat this movement posed to them. The British Union of Fascists claimed a membership that had grown to 40,000 strong within two years of being established. In a country beset by economic crisis, mass unemployment and disenchantment with the solutions offered by conventional political parties, fascism promoted itself as an energetic and seductive alternative, capable of winning support not just from those who bore the brunt of the crisis but also from individuals with money and influence. It had a serious social, economic and political programme, and, as Hitler had found in Germany, a ready-made scapegoat against whom to unite its followers.

Early hints that Mosley harboured a hostile attitude towards Jews gave way to a full-blown antisemitism. From October 1934, antisemitism was granted a starring role in the theory, strategy and day-to-day activity of Britain's fascist movement. Mosley invited a confrontation with the Jewish community, and challenged its leaders. He accused them of betraying the national interest, capturing and monopolising economic resources and driving Britain to a needless war with Germany. While thousands queued outside the Soup Kitchen for the Jewish Poor in London's East End, children in one arm and a saucepan in the other, Mosley stood on the podium at a mass rally in London's West End. And from that comfortable and privileged vantage point he unmasked and vilified "Jewish international finance" as the "nameless, homeless and all-powerful force which stretches its greedy fingers from the shelter of England to throttle the trade and menace the peace of the west... grasping the puppets of Westminster, dominating every party of the

12

state". To rapturous applause from thousands of supporters he then denounced Jewish financiers as "the enemy which fascism alone dares to challenge."[2]

The Board of Deputies of British Jews, which firmly established itself as the communal and political leadership of Britain's Jews in the 1830s (having been formed in 1760), did not appear unduly concerned by Mosley's bellicose outbursts or the actions of his uniformed activists at local level. It had a "Central Lecture Committee" to educate the public about any misconceptions they held about Jews and Judaism, and carry out anti-defamation work. It had a Press and Information Committee which could respond to wild antisemitic charges if necessary. The Board considered the work of these committees to be perfectly capable of dealing with any problems that might arise and, in any case, it had congenial relations with the police and government officials. With regard to fascism, as far as the Board were concerned, this was a legitimate political ideology, and fascism had no necessary connection with antisemitism. Jewish leaders frequently assured sceptical members of their community that Jews in fascist Italy were not only secure but prospering.

Many members of that wider community did not share this relaxed attitude about the fascists in Italy and felt even less at ease about the fascists closer to home. Becoming increasingly fearful and frustrated in equal measure, they demanded action from their leaders. They called on the Board to set up an independent body to lead a vigorous, intensive and wide-ranging campaign against antisemitism and especially against the fascist movement that was promoting it. Through the letter-pages of the Jewish press, voices warned that, "if the so-called leaders of Jewry do not take the lead, there are Jewish men and women who will".

The situation became so serious in East London that a special parliamentary debate on antisemitic terror was called in July 1936, at which the veteran local MP,

13

George Lansbury, declared: "unless this thing is put an end to – I have known East London all my life – there will one of these days be such an outburst as few of us would care to contemplate." His Labour colleague Denis Pritt (MP, Hammersmith) feared that if the government did not act there would be "pogroms in this country". Pogrom – the Russian word for murderous assaults on vulnerable communities at the hands of the mob, associated up to this point solely with Continental antisemitism – was now being used to describe to the threat posed by anti-semites in Britain.

Finally roused to the realities of the situation, and aware of increasingly strident demands for more tangible defence measures, the Board established an independent Coordinating Committee to unify and direct the community's defence work. For many ordinary Jews this was too little too late, and since the Board had been so passive and unwilling to acknowledge both the nature and extent of the antisemitic threat, and so reluctant to acknowledge its connection to fascism, significant sections in the Jewish community were unwilling to place their confidence and reliance in the Board and its responses. In the highly charged atmosphere from 1936 until 1939, several independent initiatives arose within the community. The most significant and embracing alternative was embodied by the Jewish People's Council Against Fascism and Antisemitism. This grassroots coalition emerged in the heart of the largest and poorest Jewish community in Britain at the time, in London's East End. This body openly disputed the communal leaders' particular understanding of the nature of antisemitism in Britain and of fascism, and developed a distinct analysis and set of responses which included making alliances outside the community. Its challenge to the hegemony of the established leadership on this issue was controversial but effective. The acute nature of the continuing defence debate attested to a divided community. This contradicted the view shared, ironically, by both antisemites and many Jewish leaders, that Anglo-Jewry in the 1930s was a homogeneous corporate unit.

Fascism failed in Britain, and Jews here were spared the fate that their cousins suffered in Nazi-occupied Europe. Mosley's movement won influential admirers and a degree of mass support but did not maximise its potential, or even win a parliamentary seat. That was partly down to its own internal failings and partly due to Britain's economic and political structures proving more robust than they had seemed at the height of the depression; but it was also because of the sustained collective efforts of anti-fascists who came to understand the full nature of the threat that was posed. They developed sophisticated and effective strategies of resistance that not only prevented the fascists from achieving their goals but were also able to win a number of adherents of fascism away from the cause they had once embraced with such enthusiasm.

Such strategies had to be fought for against entrenched and powerful interests, not least within the community most under attack. But they triumphed and their story deserves to be told and celebrated. Anti-fascists in 1930s Britain fully merit their place in history but we cannot afford to leave them there. For their struggles resonate powerfully in our own period when the political descendents of Mosley's movement target vulnerable minorities and offer themselves as saviours in times of renewed economic crisis, and when different elements within today's most threatened communities offer competing strategies to rid themselves of these modern-day threats.

Notes
1 *Jewish Chronicle* 20.5.1932
2 *The Blackshirt* 29.3.1935

1. Britain's Jews

When antisemites sought political support in socially and economically distressed areas of 1930s Britain, they highlighted the plight of the country's near three million unemployed, and, in the same breath, claimed there were three million Jews in Britain. By deploying this simple equation, which rested upon no factual basis, they could blame Jews for causing unemployment and suggest to their audiences a brutal but straightforward solution to their unhappy situation. Their mathematical capabilities were no more developed than their human values. The actual number of Jews residing in Britain then was approximately 330,000 among a population of forty-five million. Many Jews were unfortunate enough to work in industries blighted by casualisation. Rather than causing unemployment, they experienced long periods of unemployment themselves. Yet the Jewish community's reluctance to provide accurate statistics of its size and therefore be in a position to simply refute such outlandish claims, meant that the inventions and assertions of the antisemites could acquire unwarranted credibility. A regular *Jewish Chronicle* (*JC*) columnist, Simon Gilbert, who wrote under the pen-name "Watchman", said: "Unless we know ourselves, we cannot explain ourselves to others." He described Britain's Jews as, "a community under attack, but a community unarmed". In further articles he declared that there was:

> "...a crying need for a scientific study of Anglo-Jewish conditions. For many years some among us have called insistently at least for statistical enquiry, but this call has fallen on the deaf ears of a community which shuns figures like a pest and fails to understand their importance."[1]

On the basis of such statistical information as was collected, it was estimated that about three-quarters of Britain's Jews in the early 1930s were confined to three major population centres, with approximately 183,000 in London, 35,000 in Manchester, and 30,000 in Leeds. In her 1929 *New Survey of London Life and Labour*, Nettie Adler enumerated the London figures in more detail. She estimated that 60 per cent of London's Jews lived in East London and 52 per cent of the latter lived in the borough of Stepney alone (an area of approximately one square mile bordered by the communities of Bethnal Green, Poplar and Shoreditch).[2] Stepney was one of London's poorest boroughs, yet at the other end of the scale there were British Jews living in the finest houses in the Belgravia district of Westminster and Kensington. This colossal social divide impacted very heavily on perceptions of antisemitism and responses to it in this period. To understand this divide, though, it is necessary to examine the roots of Jewish settlement in Britain.

Historically, Britain's Jewish community comprised Dutch and Italian Jews of Spanish and Portuguese (Sephardic) descent, who settled in the 17th and 18th centuries, followed by Ashkenazi (Central and East European) Jews mostly of German descent who arrived mainly in the late Georgian and early Victorian era. The United Synagogue, the largest synagogue movement in Britain today, grew out of an amalgamation of three Ashkenazi synagogues within the City of London, and two in the West End, originally serving mainly German Jews and their descendents in the 19th century.

Many Jews in Britain in the earlier part of that century were bankers, stockbrokers, traders, and both entrepreneurs and workers within the tailoring and tobacco trades. A growing minority entered the arts, sciences and professions. In the first half of the 19th century, British Jewry's dominant groups were generally very anglicised, assimilated and prosperous. In the capital, Jews first settled close to the City of London. The Bevis Marks Sephardic

Synagogue was established in Aldgate in 1701, and remains in use today, though from the early 1800s many members of London's Sephardic communities drifted west, purchasing plush residences in Kensington and Mayfair. But a growing trickle of poorer Jews from Central and Eastern Europe also began to arrive in Britain.

Changes in the community continued apace. The middle of the 19th century saw an increasing influx of poorer Jews from Holland and northern Germany, many of whom lived a hand-to-mouth existence, wheeling and dealing as small-traders and peddlers. This was the community from which Ikey Solomon provided a prototype for Charles Dickens' character, "Fagin", in his novel *Oliver Twist*. In 1859, a Board of Guardians for the Relief of the Jewish Poor was established to meet their growing needs. Nearly 20,000 immigrants bolstered London's Jewish community between 1865 and 1881. Of these, some 12,000 came from Eastern Europe; the others from Germany and Holland.

By the 1930s though, the demography of the Jewish community had changed much more dramatically. Although the economically dominant Jews of Dutch, Italian and German descent still held most of the leading positions within the community's political, religious and cultural institutions, and were more than content to make policy and speak to the government on behalf of the whole community, they were numerically the minority. They had been surpassed by a mass influx of Yiddish-speaking Jews, fleeing antisemitic oppression and seemingly intractable economic impediments in the Czarist Russian Empire. Some arrived with several children in tow and many had large families once they were settled.

The five million Jews of Czarist Russia, who made up the single largest accumulation of Jews in the world of the 1860s and '70s, suffered a range of discriminatory laws and practices that restricted where they could live and which economic and educational opportunities were open to them. They had been thrust into a monumental crisis by the events of 1881 when a group of revolutionaries – members of *Narodnaya Volya* (People's Will) – assassinated Czar Alexander II. Those convicted of the attack included a young Jewish woman, Hessia Meyerovna Helfman. In the moments between their audacious revolutionary action and their capture and conviction, the rebels called on the people to rise up against the autocratic system they laboured under. But, exploiting Helfman's involvement in the plot, the new Czar, Alexander III, succeeded in shifting the blame for chaos and upheaval on to the Jewish minority. [3]

Within a few weeks, impoverished and vulnerable Jewish communities suffered a wave of pogroms – random mob attacks on their villages and towns, which the authorities were unwilling to prevent and were accused of unofficially instigating. In 1881, pogroms were recorded in 166 Russian towns. Some Jews decided then that a tipping point had been reached, and they sought new pastures outside Russia. After the new Czar brought in the May Laws of 1882 – a set of even more severe discriminatory rulings, dressed up as "temporary regulations" – increasing numbers of Jews followed suit and prepared to leave the country they had lived in and known for centuries. Seeking political freedom and economic security for themselves and their children, they headed westwards to America in search of the *goldene medineh*[4] – a promised land of freedom and unbounded opportunity.

The moment in which the Jewish minority in Czarist Russia felt these existential threats so powerfully coincided with the period when advances in affordable mass transport were making migration over long distances a realistic option for communities across Europe unhappy with their lot. Many poorer Germans, Austrians, Dutch, Italians and Poles travelled to new homelands. Millions of Europeans left their continent completely to settle in North and South America, Australia, New Zealand and South Africa.

Despite serious threats and deep feelings of anxiety and uncertainty, the Jews did not leave Czarist Russia overnight in a state of collective panic, but over a period of 25 years, more than a third of Russia's Jews left, heading mainly for America. Some among them who lacked the means to complete this journey arrived at temporary stopping posts in England, Scotland, Wales and Ireland, while they gathered the resources to complete their journey another day. But for many that day never came and Britain became their permanent adopted home.[5] For others, Britain was always their preferred destination. The result was that approximately 150,000 Yiddish-speaking East European Jewish immigrants augmented Britain's Jewish community over a relatively short time-span.

Most of these immigrants gravitated towards London's East End, one of London's poorest districts but a traditional refuge for the persecuted and downtrodden. The docks that were developed along the River Thames mainly in the early 19th century included a port for human cargo at Iron Gate Wharf by St Katherine's Dock. Employers gathered to recruit the "greeners" with exaggerated promises of lucrative work and comfortable accommodation, which in reality meant 16-hour shifts in a sweatshop, six days a week, and a wooden bench by a side wall of the workshop to sleep on while they dreamt of their next shift.

East European Jews were not the first persecuted minority to find refuge in the East End. In the late 1600s, an estimated 30,000 Huguenots (French Protestants) settled just east of the City of London in the streets between Bishopsgate and Brick Lane. Initially a thriving silk-weaving community, their most successful entrepreneurs occupied newly-built grand family houses, which still stand, but the Huguenots' economic boom was relatively short-lived. Unable to compete with imports of silks from France and Italy, and cheaper cottons from the very low-wage economy of Bengal shipped by the British East India company, and dealt a further blow by mechanisation, many skilled weavers suffered and left to seek their fortune elsewhere.

Their family homes were abandoned and transformed into multiple occupancy flats for new waves of impoverished immigrants. The character of the area shifted, firstly as a result of Irish settlement throughout the 19th century, especially during the "potato famine" of the 1840s, and then as the Eastern European Jews arrived en masse.

When Jews from Czarist Russia reached Britain, they might have hoped that antisemitism would be one feature of their lives they could happily leave behind in the old country. But, particularly from the 1890s, they became the target of a toxic and sustained anti-alien campaign in Britain, which culminated in the Government passing the Aliens Act of 1905. This law restricted the entry of many more Jews who wished to settle in Britain and made plain to those who had settled that they were not really wanted. Journalist and author William Zukerman described East European Jews as "sufficiently different in appearance, language, mode of life and thought from the surrounding native majority to act as a psychological irritant to a people not used to foreigners."[6]

His comment should be qualified. After all, the "native majority" now included many people of foreign Irish descent. The Irish certainly experienced great hostility too. They maintained their cultural and religious distinctiveness, but over a generation became an accepted part of London's population. Anti-Irish sentiment remained, and still reveals itself today in crude stereotyping, but it has rarely been directed against the very presence of Irish people in Britain.

At the turn of the 20th century a powerful campaign against Jewish immigration took root that crystallised through an organisation called the British Brothers' League. It described itself as "anti-alien" but left little doubt as to which aliens it saw as its principal target. Its most prominent spokesperson, Major William Evans Gordon, Conservative MP for Stepney from 1900, declared it was "a fact" that "the settlement of large aggregations of Hebrews in a Christian land has never been successful". Headed by Conservative MPs and well-supported by local media interests, such as James Silver, who owned the *Eastern Post* and *City Chronicle*, the League galvanised the poorer local populace into angry street marches calling for an end to Jewish immigration. Hoisting "Britain for the British" banners, flanked by Union Jacks, its supporters took part in intimidating marches through the East End more than 30 years before Sir Oswald Mosley first attempted to set foot there. Led by a brass band, marchers would be ferried into huge indoor rallies where fiery speeches were made asserting that Englishmen:

> "...would not have this country made the dumping ground for the scum of Europe. This was England the heart of the Empire not the dustbin of Austria and Russia."[7]

Inside the meeting hall at a League rally in the People's Palace, Mile End, in January 1902, order was maintained by 260 stewards, described as "big brawny stalwarts, dock labourers, chemical workers... and operatives from Shoreditch, Bow, Poplar" and other local areas, who physically removed any individuals who had the temerity to challenge the malicious outpourings from the platform. The marches and rallies conducted by the British Brothers' League prefigured those that Mosley would attempt with his British Union of Fascists in the 1930s, and the National Front, on similar territory, in the 1970s, the latter railing especially against the communities who had arrived as British citizens from the Indian subcontinent seeking economic improvement in the homeland of their imperial masters who had amassed such wealth at the expense of their families and communities. In a depressing continuity, each of these racist and anti-immigrant organisations enjoyed considerable support from a section of the working class in the Shoreditch and Bethnal Green areas bordering London's East End.[8]

But how did Jewish communal leaders view the mass immigration of their co-religionists from Eastern Europe? The dominant view shared by British Jewry's suited and booted leading families – the Rothschilds, Montefiores and Moccatas – was that immigrants should be allowed free entry but the Jewish community should not be seen to encourage them. Effectively, as little aid as possible was given to the aliens, especially in the first few months after they arrived, and repatriation to Eastern Europe and emigration on to America was both encouraged and assisted, through the offices of the Jewish Board of Guardians.[9] Samuel Montagu – a well-to-do Jewish Liberal MP for Whitechapel in East London, where many immigrants were settling – energetically canvassed an alternative view. While not proposing an open-armed welcome, he believed that the Jewish immigrants should be given more humane treatment from the time of landing. A third view expressed by some leading Jews who were ashamed of those arriving, actually demanded restriction. They believed that the mass influx of pauperised Yiddish-speaking Jews would provoke antisemitism and have a deleterious effect on how they themselves would be viewed as Jews by the most established and snobbish sectors of British society, whom they seemed to regard as their reference point.

Of course, Jewish immigrants would not have anticipated an over-enthusiastic welcome from the average British person whom they assumed would feel proprietorial about their country, but they might have been forgiven for expecting their fellow Jews to be on their side. Despite the ferocity of its anti-alien statements, some elements of the Jewish communal leadership were even willing to associate themselves with the British Brothers' League's campaign against poorer Jews coming from Eastern Europe. Shared ethnicity and religious practices did not imply a conception of shared interests, let alone any sense of community of fate.

The divide within the Jewish collective that was so starkly revealed then, persisted well into the 1930s, when the Jewish community would face an onslaught by a more broadly-based, enterprising and dynamic antisemitic political movement. And as that movement plumbed the depths of crude anti-Jewish sentiment, it tapped and exploited the residue of anti-Jewish attitudes developed in East London through the energetic agitation of earlier campaigners such as the British Brothers' League.

After the First World War the composition of the Jewish communal leadership had begun to alter. A minority of East European immigrant Jews had waged a successful battle for recognition, achieved a satisfactory social position and begun to find a place in Jewish representative institutions, but such bodies were still controlled principally by the old elites. The largest single group within Britain's Jewish community of the 1930s, though, were second-generation immigrants, composed mainly of workers and poor traders who grew up among the English working class. Mostly concentrated in light industry and distributive trades, especially boot and shoe, clothing and cabinet making, they possessed a distinctly different outlook from the Jewish upper and middle class. This "new community", often characterised collectively as "Jewish labour and Jewish youth", was disparaged by the wealthier and more established Jews for being largely divorced from the synagogue, uninterested in Jewish affairs, and broadly sharing the outlook and culture of its social environment. While it may have been perfectly acceptable to assimilate into middle and upper-class British society, wealthier Jews considered such processes of acculturation at the poorer end of society very disagreeable.

Zukerman believed that there was, "so much in common between the young post-war English cockney and the young East End Jew... (that) ...what goes under the name of the East End Jew is in reality no specific Jewish type at all, but a general East London labour type."[10] He probably overstates the case. The class nature of East End Jews was complex. The vast majority were engaged in working-class occupations, but a significant minority owned small enterprises. Another growing minority were entering the professions, a trend that generated much angst in the community as some feared it would lend credence to the slur that Jews were disproportionately engaged in non-productive labour.

When the *Jewish Chronicle* reported an incident in 1933 of a fight that erupted between fascists and Jews, the occupations of the four Jews concerned confirmed this class complexity. They comprised a butcher, a salesman, a traveller and an accountant. Although the "new community" was less attached to religion than its predecessors, it nevertheless underwent an extensive process of Jewish identification through childhood Hebrew and religion classes, youth clubs, societies and associations, occupational concentration, ghettoised housing and the continued, though diminishing, use of the Yiddish language.

Towards the end of the 1930s there was a further influx of Jewish immigrants, though on a much smaller scale than that which followed the events of 1881. Initially, some 11,000 Austrian and German Jews fleeing Nazism had settled in Britain. A significantly larger number arrrived in 1938-39 including thousands of children permitted to come through the *Kindertransport* rescue mission.[11] The assessment of these incomers by Jewish communal leaders was comparatively much more generous. In pleading the case for allowing German and Austrian Jews to settle, the president of the Board of Deputies, Neville Laski, displayed his own unabashedly prejudiced attitude to the earlier waves of Jewish immigrants who, together with their descendents, made up the bulk of the community on whose behalf he regularly claimed to speak. He affirmed:

> *"The greater part of these people are not as were so many of the refugees of the '80s and '90s, ignorant and uncultured, many without a trade and speaking no language save Yiddish. The vast majority of*

the sufferers today are of a class which would be an asset to any country into which they were admitted. They are cultured, speak more than one language, many of them are big industrialists and business-men... among the immigrants today are many men of high professional attainments."[12]

The Jewish community then was extremely hetero-geneous in its social, economic and cultural composition. This had profound implications for the way that different elements in the community understood antisemitism and how they chose to confront it. Communal diversity was not reflected at all well in the community's established institutions, which later sought to command the unified support of Britain's Jews against organised antisemitism. Those who had arrived in the 1880s and 1890s and their descendants, despite being disparaged by Jewish commu-nal leaders, were nevertheless expected to give unswerving loyalty to those leaders on issues that pro-foundly affected their daily lives. In the crisis years of the 1930s, one issue stood out above all others: how to organ-ise to defeat the menace of antisemitism and fascism.

The Board of Deputies

The London Committee of Deputies of British Jews was set up in 1760 when seven deputies were appointed by the elders of the Spanish and Portuguese Congregations to form a standing committee to pay homage to King George III on his accession to the throne. This committee became an instrument of the community in its struggle to acquire full civil and political rights. Around the same time, the fledgling Ashkenazi community, consisting of Jews from Germany, appointed a Secret Committee for Public Affairs and the two bodies agreed to hold occa-sional joint meetings. From 1817 the two committees united and met as one body, renamed the Board of Deputies, and this entity emerged as the "representative"

27

institution of Jews in Britain. Today, the stated objects of the Board remain the care of all external matters affecting the welfare of British Jews. It debates issues at a monthly "parliament" meeting of its members, though many observers of the Board agree that power has always resided with its officers and committees rather than through the contribution of its backbenchers on the floor of Board meetings.[13]

Apart from the matter of its internal democratic deficits, the Board's "representation" of the community has always been limited, since it has represented Jews almost exclusively as a *religious* rather than a more broadly-based ethnic or cultural minority. This corresponds with the historical model of an anglicised, assimilationist Jewry, whose distinguishing feature was when, where and how it worshipped. This model of representation, though, was rendered increasingly inapplicable by the growth of the "new community", which was largely becoming more distant from the synagogue, but intensely aware of its existential situation as constituents of a Jewish minority. By the 1930s, this incongruity had magnified considerably.

"Jewish labour and Jewish youth" were thoroughly disconnected from the Board of Deputies, but organised antisemitism in this decade made them more aware of being part of that wider Jewish community. They wanted their voices heard and, as they engaged more frequently and purposefully in community forums, they tended to align themselves with those who increasingly expressed discontent with the Board. Dissenters claimed that large sections of Jews, especially secular Jews who were members of Jewish or predominantly Jewish trade unions, effectively lacked the franchise at a time when the whole community needed to take stock of its situation and develop collective responses. One correspondent to the *JC* wrote:

> "The growth of antisemitism in this country requires an overhauling of our communal machinery. The Board of

Deputies no longer represents the Anglo-Jewish community. It is out of touch with the rank and file".[14]

Another claimed that the business of the Board was conducted in a high-handed and undemocratic manner and that it was "an unrepresentative and undemocratic institution which had no mandate on any specific issue".

The Board feared representation by Jewish trade unions, which it believed would add a definite political element to a body defining itself as avowedly non-political in any ideological sense. Increasing representation of non-religious Jewish workers through institutions such as Friendly Societies raised the danger of secularisation. The long-serving and independent-minded Board member, Bertram Jacobs, of Newport Synagogue in Wales, was often a thorn in the side of the leadership, but in 1936 he defended the Board as an institution from its critics. He argued: "The Board is far from perfect but I would remind those who criticised it that the community created institutions in its own image." That might have been true in the early 1800s but by the end of the 19th century and even more so by the 1930s, this was certainly not accurate.

In this period, East London was home to 60 per cent of London's Jews yet fewer than 12 per cent of the Board of Deputies' London-based members lived there. Several East London synagogues were represented on the Board by individuals who maintained their family ties and original synagogue membership but had long since moved to more comfortable suburbs of north and north west London. The claustrophobic East End borough of Stepney, alone, housed almost a third of London's entire Jewish population – the third most under assault from its political enemies. Stepney was home to fewer than 6 per cent of the London-based Deputies; the other 94 per cent were not at all reticent about pronouncing authoritatively on how Stepney's Jews should respond to the threats they faced.

In the mid-1930s the most prominent figures in Anglo-Jewry were people such as Neville Laski, an Oxford-educated barrister and President of the Board of Deputies; Lionel Louis Cohen, a barrister and Vice President of the Board; Robert Waley-Cohen, an oil industrialist and leading figure of the United Synagogue; the Oxford-educated philanthropist Leonard Montefiore, President of the Anglo-Jewish Association; and Hannah Cohen, President of the London Jewish Board of Guardians, who had worked as a civil servant in the Home Office and Treasury. Apart from a shared recognition of themselves as Jews, they inhabited not so much a different location, as a different universe to that of the working class Jews of East London who were bearing the brunt of antisemitic agitation at street level and on whose behalf they were urged to intervene.

Beyond their own institutions Jewish people were continuing to assert their presence in wider British society. From 1858 a Jew could sit in the House of Commons and eight years later Jews were entitled to sit in both Houses of Parliament. The Promissory Oath Act of 1871 permitted Jews to be appointed to ministerial office.[15] After the 1935 General Election, this relatively small minority, comprising barely 0.7 per cent of British society, contributed nearly 3 per cent of politicians in the House of Commons. There were eighteen Jewish members: eight Conservatives, six Labour and four Liberals. Additionally there were seven Jewish peers and five Jewish privy councillors. Significantly though, hardly any Jewish MPs sat in a constituency with a sizeable Jewish vote, and only a small proportion of the Jewish MPs hailed from the East European Jewish immigrants who comprised the bulk of Britain's Jewish community at this time.

The *Jewish Chronicle*
Since its inception in 1841 the *Jewish Chronicle* has regarded itself as "the organ of British Jewry" but it has always been an independent publication, not formally representing the community or any particular section of it. Since the mid-1980s it has been controlled by the

Kessler Foundation Trust; before then it had a succession of individual proprietors. Its editorial policy has always stayed close to the consensus of the Jewish communal leadership. This was particularly the case from 1932-36 when it was edited by Jack Rich, and not surprisingly since, at the time of his appointment, he was Secretary of the Board of Deputies. The historian Geoffrey Alderman has described the relationship between the *Jewish Chronicle* and the Jewish communal leadership as "intimately connected" and "occasionally incestuous". He has argued that Jack Rich "tailored the manner in which the paper reported events, at home and abroad to suit the purposes of the [Board] president Neville Laski."[16]

In the 1930s there existed several Yiddish newspapers, which were popular among the older generation of working-class Jews,[17] and a small number of ephemeral provincial papers,[18] but the *JC* could offer the largest and most comprehensive coverage and claim the broadest, most encompassing readership. It could be obtained in most areas of high Jewish population and also served overseas Jewish communities. By the 1930s it had achieved a considerable international reputation. An analysis of the defence debate that ensued, particularly in 1936, through its letter columns, substantiates its claim to have been widely read among most sections of the community, which makes it a particularly useful prism through which to analyse how the Jewish community confronted antisemitism in Britain in this period. Many of the quotations used in this study, voicing the perspectives of differing and often opposing elements in the community at the time, have been drawn from the *JC*.

The issue of antisemitism in Britain was profoundly important to the Jewish community, but the community's priorities and concerns stretched beyond Britain's national frontiers. A striking feature of the *JC* in the 1930s is the predominance of foreign over domestic issues, as "Palestine and Zionism" emerged as the topic most frequently covered. This period saw major international diplomatic activity in this area, in which high-ranking British government officials were centrally involved. It was an issue of relevance, if not immediate practical import, for many Jews in Britain. The identification with Jewish territorial ambitions in Palestine which came to fruition in 1948, and which many, but not all, Jews share and express today, could not be taken for granted in the 1930s. Many sections of the Jewish establishment, especially its wealthier Sephardic and German elements, were at best sceptical and in many cases openly opposed to the Zionist project and its uncomfortable implications of dual loyalty. For the wider Jewish population in Britain, compelled by circumstances to focus on bread and butter issues of daily economic survival, a Jewish state seemed an irrelevant and impractical pipe dream. Yet the *JC* had been purchased in 1907 by Leopold Greenberg, a fervently pro-Zionist entrepreneur, and this elevated news of developments in Palestine to a much higher level than was truly reflective of how the community as a whole was touched by this issue in the 1930s.

Internationally, the growth and development of Nazism, which was also frequently highlighted, was far more pertinent to British Jews, as citizens in Europe. Events in Germany were widely reported in the *JC*. This had a pronounced influence upon the way the community understood what antisemitism was, and it had a major bearing on how it viewed its domestic variety. The years 1934-37, when anti-Jewish incidents in Britain were becoming much more frequent and antisemitism was growing as a political movement, coincided with extensive editorial coverage by the *JC* of Nazism in Germany. In the year 1936, as acts of antisemitism in Britain reached their peak, more than 80 per cent of the *JC*'s domestic editorials were dedicated to this topic. From June 1936, "Jewish Defence" became a regular section of the paper in its own right, often claiming upwards of four pages in any single edition.

32

For the most part, the *JC* editorial line and the views of the established communal leadership were in harmony. On rare occasions when communal leaders were strongly criticised by the *JC*, they occasionally reacted defensively, but more commonly accepted it as friendly criticism from within. However, at the most intensive point of antisemitic agitation, in June and July 1936, relations were undeniably strained as the Board of Deputies procrastinated and vacillated over its defence policy, while the *JC* reported and reflected urgent demands which were rising with bitterness and fury from the community's grassroots.

The issue of antisemitism in Britain highlighted prolonged and deeper conflicts in the community, and the *JC* was not immune from this process. In the summer of 1936 it detailed a "special correspondent" (Maurice Goldsmith) to report from the beleaguered Jewish community of London's East End but then found that his reports frequently departed from the paper's editorial line.[19] This was most vividly demonstrated in the reporting of "The Battle of Cable Street" in October 1936.[20] The paper clearly reflected an "establishment" view, but the circumstances and conflicts of this period brought alternative views to the fore – and not merely in the form of angry and frustrated missives on the letters page.

Notes

[1] *Jewish Chronicle*, 1.10.1937

[2] Stepney amalgamated with Bethnal Green and Poplar in 1965 to form today's inner London Borough of Tower Hamlets. Shoreditch is in the neighbouring borough of Hackney.

[3] Helfman was the one member of the six convicted who escaped hanging, and was imprisoned instead because she was pregnant. She gave birth in prison and her child survived but she died shortly afterwards.

[4] Yiddish for the "golden state/country".

[5] Several accounts of Jewish immigrants to Britain record the experience of paying a fare to New York to an agent when they reached Hamburg in Germany, but actually being sold a ticket to London, realising too late that they had been tricked.

[6] *Jewish Chronicle* 12.3.1937

[7] S. Cohen, "British Brothers' League: Birth of British Fascism?" *Jewish Socialist*, No 3, 1985

[8] Speakers' notes prepared for British Union of Fascist candidates in East London at local elections in 1937 explicitly referred to the British Brothers' League as an example of how a political impact could be made locally through campaigning on an anti-Jewish programme.

[9] The Chief Rabbi at the time, Hermann Adler, wrote to his counterparts in Russia and advised rabbis there to "publicise the evil which is befalling our brethren who have come here and to warn them not to come to the land of Britain for such ascent is descent".

[10] *Jewish Chronicle* 12.3.1937

[11] The Kindertransports brought approximately 10,000 Jewish refugee children to Britain, mainly from Nazi Germany and Austria in the months before the outbreak of the Second World War. Their parents were not allowed to accompany them, and most perished.

[12] N. Laski, *Jewish Rights and Jewish Wrongs,* London 1939, pp 105-6

[13] In 1938 the Board had 355 members representing 92 London synagogues, 127 provincial synagogues, 10 colonial synagogues, and 15 lay institutions having specified Jewish interests.

[14] *Jewish Chronicle* 7.8.1936

[15] Lionel de Rothschild became Britain's first Jewish MP, representing the City of London, followed by David Salomans, who was elected as Liberal MP for Greenwich, South London in 1859. Salomans had earlier served as the first Jewish Lord Mayor of London.

[16] *English Historical Review* No 433, September 1994

[17] Especially *Di Tsayt* (The Times), edited from London's East End by Morris Myer.

[18] The provincial Jewish press became more established in the post-war era. The *Jewish Telegraph* was formed in 1950, serving communities in Manchester, Leeds, Liverpool and, eventually, Glasgow and the Midlands. A rival national Jewish paper, the *Jewish Daily Post*, which began in 1935, folded the same year.

[19] See D. Cesarani, *The Jewish Chronicle and Anglo-Jewry 1841-1991,* CUP, 1994, p151.

[20] This clash of perspectives is described in more detail on pages 214-216

2. How Jews were viewed

Antisemitism has been broadly defined as hostility to Jews as such. Because it has taken so many forms, scholars have been reluctant to claim a more precise definition, and it remains hotly debated by writers who claim, controversially, that in the 21st century there is a "new antisemitism" linked to the conflict in Israel and Palestine.[1] This study confines itself to an understanding of antisemitism and responses to it in Britain in the 1930s, particularly as it was recognised and revealed through key actors among the leadership and grassroots of the Jewish community and through its primary press outlet.

As unemployment in Britain peaked at nearly three million in 1932, much of the Jewish community was affected too, but often the difficulties for Jews seeking work were exacerbated as they encountered shop window notices announcing: "Every man on our pay-list is a British-born Christian," and adverts in the press which stipulated: "Applicants must be first-class workers, of refined manners and appearance, and Gentiles." While these discriminatory practices were common, they did not constitute the major form of antisemitism in the period. Rather, this was the organised assault upon the Jewish community, verbal, written and often physical, propagated by the leaders and supporters of a political party, the British Union of Fascists (BUF). However, the BUF did not have the monopoly on political antisemitism in this decade. Attacks of equal and often greater virulence were perpetrated by much smaller organisations, such as Arnold Leese's Imperial Fascist League (IFL) and the National Socialist Workers Party, and by individual orators such as John Penfold (who adopted the pen-name of an antisemitic historical figure, Peter the Hermit).[2]

Many disturbing assaults upon Jewry came through other outlets not directly seeking political capital but nevertheless capable of reaching large audiences, such as the clergy. There were many instances of antisemitism being propagated through Catholic newspapers and from the pulpit. These examples of frequent (but non-systematic) antisemitism indicated a climate within which an organised antisemitic force could emerge and flourish. Such incidents touched nerves. Though they paled in comparison with the force of intensive coordinated attacks, the prominence they were given in the Jewish press suggested a fear and sensitivity within the community that could not be dismissed in evaluating the threat they posed.

By the end of 1937 the BUF was in decline (though it briefly recovered strength in 1939), but in its wake there appeared a new threat to the community. This was the "aliens scare" of 1938-39, instigated mainly by popular newspapers in response to the influx of Austrian and German Jewish refugees fleeing Nazi oppression. Though it arose from external circumstances, it illustrated the potential for an internal campaign to build on the foundations that had been laid earlier by politically motivated antisemites.

Jews in Britain experienced a wide range of antisemitic incidents in the 1930s, but it was the physical attacks on people and property that they found most threatening. These occurred at varying levels of frequency and degree but reached their zenith in a reign of terror in London's East End in 1936. In several instances where offenders were arrested – often they weren't apprehended – court proceedings disclosed that they were members of the BUF. Many very young and very elderly defenceless Jews were physically assaulted – a fact that flies in the face of BUF speakers' claims, made well into 1936, that they were not antisemitic but merely opposed those Jews who used (alleged) positions of enormous power and influence to organise themselves against the national interest and against the BUF.

The foremost targets of attacks on Jewish communal property were synagogues, which were vandalised in areas such as Leeds, Gateshead, Manchester and many parts of London. In 1935, Bensham Synagogue in Gateshead was desecrated twice in a period of three weeks and posters were affixed proclaiming: "Down with the Jews". In Bethnal Green in the spring of 1939, during the festival of Passover, a pig's head was left at a synagogue. Other repeated targets were the windows of Jewish–owned shops, and frequently the Jewish shopkeepers themselves. Walls and pavements were regularly daubed with antisemitic messages, often urging people to boycott Jewish-owned shops, mimicking a practice developed in Nazi Germany. Towards the end of the decade, the slogans increased in their daring and malice. In the summer of 1938 the words "Kill the Jews" were carved into the bowling green in Bruce Castle Park in Tottenham, North London, in letters three foot long and two inches deep. And in Rochdale, in 1939, huge graffiti proclaimed: "Jewish blood will flow in the gutters".

Other incidents and practices, frequently reported in the *Jewish Chronicle* and identified through its columns as antisemitic, or as dangerous and threatening to Jews, were matters of direct discrimination, often based on antisemitic ideology. Shop-window notices and newspaper adverts for job vacancies which indicated that they would not employ Jews, were particularly common in trades in which a significant proportion of Jews were already employed, such as tailoring and hairdressing. In these cases such practices were based not on random attitudes but upon a conflict over resources that had clearly become "racialised".

One form of discrimination that investigative journalists enjoyed exposing was that conducted by leading insurance companies who classified Jews as "bad risks". One company listed "Jews" among other "untrustworthy individuals" such as "music hall artists, theatrical agents, bookmakers, foreigners", to whom they did not offer insurance. Increased premiums on car insurance were often charged in areas with high accident rates, which, it was claimed, happened to coincide with areas of very high Jewish concentration.

Social exclusion from clubs and associations had long been practised against Jews – and not just in Britain. When the comedian Groucho Marx was offered membership of a restricted country club in America on condition that his family did not use the swimming pool, he famously quipped: "My daughter's only half-Jewish – can she wade in up to her knees?" One case, in Britain, which attracted considerable publicity, occurred at Middlesbrough Motor Club in December 1933. It resulted in the president and other leading members resigning. The Motor Club committee had been "of the opinion the Jews and Gentiles do not mix socially in numbers". In mitigation a club spokesperson added: "a Jewish member was one of the first to say we had sufficient numbers".

More serious practices occurred in housing. When Jews were excluded from certain flats in Glasgow built with the aid of a government subsidy, the Glasgow Jewish community was incensed and registered its complaint, reminding the authorities that it paid its taxes alongside others. Its anger grew when the Scottish Under-Secretary then proposed a quota system. Meanwhile, in Walthamstow, East London, a property company denied Jews access to a block of flats. Dismissing any notion that it held prejudiced views, the company justified its exclusion on the grounds that its Gentile tenants objected to having Jewish neighbours and the company was merely listening and responding to their demands. Meanwhile, Jewish people in this period frequenting seaside resorts were often met with advertisements specifying "no dogs, no Jews."

Further discrimination occurred in the law courts. In a case following a fatal car accident in Leeds in July 1933 in which the driver was Jewish, Coroner J.H.

Milner contended that that the jury "was overweighted" with Jews (there were five) implying that, on account of their imputed shared identity, they would act in unison to defend their fellow Jew whether innocent or guilty. He asked three of them to step down.[3] Not only did he treat Jews as a homogeneous corporate entity, but he also assumed that tribal solidarity would trump any issues of justice and personal morality.

The incidents of ideological antisemitism which the *JC* drew attention to in this period frequently involved clergy, sometimes of high standing. After addressing his congregation at Ilford Catholic Church in August 1934 on "The evils of the unclean film industry", Canon Palmer gave an interview in which he recommended that "a strict boycott of all picture houses should be considered until such Jewish filth is swept right away".[4] Today he is remembered with pride by Canon Palmer Secondary School which, according to its website, "takes its name from a much-loved and respected Priest, Canon Patrick Palmer, who led the foundation of the Catholic community in and around Ilford", and presumably kept well away from the cinema.[5]

Although many church leaders were forthright in denouncing antisemitism, several incidents occurred which implicated the Catholic Church in particular. The central theme of its attacks was to associate Jews with the Bolshevik Revolution in Russia, which was perceived as being violently anti-Christian. The notion of an international Jewish communist conspiracy had become a popular antisemitic myth following the First World War, having evolved from an earlier notion of a Jewish conspiracy outlined in the Czarist forgery, *The Protocols of the Learned Elders of Zion.*[6]

Some prominent politicians lent credence to these theories. Winston Churchill, writing in the *Illustrated Sunday Herald* in 1920, praised Zionist Jewish efforts in Palestine and contrasted them with the allegedly malign influence of "international" and "atheistic" Jews whom he believed were part of: "this worldwide conspiracy for the overthrow of civilization and the reconstruction of society on the basis of arrested development, of envious malevolence, and impossible equality". He added:

"This movement amongst the Jews is not new... It has been the mainspring of every subversive movement during the 19th Century; and now at last this band of extraordinary personalities has gripped the Russian people by the hair of their heads and have become practically the undisputed masters of that enormous empire. There is no need to exaggerate the part played in the creation of Bolshevism and in the actual bringing about of the Russian Revolution, by these international and for the most part atheistic Jews, it is certainly a very great one; it probably outweighs all others. With the notable exception of Lenin, the majority of the leading figures are Jews."[7]

In this extraordinary article Churchill acknowledged a debt to Nesta Webster who had written a series of articles for the *Morning Post* illuminating an alleged Jewish-Bolshevik conspiracy. The previous year the *Morning Post* had claimed that Jews controlled the Russian government and that leading Jewish newspapers in Britain were supporting them and influencing Jewish immigrants in Britain to support the Bolsheviks. This provoked a response signed by ten highly placed Jewish individuals, among them Claude Montefiore, President of the Anglo-Jewish Association and Major Lionel de Rothschild MP, who assured any concerned *Morning Post* readers that, while Russian Jews might indeed be implicated in the Bolshevik revolution, British Jews were not, and they happily dissociated themselves from any Jewish newspapers taking a favourable position towards the Bolsheviks.

The *JC* reported in December 1932 how Canon Byrne, preaching at a special service in West Hartlepool Catholic Church in honour of the town's new mayor, had delivered a sermon on "Jewish materialism" in which he blamed Jews, firstly, for instigating the Bolshevik revolution, and secondly, for using their power to suppress public information about their alleged role in this revolution. Canon Byrne quoted liberally from the writings of the Vicomte de Poncins, an antisemitic preacher and writer in France.[8] The *Catholic Herald* reported a meeting in Hanwell to protest against the persecution of Christians in the USSR, in which speakers accused Bolsheviks and Jews of generating the upheavals that had dramatically worsened the position of Christians. An article in the *Catholic Gazette*, published in North West London in July 1936, headed "The Jewish Peril and the Catholic Church" was described by the *JC* as "redolent of the Protocols", and the *Catholic Times* printed an article headlined "The Jewish Plan for World Domination" by Father Denis Fahey, a Tipperary-born exponent of Jewish conspiracy theories, who later founded the ultra-conservative Catholic group, *Maria Duce*.

Such defamation was not restricted to the Catholic Church: the Church of England's Bishop of Gloucester featured on more than one occasion in the *JC*, initially with a comment on Jews in Germany in August 1933, just months after Hitler had come to power. He described the Jews as "not altogether a pleasant element in Germany, and, in particular, in Berlin life". Meanwhile, Reverend Armitage of St Leonard's Church in Bootle, on Merseyside, was preaching sermons against the "International Jew". As the danger of World War loomed in 1939, the former Dean of St Paul's, Dr William Inge, argued in a Church of England newspaper that "the danger of war is not from Germany or Italy, but from 'Reds' ready to pick quarrels, supported by the Jews who are using their not inconsiderable influence in the press and in parliament to embroil us with Germany".

Newspapers also provided the medium for other forms of antisemitism. In November 1932, the *Daily Express* granted space for a sizeable article by Joseph Goebbels, head of the Berlin section of the Nazi movement, and later its Minister of Propaganda, in which he set out his party's case against the Jews. Professing its "revulsion" against antisemitism, the newspaper justified its action by saying it gave "utmost freedom of expression to both sides of all vital social and political issues". The *JC* welcomed the fact that the paper had given space to AL Eastermann, a frequent contributor to the *Daily Express* and also the *Daily Herald*, to write a feature demolishing Goebbels arguments two days later, but commented sagely that lies, unfortunately, "fly with wings" while truth "plods behind with leaden feet".

The *Daily Express* was further reproached by the *Jewish Chronicle* for the impetus it may have given to antisemitism among the young. A children's feature describing the New Testament story told how Christ had been "put to death by the cruel Jews". Concern in the Jewish community about the possible inculcation of youth with antisemitism came to the fore again with reports about the teaching in schools of Shakespeare's *The Merchant of Venice* with its antisemitic stereotyping in the form of "Shylock". Even more disquieting for the Jewish community, though, was the revelation that German textbooks were being used in some British schools, one of which included a nefarious attack on Jews by Goebbels, and the other, excerpts from Hitler's *Mein Kampf*.

A litany of incidents could be enumerated, but the actual strength and significance of any individual statement or accusation depended on how widely it was circulated, how prominent its perpetrators were, and whether they were able to incite others or impact on policy. For example, a letter in a local newspaper might have added to the accumulation of defamation, but would have been limited in its general appeal. In 1930s Britain, however, there were people holding high positions in political or social life, or renowned through the arts, who were widely respected and reported, and their views carried extra weight. Several of them explicitly pledged their allegiance to the cause of combating antisemitism and fascism, such as Vera Brittain, Cecil Day-Lewis, Margaret Storm Jameson, Henry Nevinson and Naomi Mitchison. There were others, though, whose role in relation to antisemitism was ambivalent at best and often they displayed hostility.

The author HG Wells engaged in a series of polemics with the *Jewish Chronicle* in which he consistently denied the legitimacy of Jews as a self-defined group. He claimed that Jewish culture was narrow and racially egotistical, and that Jewish insistence on separation provided a justification for antisemitism. "It may not be a bad thing," he argued, "if they [the Jews] thought themselves out of existence altogether." The playwright George Bernard Shaw, in an interview in the *American Hebrew*, offered the following advice for Jews: "Those Jews who still want to be the chosen race – chosen by the late Lord Balfour – can go to Palestine and stew in their own juice. The rest had better stop being Jews and start being human beings."[9] Fellow author JB Priestley became embroiled in a controversy over the participation of Jews in enterprise and finance. In an article entitled "This Jew Business", which was ostensibly a reply to antisemitism, he suggested instituting a quota system through which there would be one Jew in every business, but, he added as qualification, "not at the top".[10]

Elsewhere in the publishers' lists was Douglas Reed, a former foreign correspondent of *The Times*, who emerged as a prolific and popular writer with a set of searing social commentaries, such as *Insanity Fair*, *Disgrace Abounding*, *All Our Tomorrows*, and *Lest We Regret*, which were eagerly devoured by a growing readership. Each of these eminently readable books, which ran to several reprints, typically contained at least one colourful chapter incorporating a multi-faceted attack on Jewry. Reed would attack Jews' foreignness, make allegations of clannishness, and denounce their corporate action, which, he claimed was not merely inimical to the national interest, but expressed their striving for power and dominance. "When you give Jews full equality," he argued, they "use it to become a privileged group, not to become equals". Such arguments registered with non-Jewish readers feeling economic hardship and looking for someone to blame. Through his journalistic role as a foreign correspondent he knew Berlin and other German cities very well, and although he had a low opinion of Adolf Hitler, whom he regarded as crude and unsophisticated in his propaganda, he nevertheless attempted to justify the pre-war actions of the Nazi party that had stripped Jews of their place in German society.[11]

Among political figures, Norwich MP George Hartland alleged and then attacked "Jewish control" of the cinema. He claimed that: "There are millions of boys and girls in this country... [whose] ...souls are being taken from them as blood money for a syndicate of dirty American Jews – the Hollywood magnates."[12]

Admiral George Cuthbert Cayley, a patron of the British Israel World Federation – a very right wing body claiming to defend "Christian constitution and divine destiny" – was addressing a fête held by the Berwick Conservative Association when he commented on the aspirations of Herbert Samuel by asking: "Why should we want a Jew to lead our party?" He added for good measure, "Hitler is quite right to a certain extent in getting rid of some of the Jewry of Germany. I am inclined to think we may have to do the same at home."

Other political figures focused on the popular antisemitic theme of linking Jews and communism. Lieutenant Colonel Charles Kerr, the National Liberal Chief Whip, claimed that there were "many influential people in this country supporting the Communist Party, the insidious propaganda of which is backed by the Jews".[13] Lady Ninian

Crichton-Stuart, wife of Captain Archibald Ramsey, MP for Peebles and Southern Midlothian put a similar message even more emphatically: she believed that there was "an international group of Jews behind world revolution in every single country at the present time". When challenged through the *JC*, she reiterated the charges with full backing from Captain Ramsey.

Ramsey himself, an aristocrat deeply involved with fundamentalist Christian organisations, became convinced that *The Protocols of the Elders of Zion* were true. He was unabashed by the accusation of being anti-Jewish, although he considered the terminology used by his accusers often lacked rigour. He openly acknowledged and justified his oppositional attitude to the Jews:

> *"The only correct term for the mis-called 'antisemitic' is 'Jew-wise.' It is indeed the only fair and honest term. The phrase 'antisemite' is merely a propaganda word used to stampede the unthinking public into dismissing the whole subject from their minds without examination: so long as that is tolerated these evils will not only continue, but grow worse. The 'Jew-wise' know that we have in Britain a Jewish* Imperium in Imperio, *which, in spite of all protestations and camouflage, is Jewish first and foremost, and in complete unison with the remainder of World Jewry."*[14]

The instances of discrimination and expressions of ideological conviction described above testified to the existence of a widespread belief, though held to different degrees, that Jews were an alien and disruptive force in society. The essence of their threat was seen as being rooted in Jews' corporate action. When Jews shared an activity it was evaluated differently from a group of Gentiles engaged in exactly the same activity. This was particularly the case in relation to Jews entering the professions. The Nobel Prize winner Sir Henry Hallett Dale,

Director of the National Institute of Medical Research, unwittingly caused a few eyebrows to be raised during his guest of honour speech to the 10th annual dinner hosted by the Jewish Hospital Medical Society at Piccadilly's Trocadero Restaurant in December 1937. He argued forcefully against Jews "crowding" the professions, claiming that he did not believe it more healthy for a predominantly non-Jewish people to receive all or most of their medical attention from Jews, "than it would be for a Gentile nation to be subjected to a wholly Jewish government."[15]

Notes

[1] See, for example, Anthony Julius, *The Trials of the Diaspora*, 2010, and critiques of it by Antony Lerman in the *Guardian* 27.2.10.

[2] Peter the Hermit was a monk associated with the first crusade of 1096.

[3] *Jewish Chronicle*, 28.7.1933

[4] *Jewish Chronicle* 17.8.1934

[5] http://www.canonpalmer.redbridge.sch.uk/

[6] The *Protocols*, first published by the Russian secret police in 1897, purports to be minutes of a meeting outlining a plot for Jewish world domination. It was translated into English by Victor E Marsden and published in the UK by the Britons Publishing Society in the early 1920s.

[7] *Illustrated Sunday Herald* 8.2.1920

[8] Vicomte de Poncins (1897-1976) was a devout Catholic essayist who had written several works elaborating alleged Jewish-Masonic conspiracies for world domination including *Les Juifs Maîtres du Monde* in 1932.

[9] The *American Hebrew* was a weekly Jewish newspaper published in New York between 1879 and 1956. The interview with George Bernard Shaw was discussed in the *Jewish Chronicle* on 2.2.1936.

[10] *Jewish Chronicle* 2.2.1936

[11] After the Second World War, Reed moved to Southern Africa where he doggedly defended minority white rule and became increasingly obsessed with "Communist-Zionist" conspiracies. He was one of the first to cast doubt on accepted estimates of the numbers of Jews exterminated by the Nazis.

[12] *Jewish Chronicle* 13.5.1932
[13] *Jewish Chronicle* 3.6.1938
[14] ibid 3.6.1938
[15] *Jewish Chronicle 17.12.1937*

3. The rise of Mosley's movement

During the 1920s, numerous short-lived, extreme nationalist and self-defined fascist political groups were established in Britain, such as the British Fascisti, the British Empire Union, the National Citizens Union and the Imperial Fascist League (IFL). By the end of 1932, the membership of these groups had, with the exception of the IFL, largely gravitated into the British Union of Fascists (BUF), established by Sir Oswald Mosley in October of that year. The IFL resisted Mosley's call for union and often described Mosley's party as "British Jewnion" or "Kosher fascists". Mosley in turn described the IFL as "one of those crank little societies mad about the Jews". In his study of *The Fascist Movement in Britain*, Robert Benewick argued that the IFL saw as its enemies "freemasonry, communism, Mosley and the Jews", adding that its leader Arnold Leese "attempted to show that the first three were controlled by the latter".

The BUF dominated British fascism in the 1930s, being the only party of the radical right which succeeded in obtaining wide public attention and a measure of mass support. Its membership peaked in mid-1934, and even when it took a severe dip during 1935 before rising again, it could still claim several hundred branches nationally.[1] Precise figures are unavailable but the consensus among several scholars of fascism is that the BUF enjoyed the support of more than 40,000 members at its height. Its appeal and influence, however, was more widespread, and when former leading member AK Chesterton claimed that 100,000 people had passed through Mosley's movement between 1932 and 1938, that was probably not much of an exaggeration.[2]

The BUF's major asset was undoubtedly its leader, Sir Oswald Mosley, whose personality was predominant in the movement. Educated at Winchester Public School, trained in military matters at Sandhurst, Mosley began his political career shortly after the end of the First World War, from which he returned wounded but with a distinguished fighting record. He won the West London seat of Harrow for the Conservatives in December 1918, at the age of 22, becoming the youngest serving Member of Parliament. A Sinn Fein candidate, Joseph Sweeney, elected that year, was younger still, but did not take his seat in Westminster in protest at British policy towards Ireland. He participated instead in the first Irish Assembly – the *Dail*.

It was primarily on the issue of Ireland that Mosley broke from the Tory Party. He openly admired the Irish nationalist leader Michael Collins, supported self-determination for the Irish people in a united Ireland, and opposed the use of the Black and Tans to suppress the Irish population.[3] He was also frustrated by what he saw as the lack of innovation in Tory policy in this period. Reflecting on the difficulties he endured when arguing his perspective on Ireland from the Tory benches, Mosley commented: "It became impossible to gain a hearing on my side. So I preferred to face my enemies rather than be surrounded by them."

He successfully contested the next election in Harrow as an independent. After briefly flirting with the Liberals, his political sympathies, like those of his first wife, Lady Cynthia ("Cimmie") Curzon, shifted towards the Labour Party. She hailed from the extremely wealthy family of Marquess Curzon of Kedleston and the American heiress Mary Victoria Leiter, but was inclined towards socialism, and ideologically committed at least to other people's wealth being redistributed more equitably. After failing to win a seat in Birmingham Ladywood (against Neville Chamberlain) by just 77 votes, Oswald Mosley won the nearby Smethwick seat for Labour in

1926 (a seat that achieved notoriety and media attention in the 1964 election)[4] and his wife Lady Cynthia won a Labour seat in Stoke on Trent in 1929.

It was in the course of his early years in politics that Mosley first encountered those stepping beyond the bounds of normal political engagement. A meeting in Cambridge in December 1926, in which Mosley was imparting his socialist economic and political arguments, was violently disrupted by hecklers waving Union Jacks, who belonged to a fringe fascist group. He dismissed their antics as those of "blackshirted buffoons making a cheap imitation of ice cream sellers", which is no doubt how some would have characterised Mosley's disciples just a few years later. It was not the only occasion that statements or actions he claimed as matters of principle would come back to haunt him.

Mosley's marriage to Lady Curzon in 1920 took place at the Chapel Royal by special permission of the King. Before the wedding ceremony he held a bachelor luncheon at the Ritz with two kings and two queens present. He insisted, however, in 1926, that his conversion to socialism had fundamentally altered his outlook: "When my wife and I joined the labour movement," he said, "it meant a complete break with family and former associations." That same year he declared that his father's title was "not worth taking up", but in 1928, when his father died, he decided that this title was "not worth giving up".

In 1926 the Mosleys bought an ancient manor house in Buckinghamshire, "guarded from vulgar intrusion not only by a moat but by 50 acres or thereabouts of pleasant park or meadow",[5] and that same year they purchased two exclusive town houses at 8 and 9 Smith Square, Westminster, which were converted into one house of 16 rooms. Such extravagance rankled with many in the Labour Party, including those in its upper echelons who were more firmly rooted in the party's historical attachment to the trade union movement.

Nevertheless, following that 1929 election, Mosley relished the prospect of obtaining a key Cabinet post from which to implement the "Birmingham Proposals". These were radical economic policies that he had been developing alongside colleagues in the Independent Labour Party (ILP) – then incorporated within the Labour Party and operating on its left-wing. His plans included high tariffs to protect British industries from international finance, nationalisation of key industries and a programme of public works – such as slum clearance – to slash unemployment, stimulate economic consumption and provide real improvements in housing for poorer people. He also proposed reducing the workforce, and hence unemployment, by providing maintenance grants to keep young people at school longer and pensions to provide economic security for older people. His commitment to the unemployed and the poor had been a major concern in this period. In a pamphlet penned in response to the Baldwin Government's economic policies, Mosley the Labourite had written:

"Unemployment prevails because there is no market which can absorb the goods that industry can produce. There is no market because the people are too poor to buy the full product of industry. The people are too poor because they themselves are unemployed or because the unemployment of others has been used to force down their wages."[6]

He was being tipped by several commentators as a future Prime Minister. The Labour leader, Ramsey MacDonald, conferred on Mosley the splendid title of Chancellor of the Duchy of Lancaster, and gave him the unenviable task of dealing with unemployment. [7] But he was a minister without portfolio and was excluded from the Cabinet. The Labour hierarchy clearly distrusted this charismatic aristocrat who had moved effortlessly between political parties and whose personality had already betrayed hints of authoritarian leanings.

After both Mosley's superior, James Thomas, and the Cabinet in general confirmed that they had rejected his detailed plans for economic recovery, Mosley invited 250 people who were prominent in the trade unions and political labour movement to discuss a proposal to start a new socialist party: one pledged to a form of economic nationalism through public utility corporations. The state would assume ownership of them but leave direction in the hands of trained businessmen who were currently running British industries. Unable to win sufficient backing for this plan, and cold-shouldered by those leading the Labour Party, Mosley decided to take his ball and go home, stopping just long enough on the way to denounce the "old gang" whom he believed were both responsible for Britain's economic malaise and incapable of navigating a route out of it. David Low, cartoonist of the satirical magazine *Punch*, marked this event with a memorable image of a top-hatted Sir Oswald Mosley clutching a paper entitled "Rejected Memorandum", walking behind a long line of cloth-capped unemployed workers. The cartoon caption read: "Rt Hon Dress Suit (checking the unemployment figures) – 1,739,497 1,739,498 – 1,739,499 – 1,739,500 – Good Lor! – 1,739,501!"

Claiming that there was no longer any perceptible difference between the Labour and Conservative parties, Mosley ended his formal association with Labour on 28th February 1931. The very next day he announced that he had formed a new political party, rather unimaginatively named the "New Party", which he conceived as a party of "action based on youth" that would mobilise "energy, vitality and manhood to save and rebuild the nation".[8]

The New Party was short-lived but it attracted the interest and material support of a number of intellectuals and business figures, such as printer, historian and former Unionist MP for Belfast West, WED Allen, shipping magnate Lord Inchcape, aircraft manufacturer Sir Alliott Verdon-Roe, directors of the silk firm Courtaulds, a Cheshire landowner with brewing interests called Baron Tollemache, and the car manufacturer Sir William Morris (Lord Nuffield). Morris is believed to have invested £50,000 in the New Party, having been introduced to Mosley through the proprietor of the *Daily Express*, Lord Beaverbrook.

A handful of Labour MPs, one Liberal MP and a number of ILP activists followed Mosley into the New Party, with high hopes of making a significant breakthrough against the established parties in the coming years. But the next election was sprung on them far too soon for a party still finding its feet, and all the New Party candidates who had formerly been MPs, including Mosley, lost their parliamentary seats. Apart from Mosley himself gaining a vote of 20 per cent in Stoke, and a candidate in Merthyr Tydfil scoring well, most of the New Party's twenty-four hopefuls gained a derisory vote.

The significance of the New Party, though, as a nucleus and ideological pre-figuration of the BUF, lay in its advocacy of the corporate state, which became central to the BUF's national economic and social strategy, and in its overt challenge to the system of liberal democracy. In the first issue of its short-lived newspaper, *Action*,[9] Mosley wrote:

"We must create a movement which aims not merely at the capture of political power, a movement which grips and transforms every phase and aspect of national life to post-war purposes, a movement of order, of discipline, of loyalty, but also of dynamic progress; a movement of iron decision, resolution and reality, a movement which cuts like a sword through

54

*the knot of the past to the coming of the modern
state... We stand for the new England. We stand for
the future of British purpose... We believe that within
a measurable time this country will be exposed to the
dangers of a proletarian revolution... (which) ...will
mean massacre, starvation and collapse. We believe
that the one protection against such a disaster is the
corporate state."*[10]

In the following issue, Mosley set out, in rather chilling
language, how the New Party conceived of the state. It
would be "coordinated, cooperative and controlled... as
compact and as self-conscious as the human body... no
dead limbs and no parasites".[11]

If the wreckage of unbridled capitalism had spurred
Mosley's efforts to develop an economic policy for the
Labour Party that would solve unemployment, his fire
was now turned on what he saw as the perilous threat
from communism.

*"We shall meet communism in the street if need be
not only by the negation of force opposing force but
with a faith and idea greater, nobler, more powerful
and more victorious."*[12]

He argued that "Communism must be met not by a flabby
negative but by a virile positive," which was the corporate
state, an idea he claimed was "probably capable of
greater understanding and development by the British
character than by any other nation in the world."[13]

It was in this period that Mosley foreshadowed the fascist approach to government when he stated: "We believe
in a strong government by a small central executive of not
more than five persons," and expressed his desire that
this government must be given "powers of rapid action"
through a "General Powers Bill". The willingness to use
violence for political ends, which came to the fore later
through the BUF, was also rehearsed in this period.

Mosley employed as bodyguards the England Rugby Captain Peter Howard and a young Jewish boxer Gershon Mendeloff (well known in his native East London as Ted "Kid" Lewis), and they were handed the brief of training a physical force to maintain order at meetings. Looking to the future, Mosley saw his "Biff Boys" as the advance guard of a force that could provide muscle against the communist threat that increasingly dominated his fears.

He translated these real or politically manufactured fears into apocalyptic visions for his followers, arguing, "While there is time we organise the youth and the manhood of Britain." In the final issue of *Action*, Mosley stated: "We shall be a movement born of crisis and of ordeal, or nothing. If that crisis does not mature we shall be nothing, because the country for perfectly good reasons will not require us."[14]

Although Mosley was rooted in conventional British politics, the building blocks of his new political programme were inspired by theorists and propagandists in Continental Europe. At the beginning of 1932 he travelled to Germany, and met leading Nazi officials, though not Hitler himself, and then to Italy, where he had a long audience with Mussolini. He returned animated much more by the example of Italian fascism in power than by Germany's incipient rulers, though some of his supporters certainly had a penchant for Hitler's model. In August 1932 a New Party member was convicted for fly-posting leaflets proclaiming: "Expel all the Jews from the country." When the *Daily Herald* asked the New Party's assistant director, Leslie Cumming, to comment on this case, he said: "We neither approve nor disapprove".[15] Confirming that the New Party had "no official attitude to the Jewish question", he simply added that the member in question "was not authorised" to carry out the action for which he was prosecuted.[16] In April 1932, Mosley himself chaired a meeting of the youth section of the New Party, NUPA (a contraction of New Party), at which the speakers were Henry Hamilton Beamish of the Britons Society (which had translated and reprinted the seminal antisemitic text, *The Protocols of the Elders of Zion*) and Arnold Leese of the Imperial Fascist League, who were addressing the topic of "The Blindness of British Politics Under the Jewish Money Power".[17]

Mosley's fascism of choice, though, was Mussolini's model. He was enamoured and inspired as much by its cultural adornments and symbolic trappings as its economic and political practices. The former radical socialist, Benito Mussolini, was consolidating a self-proclaimed "fascist" corporate state with a paramilitary organisational basis, complete with uniforms, a salute and an emblem: the Imperial Roman "fasces" symbol – an axe protecting a bundle of rods, representing power and jurisdiction. Mosley set out to replicate the content and style of Italian fascism on British soil as the New Party transformed itself into the BUF in October 1932.

The final stretch of Mosley's extraordinary political journey from socialism, with its egalitarian and democratic impulse, to fascism, with its impulse towards unquestioning hierarchical authority, came as a shock to some, such as former members of the Independent Labour Party, John Strachey and Allan Young, who jumped ship having travelled much of the way with Mosley. They had sincerely believed that his creation of the New Party heralded a new modern movement of the Left. Other similarly deluded people might have abandoned Mosley earlier had they heeded the warnings of Cecil Melville's extraordinarily prescient text: *The Truth About the New Party*, which, in September 1931, identified the common trajectory of Mosley and Hitler, and the

57

artist Wyndham Lewis, towards the menacing and tyrannical ideology of National Socialism.[18]

The BUF developed a rigidly hierarchical structure with a host of departments and officers. In general it had an educated middle-class leadership, including several individuals who had gained experience within other political parties and groups. Among them were the journalist AK Chesterton, the former member of the British Fascists, Neil Francis Hawkins, American born William Joyce, who had been a fellow traveller of this group too,[19] the philosopher Alexander Raven-Thomson whose early political involvements included a spell in the Communist Party, William Allen, the former Ulster Unionist, heir to a family printing empire, and an early enthusiast for the New Party, and former Labour MP John Beckett, who had once shared accommodation in Limehouse, East London, with Clement Atlee.

Scholars of fascism still struggle to isolate its distinct ideology because its philosophy and programme contain contradictory elements that occur within a range of other political and economic systems. The principal components of Mosley's movement at its inception were nationalism, corporatism and anti-communism, and these elements were unified through their absolute opposition to sectional interests. Michael Billig, author of a 1978 study of Britain's post-war fascist movement, added a crucial component, contending that the fascists' ideology "is expressed in a manner which poses a threat to democracy and personal freedom".[20]

By 1934 the distinct elements that comprised the core of the BUF's ideology were synthesised through an all-embracing antisemitic doctrine and this provided the basis upon which it embarked on its major period of agitation until 1937, after which it declined. Every enemy that Mosley had perceived as a barrier to Britain solving its economic crisis and making political progress, which in an earlier phase he might have described as "old gang politicians" or "non-productive international finance" or "the yellow press", ultimately became reduced by his movement to one word: "Jews". His speeches didn't get any shorter though – he was capable of addressing his audience for 90-100 minutes at a time – but the content of his utterances and the target of his venom narrowed considerably.

The BUF enjoyed a brief revival in 1939 as the anti-war party of Middle England, on the eve of a new global conflagration that was to claim the lives of so many millions of combatants and civilians. True to the convictions it established in the mid-1930s, Britain's fascist party depicted this imminent war, during which Nazism would take six million Jewish lives, overwhelmingly civilians, as a "Jews' quarrel" that would be fought only so that "international usury may draw its dividends".

The BUF could not have entered the political scene under more favourable conditions. Unemployment had risen rapidly from less than 1.5 million in 1929 to almost 3 million in 1933 – more than 20 per cent of the working population. In some major industrial areas, such as Glasgow, unemployment hit 30 per cent, and in Jarrow in the north east of England it was more than double that figure. It was not until 1937 that unemployment nationally dipped below 2 million and it rose above that threshold again in 1939.

The government lacked confidence and responded weakly to the crisis that people faced on a day-to-day basis as their living standards plummeted. In the late 1920s and early 1930s, while Britain lost national prestige and influence and its people suffered hardship, fascist leaders in Italy boasted that they had solved the crisis of unemployment, while in Germany the Nazis were making rapid political progress. One of the major challenges to anti-fascists in this period was to unearth the true economic story of working people under fascist regimes and to show how, despite bold claims, the living standards of many workers were actually suffering in fascist countries.[21]

Mosley and his movement presented themselves as saviours, uniquely capable of delivering the British people from their catastrophic circumstances. His most direct vehicle for winning support was his party's newspaper – *The Blackshirt* – which began as a monthly but was soon published weekly. It was augmented in 1936 by other less frequent BUF publications such as *Action* and *Fascist Quarterly*, though these titles were written more for those already operating inside the fascist tent. *The Blackshirt* was more overtly aimed at winning support from the uninitiated, as well as serving to reinforce the ideas of those already committed to its worldview. It addressed itself to different, even competing sectors in the society. Many quotes in this study, illustrating the politics of Mosley's movement, are drawn from this paper, which appeared continuously from 1933 until the end of the decade.

The first issue of *The Blackshirt*, published in February 1933 did not pull its punches. It proclaimed: "On to Fascist Revolution: drastic action or disaster" and warned: "If our present political system muddles to collapse, Fascism alone can stand between the country and anarchy. We must be prepared to save Britain by force." Might this mean dictatorship? Mosley moved to assuage potential critics:

> "*It is true that we suggest for Britain authoritative government... the endless blether of the parliamentary system is paralysing the action that is necessary. But our authoritative government... would not be a dictatorship but it would be a government which... would act rapidly through Orders in Council, and would be free from the daily obstruction of a party opposition.*"[22]

However, in his book, *The Greater Britain*, launched in parallel with the BUF, Mosley more explicitly advocated and defended dictatorship but claimed that it was not "dictatorship in the old sense... which implies government against the will of the people"; rather it was dictatorship "in the modern sense... which implies government armed by the people with power to solve problems... By dictatorship we mean leadership. By dictatorship they mean tyranny."[23]

Its appeal for a "national awakening" and the novelty it claimed for its style of politics was targeted particularly towards youth, an orientation firmly established by the New Party. Though its own leaders had left their adolescence far behind, it called on youth "to show the way to the older generations". According to the BUF, "Other parties have always neglected youth until they found occasion to call upon them to immolate themselves on the battlefield." The BUF, on the other hand, was "the only party that understands youth and can offer it the chance and honour to serve the home country in times of peace". The BUF described its members as "young, clean, vigorous and healthy", elevating these features while simultaneously implying that such traits were typically absent among their opponents. It looked to a particular social class for its youngest recruits and successfully established student branches in twenty public schools.

In a perceptive contemporary study, *Why They Join the Fascists*, Lionel Birch recognised the immensely powerful and attractive blend of "revolutionary and patriotic" idealism that Mosley's movement offered its recruits.[24] In the BUF they would find: "a comradeship of struggle" that promised to be "epic, heroic and legendary," and in which service, devotion and sacrifice would be rewarded with a collective sense of strength, unity and power. Mosley himself underlined this in *The Greater Britain*, in which he says of potential converts to the cause: "We can only offer them the deep belief that they are fighting that a great land may live."

However, the BUF failed to capitalise on what appeared to be such promising circumstances. It had originally attempted to build on a national basis and it created hundreds of branches, but its sustained impact was limited to a few areas, and these were not necessarily the most distressed localities, where the most desperate, disempowered people yearned for an alternative to the failures of established politics. Seeking membership from a cross section of the population, it made distinct propaganda appeals to particular sectors, such as cotton workers in Lancashire, coal miners in the North East and Wales, farmers in Dorset, shopkeepers and the self-employed in smaller towns, with varying degrees of success. It held meetings in towns that traditionally contributed many workers to the army, navy and airforce, large numbers of whom had fallen into the ranks of the unemployed. The BUF set up its own Fascist Union of British Workers to take up unemployed workers' demands for jobs, and the plight of the low-paid, as they campaigned to meet the needs of what they, as much as their opponents, sincerely described as "Hungry England".

Mosley meeting in Manchester

Towards the end of 1933 and early in 1934, Mosley sought support for the BUF from a very different sector to those suffering physical pangs of hunger who could hardly be expected to deliver large amounts of money for the party's coffers. In this period Mosley made great efforts to court various powerful and well-fed establishment figures – business magnates, newspaper proprietors, intellectuals and politicians. His vehicle was the innocuously named "January Club". This was a regular wining and dining event, chaired by Sir John Squire, editor of the *London Mercury* – a leading monthly literary journal – which took place at exclusive venues far beyond the reach and experience of the workers whose interests Mosley claimed to champion. This club would meet in the finest hotels, such as the Ritz and the Savoy, where they would discuss the merits of the corporate state and other fascist-inspired proposals. In these plush surroundings Mosley would gauge how much support and commitment he could obtain from these powerful individuals for his radical ideas and the authoritarian political instrument through which he intended to bring them to fruition. Such influential figures, were doubtless making a counter-assessment of Mosley and his movement. They were calculating the extent to which his political philosophy, and the foot soldiers he was recruiting, might defend their social and economic interests in a period when critiques of capitalism and class divisions were coming to the fore; when socialist ideas of egalitarianism and redistribution of wealth were inspiring a new wave of intellectuals whose voices were increasingly heard; and when militant left-wing oppositional forces such as the Communist Party and Independent Labour Party, the trade unions and Unemployed Workers' Movement were attracting growing support and enthusiastic interest.

Mosley won the confidence of several business leaders and he claimed that his party enjoyed financial support from highly placed individuals within several companies – though evidence of their donations is elusive. Regular attendees of the January Club included General Sir Hubert de la Poer Gough, a director of Siemens and of Caxton Electric Development; Vincent Vickers of Vickers Electronics and a director of London Assurance; Colonel Middleton, director of Yorkshire Insurance; and JF Rennell Rodd, a partner in Morgan Grenfell merchant bank. On a smaller scale, *The Blackshirt* newspaper frequently carried advertising by Watney's brewery, J Chandler's wines and spirits, Mitchell and Butler's brewery, Jubilee Cars' "expert driving tuition" and John Bull's shaving products – no doubt extremely useful for keeping neat and tidy the moustaches that were becoming fashionable among male BUF members in the mid-1930s.

Wealthier fascists might also have wished to relax at the end of a long day of propagandising against Jews and communists, in a comfortable chair from the "exclusive hand-made furniture" range of Mayfair-based *Blackshirt* advertiser, Thomas Prior. Despite constantly exhorting his supporters to "Buy British", Mosley was rather successful at obtaining regular funds from abroad. It is believed that Benito Mussolini's government in Italy subsidised the BUF to the tune of more than £35,000 a year until late 1936. Mosley's opponents in the Communist Party complained through anti-fascist handbills: "Don't you think Mosley gets his share of the 'International finance' that he's always talking about? Enough to buy £2000 Bentley cars with."

January Club events were also attended by some wealthy Jewish individuals, such as the historian and biographer Sir Philip Montefiore Magnus, and Major Harry Nathan, Liberal MP for Bethnal Green in East London and chair of the Anglo-Chinese Finance and Trade Corporation. Just a few months before this association with Mosley, Major Nathan had been a contender for the presidency of the Board of Deputies of British Jews. Such associates among Jewish individuals proved a useful foil for Mosley when his opponents accused him of antisemitism, though they also caused him grief from rivals within the world of fascism, such as the Imperial Fascist League, who labelled Mosley's movement "Kosher Fascists" and ultimately accused Mosley himself of being Jewish. Leading fascists angrily denied charges that they were trading in antisemitism, but recoiled with horror when any of their own were accused of being Jews. In 1937 a local BUF paper in East London carried the headline "Reds Attack Dead Woman". Rather than being the stuff of macabre rituals, it was a reference to a Communist leaflet that mentioned the late Cynthia Mosley and apparently perpetrated "the deliberate lie that she was a Jewess", which was "an attempt to hurt Mosley by insulting the memory of a dead woman who can make no answer."[25] In garnering the support of influential figures, Sir Oswald was ultimately much more concerned with what any individual could bring to the table than with the intricacies of their ancestry.

For Mosley, the icing on the cake as far as domestic financial and political support was concerned, was the support he received from a distinctly non-Jewish press baron – Viscount Rothermere of the *Daily Mail*. After Rothermere's brother, Lord Northcliffe, died in 1922, Rothermere took complete control of this mass circulation daily and its sister publications the *Sunday Dispatch* and the *Evening News*. Rothermere was a longstanding Conservative but he had shown a willingness to dabble independently in politics in the late 1920s by giving active support to a party slightly outside of the mainstream – the short-lived United Empire Party (UEP), which supported the British Empire but also argued for it to become a free trade bloc. In 1930 the *Daily Mail*'s support helped the UEP win a parliamentary seat in Paddington South at the expense of the sitting Tory MP. Mosley also noted both the content and tone of Rothermere's editorial of July 1933, entitled "Youth Triumphant", in support of Hitler's movement in Germany, and relished the opportunity that support from a popular daily newspaper might bring his own fledgling movement. Rothermere had written:

"The indulgence, or indifference, with which the British public allows worn out party leaders to cling to political power is one of the main causes of the muddle in which our national affairs have so long remained. Until the younger generation asserts itself in Britain, as the youth of Germany and Italy has done, the self-satisfied soothsayers now in office... will continue to exercise their disastrous sway... The world's greatest need today is realism. Hitler is a realist. He has saved his country from the ineffectual leadership of hesitating, half-hearted politicians."

Like Cecil Melville before him, Rothermere saw in Mosley another potential Hitler. For Melville it was a doom-laden prophesy. Rothermere, on the other hand was exultant. On 15th January 1934 the *Daily Mail* gave Sir Oswald Mosley his finest media moment. It published a double page spread entitled "Hurrah for the Blackshirts". Rothermere had warmed especially to Mosley's emphasis on young people:

"Youth is a force that for generations has been allowed to run to waste in Britain. This country has been governed since far back in Victorian times by men in the middle 60s... The Blackshirt movement is the organised effort of the younger generation to break this stranglehold."

He was also willing to submit to Mosley's arguments about creating new and authoritarian political instruments based on examples elsewhere in Europe:

"Blackshirts proclaim a fact which politicians dating from pre-war days will never face – that the new age requires new methods and new men... they want to bring our national administration up to date. This purpose does not rest on theory alone. It

66

can be justified by the gigantic revival of national strength and spirit which a similar process of modernisation has brought about in Italy and Germany."

Rothermere concluded:

"That is why I say, Hurrah for the Blackshirts! They are a sign that something is stirring among the youth of Britain... hundreds of thousands of young British men and women would like to see their own country develop that spirit of patriotic pride and service which has transformed Germany and Italy. They cannot do better than seek out the nearest branch of the Blackshirts and make themselves acquainted with their aims and plans... they will find the loyalties and aims of the Blackshirts as British as their membership and, as a striking contrast with the hesitations and compromises of all other parties, they will discover that black shirts do not cover faint hearts!"[26]

Below this article Rothermere signposted his readers to take the next bold but logical step: "Young men may join the British Union of Fascists by writing to the Headquarters, Kings Road, Chelsea, London SW." His newspapers even ran a letter-writing competition where entrants could win £1 for sending in the best letter that opened with the words: "Why I like the Blackshirts".

The open support for Mosley from figures more firmly rooted and more comfortable within traditional right wing Conservatism ran into the buffers in the summer of 1934 in the aftermath of the extraordinary events at a major public rally for the Blackshirts that was held at the Olympia Exhibition Centre. This was to be the BUF's second major show of strength in an indoor arena in central London. In April 1934 it had mounted a rally for several thousand supporters at the Royal Albert Hall in

London which won enthusiastic plaudits from the more traditionally Conservative sections of the press. At the Albert Hall rally, which coincided with the start of a three day diplomatic visit for meetings with government ministers by Signor Suvich, the Italian Under-Secretary for Foreign Affairs, Mosley spoke for nearly ninety minutes, and then answered written questions submitted from the floor for a further hour. Even those who were not his traditional supporters acknowledged that he held his audience spellbound.

The *Daily Express*, an unwavering bastion of traditional Conservatism, which had the distinction of being the first British newspaper to carry a crossword, and whose circulation consistently outstripped its middle market competitors, focused on the style as well as the content of Mosley's speech:

> "*The peroration was perfect. Sir Oswald, his voice rising and falling, talked of the makers of the Empire and the Union Jack, the constitution and history. The silence in the hall was intense. Suddenly Sir Oswald's voice ceased... the cheers and the hand-clapping rose to a storm.*"[27]

The *Evening News*, part of Rothermere's stable, unsurprisingly wrote:

> "*Last night's great Albert Hall meeting was a notable triumph for Sir Oswald Mosley and for the Blackshirt movement of which he is the paramount leader. Many, if not the majority, of the vast audience that listened so attentively... came there with open minds. They left convinced that here was a new party that really mattered, a new power and inspiration in the political land. Many of them are already telling their friends that here is the sort of party that the country needs... And they are right.*"

The more nuanced commentary in the *Manchester Guardian* noted the three occasions in particular during his speech when the applause became "almost rapturous":

> *"The first was when he said that Fascism in Britain was growing faster than anywhere else in the world. The second was when he stated that Fascism would give a man a job in government and full power to get on with it, but would dismiss him if he failed. The third was when he said that Jews would be expected to put Britain before Jewry."*

The *Manchester Guardian* went on to comment that: "This reference to the Jews suggested a closer relationship to Continental Fascism than Sir Oswald publicly admits and he was at pains to justify Hitler and Mussolini against the charge of tyranny."[28] *The Times*, on the other hand, gave a short, rather uninspiring, factual account of a few points from Mosley's speech and offered no independent comment on it.

Following that triumphant meeting, the BUF held an even more ambitious event in June at Olympia. Among the 15,000 strong audience sat many Members of Parliament. The *News Chronicle's* political correspondent estimated that 150 MPs, mainly from the Conservative benches, were present, as well as members of the Lords. He also noted how some prominent political figures, such as Lord Erroll, Sir John Rhodes and Sir George Duckworth King, came suitably dressed for the occasion, wearing their black shirts.

Outside the hall a noisy protest led by the Communist Party and the Independent Labour Party made its presence felt. The *Daily Mail* described the protesters as "a disorderly red mob filing the air with obscene and blasphemous cries", adding that this "mob" was "largely composed of aliens". It contrasted them unfavourably with those sitting "patient and hushed" inside the hall waiting for the leader to walk under a spotlight up to the

podium amid a fanfare of trumpets. The podium was surrounded by fifty-six Union Jack standard bearers in
blackshirt uniform and twenty-four microphones.
According to the *Daily Mail*, the assembled crowd
included "many people well known in various walks of
life" who were "representative of the best elements of the
British nation."[29]

Not all the guests were welcome though. Significant
numbers of political opponents managed to obtain tickets
and came with the express intention of disrupting the
meeting in order to show that there was determined
opposition to Mosley's ideas and to expose the fascist message as fundamentally opposed to democracy and
progress.[30] Mosley's opponents knew that his guard of
honour would be kept on a short leash but anti-fascists
anticipated that, in the worst case, they would be summarily ejected from the meeting, having successfully
attempted to intervene. The manner in which they were
actually dealt with delighted some of Mosley's more wild-
eyed and bloodthirsty supporters but shocked many of
Mosley's more conservative backers, not least several of
the wealthy contributors he was grooming through the
January Club.

When serious heckling occurred, Mosley stopped
speaking, and spotlights were trained on the hecklers. A
large group of Blackshirt stewards pounced on the disruptive individuals, dragged them from their seats and
inflicted repeated kicks and blows.[31] The hecklers,
having already been set upon by large numbers of stewards, were thrown out of the doors of the auditorium,
and were savagely beaten in the corridors and the foyer,
while the police remained outside the building unwilling
to intervene. Over tea the previous day, the
Metropolitan Police Commissioner, Viscount Hugh
Trenchard, had been assured by Mosley that his
Blackshirts were more than capable of stewarding the
meeting effectively, so he had agreed that police would
not enter the actual meeting hall.

The events in and around the building that night so shocked many individuals who had attended that they later gave their testimonies to various organisations, such as the Union of Democratic Control[32] and National Council for Civil Liberties, which collected and published them to warn the general public about the dangers of Mosley's movement. Some of these individuals giving testimony were named; others, scared of physical reprisals, preferred to just give initials.

> "...there was the sound of someone shouting something – and before one could look up a mass of Blackshirts were on the man. I counted a dozen... they beat constantly for several minutes at someone they had on the floor and finally dragged him out by the arms."

> "The young man rose from his seat and shouted 'Fascism means war'. At once between 8-10 Blackshirts pounced on him... pummelling him with their fists."

> "I counted 20 cases in which those being ejected were offering no resistance but were being pummelled, beaten, kicked or hit by 10 or more Blackshirts."

> "Young men and women came out in a very distressed condition. Many women were holding their breasts and their faces displayed signs they had been clawed by fingernails... One man looked as though an animal had attacked him, his face was mauled, and his legs were dangling and his clothes were torn. Practically all of them had smashed faces, not just bruised faces, but smashed faces."

> "...where I was most of the audience was fascist in sympathy. They cheered and waved when interrupters were beaten... the most revolting part of the

meeting was the bloodlust on the faces of those around me, as each person was beaten. It made the tales I had heard of Austria and Germany become real." [33]

Several of the regular staff who worked at the Olympia venue gave testimony too. One of them described it as:

"...one of the most brutal affairs that any human being can witness. People ... were pounced upon by the Blackshirts ... when they fell there were about 20-30 of these villains assaulting them. Their arms were twisted behind their backs while (they) received) about 20-30 punches and (they) kicked them about on the floor till they were helpless."

The Blackshirts then instructed their victims to leave the building. "But when they proceeded to the outer yard, there another gang would do the very same actions."[34]

Another employee of Olympia who deposited a signed copy of his testimony with a solicitor wrote:

"I am prepared to swear that I saw Blackshirts armed with knuckledusters which were hidden under bandages or gloves. This I saw because several times they removed the gloves in order to straighten the knuckledusters on their hands."[35]

More experienced opponents of the fascists were shocked by the scale of the assaults but not by the appearance of strong-arm tactics. The film director and critic, Ivor Montagu, who was active in the Communist Party, wrote a pamphlet quoting several other witnesses to the events at Olympia. He remarked: "Blackshirt meetings up and down the country during the last 12 months have left behind them a long trail of records of violence... Olympia was notable because it was the first occasion on which such violence found victims among, and was carried out under the eyes of, respectable members of the bourgeoisie."[36]

The police concentrated their efforts on maintaining order outside the meeting, before completing their tasks for the night by escorting uniformed fascists to safety in groups of four, as they left the premises at 11.30pm. During a lively and continuous demonstration on the streets near Olympia, more than twenty anti-fascist protestors had been arrested, while those perpetrating vicious assaults within the building remained free from the attentions of the authorities.

Many hecklers who had been violently ejected from the hall needed medical assistance. A doctor from Highgate who was helping to treat the injured and was later interviewed by *The Times* contradicted Mosley's claim that it was actually his stewards who had been the target of violence. Dr Peter Gorer confirmed that he had been personally aware of more than seventy individuals needing medical attention after attending the meeting, one of whom had lacerations caused by "sharp cutting instruments", another with scalp lacerations probably resulting from being assaulted with a fire extinguisher. Dr Gorer stated that none of the people he and his medical colleagues treated had been wearing black shirts. In testimony to the Union of Democratic Control, he revealed an interaction with the police near the entrance to Olympia: "I went up to the constable and said I was a doctor and thought I better stand near the door and he used insulting language and invited me to return to Moscow."[37]

At the very moment when Mosley was forging unity between his hard-core fascist supporters and those more comfortable within conventional right-wing politics, the tactics he sanctioned at Olympia split this tentative alliance. But commentary on the manner in which the BUF had handled the Olympia meeting in Parliament and the mainstream press was by no means completely hostile to Mosley, who argued a case of self-defence. He claimed that opponents of his movement had long been carrying out violent assaults on his members and supporters. Mosley was very keen to point out that Jews were prominent among those who were responsible for such assaults – a theme taken up enthusiastically by Tory backbenchers in a parliamentary debate on 24th July 1934, several weeks after the Olympia disturbances. William Greene, Conservative MP for Worcester asked: "Is it not a fact that 90 per cent of those accused of attacking Fascists rejoice in fine old British names such as Ziff, Kerstein and Minsky?" Frederick MacQuisten, Conservative MP for Argyll enquired: "Were some of them called Feigenbaum, Goldstein and Rigotsky and other good old Highland names?"

These surnames were not plucked out of the ether. They had been published in the BUF's *Blackshirt* newspaper, within a more extensive list of individuals who had been convicted and received prison sentences in the previous year for assaults on BUF members – not in MacQuisten's constituency in Argyll, where Jews were indeed something of a rarity, but in London. MacQuisten's concerns clearly extended well beyond parochial matters. A list of twenty-five names, mainly Jewish, had also appeared in a crude antisemitic pamphlet, *Fascism and Jewry*, by William Joyce which Greene and MacQuisten might have used for their source material. Just beneath the list, Joyce wrote: "These little sub-men are a nuisance to be eliminated, but their wealthy instigators... are, in sum, a criminal monstrosity, for which not all the gold of Jewry, can pay the just compensation which we will demand and obtain."[38]

In the immediate aftermath of the Olympia meeting, the *Daily Mail* and *Sunday Dispatch* both published spirited defences of Blackshirt tactics at this rally, as did the *Morning Post*. But the events that night were greeted with much less enthusiasm, and even outright criticism in Conservative publications such as *The Times* and the *Daily Telegraph*. Olympia was clearly troublesome for those of Rothermere's ilk and other backers much more at ease with traditional Conservatism, and it tempered their desire to deepen their association with a political movement that was so willing to demonstrate physical brutality, rather than promote a culture of patriotic values and use its intellectual force to defeat its opponents. It did not lead to immediate denunciation and disengagement, rather a gradual distancing that took more concrete form through a public exchange of letters between Rothermere and Mosley some six weeks after Olympia. The content of Rothermere's separation letter did not rule out a later rapprochement around common aims more closely tied to mainstream Conservative Party goals.

Clearly such figures did not want the political ideas they were supporting to be damaged by association with violence, although Rothermere et al demonstrated or feigned extreme naivety about both Mosley's tactics and his ideological convictions. He probably knew as surely as committed observers such as Ivor Montagu did, that this was not the first time Mosley's "Biff Boys" had meted out such treatment. They had first shown their hand – or rather their fists and knuckle-dusters – at meetings in Oxford Town Hall in November 1933, and in Carlisle in April 1934, where a small group of demonstrators who shouted "Down with the persecution of the Jews" and "Down with fascist brutality", were treated to a classic example of what they were protesting about as they were kicked and battered by up to forty fascists. Knuckle-dusters were used against hecklers at a meeting in Bow in London's East End in early 1934. In the run-up to the Olympia meeting there had been physical skirmishes between supporters and opponents of fascism in Finsbury Park, north London.

Lord Rothermere claimed that Mosley's turn towards explicit antisemitism was also intolerable. He wrote to Mosley on 14th July 1934 stating how he had "made it quite clear in my conversations with you that I could never support any movement with an antisemitic bias". This statement, however, rings hollow for a man who

75

would have understood the power of the media extremely well. Just a few weeks before Rothermere openly gave the Blackshirts his blessing with such remarkable enthusiasm, he would surely have noted a front-page headline on *The Blackshirt* newspaper asking: "Shall Jews drag Britain to War?" which could hardly be considered coy about its attitude to the Jews:

> "*Modern conservatism in Britain is entirely subservient to the international finance of the City of London which is of course largely Jewish. Socialism too is dominated by so called intellectuals many of whom are Jewish, while the rest are invariably under Jewish influence... the Jews have now organised as a racial minority within the state to conduct a furious agitation with all the force of their great money power.*"[39]

At the Olympia meeting itself, Mosley's speech poured derision on his socialist opponents who drew their inspiration from "the German Jew Karl Marx", on opponents in the Conservative Party who drew inspiration from the "Italian Jew Benjamin Disraeli", and those among the Liberals admiring "that typical John Bull Sir Herbert Samuel". And Mosley described those who had created disorder at the rally as "razor gangs from the ghettoes subsidised by Moscow gold... the hirelings of Moscow finance" and "dupes of alien interests" who were "carrying weapons never seen before the ghettoes were emptied on these shores."[40]

Just a few days after the Olympia rally, the *Daily Telegraph* reported that Julius Streicher, editor of the leading Nazi paper *Der Stürmer*, had expressed satisfaction that "the Mosley movement has positively defined its attitude towards the Jewish problem."[41] But it apparently took Rothermere a further five weeks to notice anything untoward in Mosley's attitude towards Jews.

In May 1934, a few weeks before the Olympia rally, William Joyce had written in *The Blackshirt* recommending BUF public speakers to read Hitler's *Mein Kampf*. Indeed, Rothermere was already a firm supporter of Hitler. Six months after Hitler became Chancellor, he told his readers how Hitler had saved Germany from its enemy within:

> *"The German nation was rapidly falling under the control of its alien elements. In the last days of the pre-Hitler regime there were 20 times as many Jewish government officials in Germany as had existed before the war. Israelites of international attachments were insinuating themselves into key positions"*[42]

Whatever misgivings he claimed about Mosley's attitudes to Jews, Rothermere maintained his friendship with Adolf Hitler throughout the decade, and could hardly have been unaware of the policies and practices that regime had already enacted towards the Jews.[43] He sent a telegram to the German leader in October 1938 supporting Germany's invasion of the Sudetenland in which he expressed the hope that "Adolf the Great" would become a popular figure in Britain.

At Olympia, the fascists won the physical war but the anti-fascists largely won the propaganda war. Despite the battering Mosley's opponents took, they then found it easier to mobilise in numbers in oppositional activity. The *Daily Worker*, organ of the Communist Party which had played a leading role in the demonstrations both outside and inside Olympia, quipped: "Mosley might have the millionaires but he hasn't the millions, that's clear." The third London rally, due to take place at White City at the beginning of August, in a grand spectacle preceded by boxing matches, was called off. Rethinking his strategy, Mosley prepared instead for an open-air rally in Hyde Park a month later. At that event, nearly 5,000 fascists were outnumbered more than twenty to one by anti-fascists. Press photographs from the event depict the fascists surrounded firstly by a ring of police, and secondly, completely encircled by much deeper rows of opponents who drowned out the fascists' speeches.

With the loss, or at least a fading into the background, of establishment support and a relative upturn in the economic fortunes of the country making it harder for Mosley to make headway on a national basis, the BUF's activities became concentrated on building a belligerent street-level populist movement of agitation and provocation in predominantly working class areas surrounding Jewish populations, in Manchester, Leeds, and most of all in London's East End.

Its strategy and tactics in these districts were executed through public meetings and mass rallies (both indoors and outdoors), marches and demonstrations, public sales of *The Blackshirt*, and distribution of leaflets and pamphlets. Its public rallies were notorious for the brutality of stewards towards any opposition but, from the Jewish community's standpoint, the greatest menace was felt from the BUF's street activities – its open-air meetings and acts of physical intimidation. The *Jewish Chronicle's* special correspondent concisely described the BUF's technique: "intimidate opponents, arouse public excitement, make inflammatory appeals and then intrude the most sensitive areas".

It was a grave setback at such an attempted invasion in October 1936 that began the BUF's decline as a political force. Intending to march through the most sensitive areas of the East End of London, its uniformed columns were blocked at Gardiners Corner in Aldgate and at Cable Street by the opposition of hundreds of thousands of East Enders; eventually the police advised that its planned march be abandoned. A week later, the BUF responded with a night of antisemitic terror in East London in which a Jewish man and child were thrown through a shop window, fifty Jewish shops on the Mile End Road were raided and smashed up, and a car was overturned and set alight. In a separate incident earlier that week, around one hundred young Blackshirts invaded an East End estate populated almost entirely by Jews, and intimidated, abused and assaulted its inhabitants.

Given its emotive appeal, the BUF set great store upon its image. The events of Cable Street severely damaged its confidence and in the following months many leading activists resigned. The action of the Government in passing the Public Order Act, which forbade the wearing of political uniforms and considerably extended police powers, accelerated this decline. In the weeks immediately following the Battle of Cable Street, the BUF claimed to have recruited many new members, but these were overwhelmingly young men temporarily attracted by the prospect of street fights. In the opposite direction, Mosley was shedding politically experienced, ideologically committed members, who had lost faith in his leadership qualities or finally recognised that neither the BUF as a movement, nor its leader, were invincible. Despite upheavals within its membership base, the BUF's antisemitic incitement continued and increased in its malevolence. For a period in 1937, it attempted to hold meetings in streets that were overwhelmingly populated with Jewish people, which ultimately met with banning orders.

One prominent defector, Charles Wegg-Prosser, commented that the BUF's "best propagandists and most dedicated workers have gone leaving only careerists and thugs". Wegg-Prosser had been appointed District Organiser of the BUF's Shoreditch Branch in February 1936, and was one of six carefully selected BUF candidates contesting local council seats in East London in March 1937 – which was effectively Mosley's last throw of the dice in that area. Very soon afterwards Wegg-Prosser, who acknowledged that he had become committed to the movement because he saw it as a dynamic force aiming for "social betterment", came to question the whole enterprise and switched sides.[44]

By 1938 Wegg-Prosser was writing exposés of the BUF for anti-fascist publications, in which he lambasted the internal regime of the BUF as "a movement where discussion is banned and criticism is banned and loyalty to a leader replaces loyalty to a cause."[45] He regarded

Mosley's antisemitism as fundamentally opportunistic:

> "*In 1931 the New Party took part in the General election... where the Whitechapel candidate was a well known Jewish boxer [Ted "Kid" Lewis]* [46] *... to those same streets where now he goes to bring hatred and provocation Mosley then went hat in hand for Jewish votes. In those same Jewish buildings which fascists now daub with 'PJ' slogans,* [47] *Mosley once stood and urged Jewish electors to begin the regeneration of Britain by sending a Jewish Mosleyite to Westminster.*" [48]

The political defeat of the BUF in East London after three years of concentrated efforts was underlined by its failure to win any of the six East London seats in three boroughs that it contested enthusiastically in the local elections of 1937. Wegg-Prosser stood for a Limehouse seat alongside Ann Brock Griggs, described in the BUF publication, *Action*, as "the wife of a well known architect and mother of two charming children". [49] In Bethnal Green the candidates were philosophy graduate and ideologue Alexander Raven-Thomson, and a provocative street orator EG "Mick" Clarke. In Shoreditch, local furniture worker JA "Bill" Bailey was standing with another BUF heavyweight parachuted in, Director of Propaganda and inveterate antisemite, William Joyce.

Having talked up its prospects in *The Blackshirt* – "Great Election Rallies. Mosley Opens the East London Campaign. The March to Victory Begins" – in the end the BUF had to settle for returns ranging from 14.8 per cent to 23 per cent, and did not win any of the seats it contested. *The Blackshirt* blamed its failure on Jewish voters in these constituencies. "Mosley chose deliberately to commence his attack in the strongholds of the Jewish race. The Jew is a wily politician and replied by plumping solidly for Labour candidates whom he considered in those constituencies to be most likely to defeat the

Blackshirt", it reported. The BUF comforted its activists and supporters with the assessment that, "the Englishman does not take readily to new movements".[50]

The BUF's failure in East London and in the country as a whole must also be seen in the context which had contributed to its early potential. Its central policy of corporatism was developed as the response to "the crisis". But although many people experienced very hard times, the truly deep "crisis" was comparatively short-lived, with Britain's economic recovery occurring more rapidly than in other European countries and this was followed by a period of increasing domestic stability. This militated against the success of a party such as the BUF. However, despite its political failures, it was able through intense activity to play a major role in exacerbating the existing level of antisemitism in certain areas and in winning new adherents to antisemitism, particularly among younger people.

Notes

1. Mosley claimed that the BUF had 472 branches just before the General Election of 1935, which the BUF chose not to contest. Its slogan in 1935 was "Fascism, next time". A functioning branch, recognised and supported by the party centrally, would need a minimum of fifty members. It is unclear how many of these branches were still fully functioning in 1935.

2. AK Chesterton, cousin of the prominent English writer and poet GK Chesterton, remained in far-right politics after the war. He established the League of Empire Loyalists in 1954 and was a founder member of the National Front in 1967.

3. The Black and Tans, who were widely condemned for terrorising Ireland's civilian population, were effectively a mercenary force of 8,000 former British soldiers recruited to assist the Royal Irish Constabulary against Irish nationalists and rebels.

4. The Tory candidate, Peter Griffiths bucked the national trend in the 1964 election to pull off an unexpected victory here after a widely condemned campaign in which his supporters used the slogan "If you want a nigger for a neighbour, vote Labour."

5. *Fascist Promise and Fascist Performance*, Labour Research Department, 1934

6. *Sir Oswald Mosley MP replies to Mr Baldwin on Industrial Problems and the Socialists*, ILP, 1929

7. In 1909 the incumbent in this post had been Britain's first Jewish Cabinet Minister, the Liberal Party MP, Herbert Samuel.

8. The sexual politics exemplified by Mosley's emphasis on "manhood" in his New Party phase continued through into the BUF, when he typically dismissed mainstream political parties as "organisations of old women, tea fights and committees." In decrying attacks by these parties on freedom he described the country as "hag-ridden".

9. *Action* was published weekly from 8th October to 31st December 1931, then closed in a rationalisation step before Mosley and close associates embarked on travels to Italy and Germany. In 1936 the BUF launched a monthly publication, also called *Action*.

10. *Action* 8.10.1931

11. *Action* 15.10.1931

12. *Action* 5.11.1931

13. *Action* 26.11.1931

14. *Action* 31.12.1931

[15] *Daily Herald* 20.8.1932

[16] In the same interview Cumming told the *Daily Herald* reporter "We have definitely embraced the fascist philosophy... The young men in our clubs and Young Men's Institutes throughout the country will undoubtedly form the nucleus of 'storm troops'."

[17] See Stephen Dorril, *Blackshirt*, 2006, p203

[18] Cecil Melville, *The Truth About the New Party*, Martin Lawrence, 1931

[19] The British Fascists, originally calling themselves British Fascisti were formed in 1923, as admirers of Mussolini's economic and political programme, though they included racial politics in their platform too. They called for the "purification of the British race" by "restriction of alien immigration" and for excluding from public office "those not of British birth or parentage".

[20] See *Fascists: a Social Psychological View of the National Front*, Academic Press, 1978. This study is based on interviews with middle-rank officials of the National Front, which was formed in 1967.

[21] Individual trade unions, and bodies such as the Labour Research Department and National Labour Council, brought out a series of well researched leaflets and pamphlets providing this information.

[22] *The Blackshirt* No. 1, February 1933

[23] *The Greater Britain*, BUF Publications p26 1932

[24] Lionel Birch, *Why They Join the Fascists*, People's Press, 1936

[25] *East London Pioneer*, January 1937

[26] *Daily Mail* 15.1.1934

[27] *Daily Express* 23.4.1934

[28] *Manchester Guardian* 23.4.1934

[29] *Daily Mail* 14.7.1934

[30] Some had won tickets by sending in spoof letters on "Why I like the Blackshirts", for the competition run by the Rothermere press.

[31] There were 2,000 Blackshirts among the audience and half of them – mostly men but also some women – were acting in a stewarding capacity.

[32] The Union of Democratic Control was created by radical liberals and members of the Independent Labour Party in 1915 as a pacifist organisation seeking democratic control over foreign policy. In the 1930s it turned its attention to exposing fascism.

[33] *Eye witnesses at Olympia*, Union of Democratic Control, 1934

[34] ibid

[35] *Fascists at Olympia,* Ivor Montagu, Gollancz, 1934

[36] ibid

[37] *Eye Witnesses at Olympia*, op. cit

[38] In Joyce's crude pamphlet, Feigenbaum and Goldstein's names appear next to each other, as do Ziff and Kerstein's.

[39] *The Blackshirt* 4.11.1933

[40] *The Blackshirt* 15.6.1936

[41] *Daily Telegraph* 11.6.1934

[42] *Daily Mail* 10.7.1933

[43] In April 1933 Nazi stormtroopers began intimidating shoppers to boycott Jewish businesses, and the Reichstag passed laws to remove Jews from civil service jobs, restrict Jewish lawyers, judges and physicians, and establish a quota system limiting Jewish student participation in schools and universities. From May 1933 the authorities approved public book-burnings of material produced by Jews and others the Nazis saw as their enemies. In September 1933 Jewish writers, musicians, conductors and other artists were stripped of their positions.

[44] Wegg-Prosser became active in the Labour Party in West London after the war, unsuccessfully contesting the Paddington South seat at three general elections. He was also co-founder of Britain's first neighbourhood law centre, in North Kensington in 1969.

[45] For example, he wrote for *Vigilance*, the publication of the Jewish People's Council Against Fascism and Antisemitism. For further discussion of the Jewish People's Council see Chapter 7.

[46] Ted "Kid" Lewis, born Gershon Mendeloff, was a welterweight boxer and bodyguard for Mosley during the New Party period.

[47] PJ stood for "Perish Judah" – this slogan, initially used on the letterhead of a fringe antisemitic group, the Nordic League, became more widespread through activists at street level.

[48] *Vigilance*, Jewish People's Council, September 1938.

[49] Brock Griggs was charmed in turn by Hitler's regime in Germany, reporting May Day in Germany 1936 for *Action*: "All is joy, cheerfulness, good humour and hope for the future of a great race... free to enjoy the traditional festival of May without fear of treachery in their midst."

[50] *The Blackshirt* 6.4.1937

4. Antisemitism and the British Union of Fascists

Within weeks of its inception, the BUF vigorously denied that it was in any way antisemitic and claimed that it was recruiting some Jewish members. It positioned itself as a new political party, proudly subscribing to a fascist ideology whose central notion was the corporate state and opposition to sectional interests within the state. This opposition carried the germ of a threat to many particularistic groups in society, including the Jews. The term "fascist" already carried baggage. Any movement embracing this ideology was suspected of harbouring a dubious position on the Jewish question because of the statements and activities of organisations self-identifying as fascist that predated the BUF, and because of developments in Germany. Mosley moved quickly to dispel any association of his party's ideas with anti-Jewish prejudice. Issue four of *The Blackshirt* carried a front-page article on "Fascism and the Jews", which confronted the issues of antisemitism in Britain and under existing fascist regimes. It praised the "single-mindedness" of Mussolini who, in pursuit of his corporatist project, "avoided conflict with Jews", and pointedly criticised Germany's Nazi government: "The issue of fascism has been obscured in Germany by the irrelevant Jewish question," Mosley explained. "The great case of fascism should not be obscured by sideline or irrelevance."

And yet, by elaborating tendentiously on Germany's context in the same article, he provided more than a hint of justification for Nazi hostility to Jews:

> "...in Germany Jews are conspicuously associated at one extreme with the Communist and Socialist movements, and at the other extreme with international finance. Jews have been associated economically and

86

politically, apart from every consideration of race, with the two main enemies of the fascist movement."

Nevertheless, the article reminded readers that "Jew-baiting in every shape and form was forbidden by order in the British Union of Fascists, before the Union had been in existence two months". It insisted that, "the Jewish question is no issue of fascism".[1] Mosley emphasised this point in personal correspondence with a prominent member of the Jewish community, Lord Melchett, a contemporary from his days at Winchester public school and a fellow enthusiast of Mussolini's corporate state.[2] Mosley wrote to Melchett on 6th January 1933 assuring him that: "antisemitism forms no part of the policy of this organisation and... antisemitic propaganda is forbidden in this organisation."

An editorial in *The Blackshirt* six weeks later returned to the theme, stating its disappointment and annoyance that many Jews had adopted anti-fascist positions. It blamed them for allying with communists in physically attacking BUF members. Nevertheless, the editorial reiterated:

"There is only one menacing danger to Jews in England, and that danger arises from the communist company that many of them keep... Antisemitism is no issue of fascism and is unknown to fascism outside of the Teutonic races. In Germany antisemitism is a symptom, not of fascism, but of Germany."[3]

Sounding a clear warning, or perhaps clearing the ground for battles to come, the editorial concluded: "The future position of their race rests upon the leaders of English Jewry. We have not sought any struggles with them, but we do not shrink from struggles which are forced upon us."

Was the BUF perhaps seeking to goad Jewish leaders and propel them towards an open conflict? If Jews as a whole were being blamed by the BUF for exhibiting carelessness in choosing their friends, and were increasingly typecast as intermeshed with communists whom the BUF had declared their principal enemy, it was a connection Mosley had gratuitously encouraged in his movement's formative period. At a public meeting in the Memorial Hall in Farringdon Street, London, in the very month that the BUF was launched, Mosley ridiculed a group of hecklers before they were violently removed by his Biff Boys. He branded those who had the temerity to disagree with the content of his speech as "three warriors of the class war", adding for good measure, "all from Jerusalem". In March 1933 *The Blackshirt* reported that fascists walking home from a public meeting in Manchester were attacked by a group of political opponents led by "a boy of the bulldog breed from the local ghetto".

Having claimed initially that "antisemitism was no issue of fascism", and was forbidden in their movement, the line began to be subtly modified. Denials of antisemitism became conditional, subject to the qualification that Jews should not act in any way that was inimical to the "national interest" – as defined by the BUF. "Any British citizen, Jew or Gentile who is loyal to Great Britain will get a square deal from us," the party stated. The treatment that would be meted out to Jews who did not conform to the BUF's requirements was initially left vague. Gradually it adopted the position that such dissenting Jews would be treated as aliens and denied substantial civil and political rights. The BUF's newspaper began drawing distinctions between "good" and "bad" Jews, and increasingly associated the latter with all kinds of evil. A *Blackshirt* article in August 1933 castigated "alien drug-traffickers and white slavers who flourish like fat slugs on the decayed body of bourgeois society." For confused or uninitiated readers pondering precisely which group of foreigners these "aliens" referred to, the writer added:

"The emotional persecution of Jews in Germany will not be repeated in fascist Britain, but it is high time that the traffickers in misery, those who have bought and sold the well-being of the nation on the stock exchanges of the world, were brought to book."[4]

Though still preferring to use codewords, the language depicting "bad" Jews became more menacing:

"The unscrupulous monopoly holder, the gambler against British interests, the white slave-trafficker and the wage-slave trafficker are all traitors to Great Britain. Under a fascist government they will pay for their crimes".[5]

In September 1933 *The Blackshirt's* front-page headline declared: "Britain for the British. The Alien Menace." The lead article began:

"A grave alien problem exists in this country. At a time when over 2 million Britons are unemployed, thousands of aliens are enjoying a good living in our midst... While Britons are unemployed not a single alien should be admitted into this country. More than this: while Britons are unemployed, the aliens who now hold jobs should not be permitted to retain them."[6]

The net of enemy aliens widened but Jews topped the list of undesirables. The BUF claimed that "the very lowest types of the modern world", have been "admitted to our shores by Old Gang governments. The foreign Jew, the Polish criminal, the Lascars who displace Britons in their natural element, the sea, will have no place in Britain under fascism. The alien financier who has used the City of London, to finance our competitors abroad and to damage British industry by financial manipulation, will be deported."[7]

Nevertheless the BUF still felt constrained to remind its readers: "The British Union of Fascists is not anti-semitic because antisemitism is not only unfair but also undiscriminating and ineffective. The low type of Jew who has come into this country from abroad and should be sent back... is not by any means the only alien who threatens our standard of living. Also there are good Jews as well as bad Jews."

This article insisted that the latter alone were its real target: "Many Jews have fought for this country, and some of their families, through years and centuries, have proved themselves to be loyal citizens of Britain. Such men have nothing to fear from fascism. On the other hand, the low type of foreign Jew... will be run out of the country in double-quick time under fascism... the better type of Jew, who in the course of years has become very British in outlook, will be very glad to see them go."

Lest anyone think that it was the BUF that was responsible for stirring up animus against the Jews, it added: "these aliens are the people who bring discredit to the Jewish race and arouse feeling against them."[8] The notion that any antisemitism was caused by the Jews themselves would soon become a recurrent theme in speeches by BUF ideologues.[9]

The Blackshirt of 18th November 1933 published an anonymous poem allegedly submitted by a reader. The paper commented: "The policy of the British Union of Fascists towards the Jews cannot be set out more clearly than in the following poem." The poet declares at the outset: "I refuse to condemn a man for his race," and then praises the Jew, "born in this dear old land" who "loves her soil" and "stands for fair play" who are "far more English than they are Jew". But these qualities are eluc-idated essentially to distinguish such fine, welcome specimens from:

"The oily, material, swaggering Jew
The pot-bellied, sneering, money-mad Jew

Who sells his country and soul for gain
Who sweats his fellows, whose life is vain."

The poet concludes: "There are Jews and Jews."

Towards the end of 1933, the BUF was typically blurring the distinctions it had previously emphasised, and it began referring to the Jews as a homogeneous body by using the umbrella term, "Jewry". When several Jewish organisations combined to promote a boycott of goods from Nazi Germany, the BUF demanded that:

> *"Jewry in England must decide whether its members are of British nationality or not and must acquaint the world with its decision. If Jewry in Britain is British and places the interests of Britain first, then it is utterly unjustified in interfering with the internal affairs of Germany by declaring a boycott of German goods."*[10]

The BUF seized on this boycott movement to show how Jews were acting counter to the "national interest". It argued that boycott, in defence of perceived Jewish interests, caused unemployment, especially in Lancashire:

> *"Germany can pay for Lancashire goods only through exports, and this is not the moment when Lancashire can find other markets. Nor will they be found for her by her government, bound as it is in the shackles of Jewish international finance... Jews expect to satisfy their hatred of Germany at the expense of 30,000 Lancashire workers."*[11]

Especially in the early months of the movement, the BUF promoted fascist Italy as a shining example of a government that advanced nationalism and promoted the corporate state, without displaying a negative attitude to Jews. It compared Italy's government under Mussolini favourably with Nazi Germany, which was much more fixated on the Jews. Towards the end of 1933, however, convincing themselves and seeking to convince others that Jews were organising as a separate and antagonistic "racial interest", the BUF banned Jews from membership of the party (though they had hardly been queuing in droves to join). In May 1934, William Joyce, an ardent antisemite, well placed within the BUF's propaganda directorate, encouraged the party's public speakers to acquaint themselves with three key books: James Drennan's *BUF, Oswald Mosley and British Fascism*, which had just been published; Mussolini's 1928 autobiography, *La Mia Vita*; "and Hitler's *My Struggle*, better known through its German title, *Mein Kampf*', adding: "The latter work is of remarkable interest to speakers who will find that Adolf Hitler has a shrewd appreciation of their problems." For Hitler the greatest "problem", overshadowing any others, was that of the Jews.

During 1934, as the BUF intensified its public activities through meetings and rallies, so the opposition to it grew. The BUF initially described its opponents as "reds" or "communists", and it berated individuals "from the ghetto" for associating with the communists. Through 1934, BUF speakers and newspaper comment increasingly portrayed "reds" or "communists" as tools of Jewish interests. Aware of the depth of opposition by the Communist Party through its mass leafleting campaigns and its newspaper, the *Daily Worker*, the BUF began to speculate about who might be footing the propaganda bill. It asked: "Who pays, Moscow, Jews, or both?"

The BUF began to list names in its newspaper of those convicted of and sentenced for attacks on Blackshirts. One list published in *The Blackshirt* in June 1934, contained seven names, six of which were recognisably Jewish. Triumphant reports in *The Blackshirt* of a Mosley rally in Manchester in early October 1934, against which political opponents forcefully demonstrated, carried the headline: "Alien Yiddish finance is ruining British industry". Mosley's most powerful statements railing against "international finance" and its capacity for controlling Britain were picked out in bold type in *The Blackshirt*'s report of the meeting, such as:

> *"The organised corruption of press, cinema and parliament, which is called democracy, but is ruled by alien Jewish finance – the same finance which has hired alien mobs to yell here tonight."[12]*

The growing tendency of the fascists to attribute immense power to Jews and impute a conspiratorial method was evident in a further meeting addressed by Mosley in Manchester in November 1934, in which he accused "Jewish international finance" of "exploiting Oriental labour to destroy Lancashire for the profit of the City of London".

In this same speech he berated the "force which is served by the Conservative Party, the Liberal Party and the Socialist Party alike, the force that has dominated Britain *ever since the war*, the force of international Jewish finance" (my emphasis). This was a very revealing statement given that, just months before, he had argued that Jews had nothing to fear from fascism if they supported "British" rather than "Jewish" interests. Clearly he deemed them incapable of doing this since they were already locked into a longstanding process in which they continued to serve their own narrow "racial" interests.

Mosley followed his Manchester rally with large meetings in Burnley, Accrington and Bury, appealing especially to unemployed workers. He told them:

> *"As long as you tolerate the organised forces of financial Jewry operating from the City of London against the country of its adoption then you will continue to see... the Indian being sweated in the mills of Bombay and Madras in order that you can line up in the unemployment queues in Burnley."[13]*

Concerned, though, to maintain a cross-class appeal and not appear purely as a champion of workers' interests in the North West, he acknowledged that: "The owner occupier firm, the small shopkeeper and the individual industrialists enrich the nation by their activities as well as themselves." He reassured local entrepreneurs: "We are not against private enterprise or private capital. The capital we are up against is the great accumulation of wealth in a very few hands, usually alien, employed not to develop the nation but to hold it to ransom."

In March 1935 *The Blackshirt* left readers in little doubt about which particular minority group it was fingering when it described the financial power of the City of London, "demanding its pound of flesh with all the severity and vengeance of Shylock."[14] At a major public meeting at the Albert Hall that month, Mosley propelled his party's policy on the Jews one step further when he declared that the Jew must "put Britain first or be deported". He described Jews as:

"The nameless, homeless and all-powerful force which stretches its greedy fingers from the shelter of England to throttle the trade and menace the peace of the West... grasping the puppets of Westminster, dominating every party of the state".[15]

His proclamation that international Jewish finance was "the enemy which fascism alone dares to challenge" was greeted with enthusiastic and prolonged applause. A throwaway comment in the same speech seemed to confirm that, despite frequent denials, antisemitism had formed part of Mosley's worldview from his party's very inception: "We know the enemy and we know what we are up against. *We knew it when we began this battle.*" (My emphasis.)

The elements among Jewry that Mosley charged with acting against the national interest were those engaged in non-productive international finance and those sup-

94

porting international political movements embodied *par excellence* by the Communist Party. Mosley previously attacked both of these elements whilst simultaneously denying that he harboured antisemitic attitudes. Fascism, he argued, opposed both finance capital and communism. As the movement developed, though, it increasingly identified Jews as the origins of both, and began to associate these contrary elements together within a conspiratorial framework. Rather than representing "disloyal" elements within Jewry they came to be seen as representing Jewry itself as a single, integrated, corporate group. In the BUF scheme, it eventually became impossible for Jews as a whole to be other than an utterly alien element, necessarily seeking to undermine fascism and the British "national interest".

The Blackshirt continued to portray the BUF as the victim of unwarranted Jewish attentions and claimed it was retaliating in self-defence. But its rationalisations for its responses became more inflected with the biological themes that typified Nazi antisemitism. In May 1935 the paper declared: "Jewry attacked us; we have retaliated, and shall continue to retaliate until this *pestilence* is at an end" (my emphasis).[16] In his column the following month, Cuthbert Reaveley characterised the Jews as wholly alien and destructive: "Like some evil cancer he eats his way into the trade unions and governing organisations alike." He railed against "the repugnant odour of the Izzies and the Ikes" and concluded that "the dead weight of Jewry lies inert upon our land, like some monstrous stone."[17] What solution did they have for this pestilence, this cancer? William Joyce spelt it out to hundreds of BUF supporters at an open air meeting in Stoke Newington, North London in the summer of 1936: "We pledge ourselves to rid the country of the Jews" adding, "Karl Marx said 'Workers of the world unite. You have nothing to lose but your chains.' Workers of Britain you have nothing to lose but your Jews."[18]

The ideological armoury mobilised against the Jewish community comprised many elements. The chief target was "international Jewish finance" as this was the key to a host of more specific accusations: that five Jewish firms determined the price of gold; that the Bank of England was under Jewish influence; that the British Chamber of Commerce was "Jew ridden"; and that the press and big business were victims of organised Jewish blackmail. Some rival fascist groups asserted that the press was directly under Jewish control, but this claim was easily refutable by empirical evidence, so the BUF postulated a more complex relationship, whereby Jews did not own the press but controlled it by threatening to boycott advertising unless newspapers promoted "Jewish interests". This was powerful, precisely because it could not be simply disproved. Its refutation rested purely on denial by the press controllers. And by suggesting that Jewish financial machinations were so significant that their absence would have serious consequences, it reinforced mythical notions about the nature and extent of Jewish financial power. When Lord Rothermere publicly fell out of love with the BUF, Mosley claimed that he had done so under duress – that he had been pressured by Jews who had threatened to implement a boycott of advertising in the *Daily Mail*. However, given Rothermere's open admiration for Hitler, he was unlikely to have remained silent on this matter if it really was the case.

"International finance" could also account for the Jewish community's alleged political power. The BUF denounced mainstream political parties as "the parties of organised Jewry". Fascists did not need to show a large, overt representation of Jewish MPs in order to assert that the political parties served Jewish interests. The principal issue on which the BUF claimed that Jews controlled the British political establishment was foreign policy towards Nazi Germany. "Shall Jews drag Britain to war?" asked *The Blackshirt* in November 1933. The BUF later popularised the slogan, "We will not fight in a

Jewish quarrel". In 1938, Mosley claimed that the Labour Party was attempting to drag Britain to war "at the instigation of its master – International Jewish Finance".

The core of the BUF's ideological attack was indirect. It charged Jews with exerting a powerful and negative influence over society, and could link it to very specific issues, as was demonstrated particularly by BUF activity in northern industrial towns. Speaking in Ashton-under-Lyne in 1935, Mosley declared: "The international Jew sits in London and ruins Lancashire," while in Leeds he concentrated his attacks on alleged Jewish control of the British wool and furniture trades.

On a grander scale, the BUF accused Jews of owning the Empire, often coupling this accusation with the charge that Jews had not fought for it. This appealed to a notion of reclamation that the BUF used extensively in local propaganda. It identified assets which, it asserted, had once been "English property" but had fallen into the hands of Jews, who then maintained an exclusive stranglehold upon them. A BUF pamphlet claimed:

> "Not so long ago East London was the home of British stock. The cabinet-maker, polisher and tailor were Englishmen. Today the Englishman in East London is the slave of the Jewish master."[19]

Whilst the Englishman fought in the war, the Jew, said the BUF, was stealthily profiteering, poaching jobs and acquiring property. This indirect attack upon a barely visible enemy could be potent. It erects an absolutely flexible and logically irrefutable system capable of explaining all cases. As the demonstration of objective reality undermines successive layers of the argument, so the explanatory key, the hidden hand, becomes even more elusive and thus even more powerful. It constitutes a comprehensive and consistent view of social reality. Its weakness, however, is that, though it is difficult to negate, it is equally hard to prove. After Mosley made his initial allegations against "Jewish finance", Jewish community leaders called his bluff and publicly demanded that Mosley "name the names" – he ducked this challenge.

By 1937, though, the BUF had lost any inhibitions. The party initiated a campaign of gross personal slander against individual well-known Jews. It associated genuine social evils, such as racketeering and slum landlordism, with particular Jewish names, and then sought to accuse Jews in general of being responsible for them. It might have been plausible to believe in the controlling force of a hidden group, but this could not satisfy the demands and the experience of the demographic entity the BUF was mobilising most enthusiastically. East London, where the campaign was concentrated, was overwhelmingly a working class area. The Jews who lived there alongside non-Jews were patently not international financiers but ordinary workers who lacked political or economic power. Many lined the streets in the same queues for the Labour Exchange as non-Jews. There were, however, a number of Jewish employers, particularly in the clothing and furniture trade, and the BUF lost no opportunity to accuse them of victimising fascists or to reproach them with a range of disreputable business practices, usually undercutting prices to ruin non-Jewish rivals and sweating their employees.[20]

Jewish workers were accused of "crowding" occupations and of excluding "native Britons", as the BUF targeted its appeals to workers in industries where high proportions of Jews worked. Writing on the furniture trades in the BUF's local monthly broadsheet *East London Pioneer (ELP)* , Henry Gibbs claimed that

> *"...during the past 10 years Jews have obtained a monopoly of the businesses in East London. Unless the workers accept the terms offered then they get no job... (and) ...the labour of relatives of the Jewish bosses from Germany – the cheapest labour in*

London today – is used as a weapon to force down the wages to the lowest possible level."[21]

Gibbs penned further pieces for *ELP* making similar claims about the tailoring industry. In 1938, Mosley championed the cause of "English-born taxi-drivers" against what he described as their "alien competitors".[22]

The principal political allegation that the fascists levelled against working class Jews was that they were communists. The BUF portrayed them as serving another country's government (the USSR) as well as subscribing to an ideology motivated purely in the interests of one class rather than in the national interest. Overall, however, the BUF gave more prominence to the physical rather than the political activity of working class Jews, repeatedly accusing them of "declaring war on fascism". It made constant references to "Jewish razor gangs" and produced statistics to demonstrate that Jews were the principal offenders among those convicted for assaults on fascists. The images of Jewish savagery that were conjured up, were frequently accompanied by crude sexual innuendo and accusations that Jews exploited sexual vice. At Bethnal Green, in August 1936, a popular local BUF street corner speaker, "Mick" Clarke, urged the crowd to take up the struggle against Jews and communists, otherwise, he warned, they would witness their "churches pulled down", their "children's eyes torn out and nuns carried through the street and raped".

The BUF's broad ideological onslaught assailed the widest and most diverse elements in Jewish society. Through a calculated strategy of stereotyping and scapegoating, it extended its attack to ever increasing numbers of Jews. Nevertheless, the BUF persisted in claiming that opposition to Jews was a political response to their activities and not to their existence; that it "does not attack Jews by reason of what they are but by reason of what they do". It accused Jews of constituting a foreign body that had organised itself as a racial interest group. This implied a response to acts of will rather than a response based on the pseudo-scientific biological determinism that characterised Nazi-style racial ideology. But, particularly in the most intensive period of antisemitic agitation during 1936-37, and especially through street-corner meetings at which their speakers addressed large crowds, use of racial language became more common, even if the BUF's racial ideology lacked coherence.

The party's initial statements of hostility against Jews, denoting them as "alien", owed more to geography than biology, but this came to be elaborated in terms of an "alien type". At first, BUF speakers were rather coy about using the word "Jew", and they frequently substituted "Eastern", "Levantine" and most commonly "Oriental". It was necessary, argued BUF speakers to "purge from our lifeblood the Oriental element". But "Oriental" indicated more than a cultural phenomenon. In claiming that "an Oriental merchant can sentence a British man or woman to starvation", they stated that Jewish finance had "no sense of kinship with Western peoples". A popular BUF speaker at open-air meetings in Stoke Newington in 1936, called Pipkin, was fond of declaring that: "those who oppose fascism are not of our flesh and blood". In a further speech he railed against "aliens who have no British blood in them who are receiving the hospitality of Britain". Such "aliens", though, would surely have been hard-pressed to recognise attitudes like his as fine examples of British "hospitality". Pipkin's "flesh and blood" theme was appropriated in July that year by the BUF's leading propaganda officer, Raven-Thomson, and his fellow street corner demagogues, at a series of open-air meetings in the East End, shortly after they announced that they would be contesting seats in the district at the next local elections. The speakers saluted their audiences: "You English are blood of our blood, flesh of our flesh", and warned: "The gloves must be taken off – it is gentiles v Jews, white man v black man".[23] In late 1936 it became increasingly common for BUF speakers to refer to

100

their audience as (superior) "white men". William Joyce emphasised the racial categorisation of Jews as non-white when he warned that "a dirty negroid Jewish culture is sweeping over the whole country".[24]

BUF speakers at Duckett Street, Limehouse, in the summer of 1936, sought to dehumanise Jews by labelling them "rats and vermin from the gutters of Whitechapel", borrowing phraseology popularised in Nazi Germany. At a street meeting in Bethnal Green, William Joyce declared: "Jews are Oriental sub-men... an incredible species of sub-humanity... a type of sub-human creature". It was in the more salubrious surroundings of Hampstead Town Hall that Joyce described Jews more graphically as "crawling vermin" and "simians with prehensile toes". He wasn't praising their agility.[25] If rank and file members of the BUF had trouble keeping up with precisely which animal the Jews were most akin to, and whether they possessed two, four or six legs, they would have been further confused by a BUF speaker called Perrin addressing a meeting of 250 supporters in September 1936, when he ventured that politicians were "all under the control of Jewish finance – a giant octopus which is gradually extending its tentacles all over the British Empire and squeezing the last drops of blood of the British people".

When the BUF expanded its name to "The British Union of Fascists and National Socialists" in early 1936, this marked a significant shift away from Mussolini's template towards embracing the Nazi model of the "modern movement", and revealed its increased kinship with Hitlerian modes of thought. From 1936, Nazi conceptions of the nature of the "Jewish problem" became more dominant within the BUF. But to assume an inexorable logic towards a more pronounced racial ideology would be to underestimate the differing nature and levels of adherence to antisemitism within the organisation as a whole.

Historians continue to debate the development of antisemitism in BUF ideology and Mosley's personal beliefs about Jews. Charles Wegg-Prosser, the defector from the fascist movement who was referred to earlier, highlighted these contradictions.[26] He believed that antisemitism was a tool of convenience in Mosley's hands, utilised very cautiously at first, and only after previous "crusades" had fallen flat. He recalled that, at the same time that Mosley was introducing antisemitism into his public meetings, at private gatherings he would admit that he had Jewish friends whose abilities he greatly admired. Wegg-Prosser also described "Mick" Clarke – who justifiably earned his reputation as one of the most crudely antisemitic street speakers in London's East End – as "another man who has not always avoided Jewish company".

Roger Corbet joined the BUF in 1936 at the age of 18 and became the Deputy District Leader in Birmingham. When he defected in 1938 he reflected on how he and others had been persuaded to adopt an antisemitic outlook:

> *"Six months ago I was speaking and feeling heatedly about Britain's Jewish question. Today, looking upon it with a mind unbiased and unfed by the fires of false propaganda I know that the problem is largely the figment of twisted minds. The danger is that young men and women who enter the movement... are constantly in contact with anti-Jewish sentiments. The vast majority that join feel neither one way nor the other in response to the Jews but sooner or later the constantly hammered statements of their leaders are taken without question and an antisemitic philosophy is developed. So long as they remain in the fascist ranks it stays. As soon as they leave it and think for themselves, it vanishes."*[27]

There is agreement that, at the outset, the BUF was not overtly antisemitic, though it certainly contained antisemites among its early recruits. Some of them had previously been members of other organisations such as the Imperial Fascist League or the British Fascisti, for whom antisemitism was already part of the ideological armoury. And Mosley knew what kind of views these individuals held with regard to Jews when he recruited them. The novelist Nicholas Mosley has claimed that his father, Sir Oswald, had wanted to introduce a challenge to "international Jewish bankers" into the programme of the New Party when it launched itself in 1931 but was dissuaded by his close collaborator at the time, Harold Nicholson.[28]

The overt oppositional politics of the New Party and then the BUF stressed anti-communism from the beginning. Several historians view the shift in emphasis from anti-communism to antisemitism as primarily opportunistic. It was, they say, an instrumental act of a desperate movement seeking greater working class support. They argue that, rather than elaborating a racial ideology, the BUF exploited political racialism in a strategic and tactical manner to recover and increase its support. A more complex view sees antisemitism as being progressively incorporated into an existing ideology that was fundamentally anti-democratic and, despite Mosley's enthusiasm for science and technology and his often stated desire for dynamic progress, actually ambivalent about modernity. This analysis argues that it was a small ideological step for this movement to identify Jews as the "modern menace" that threatened humanity's wellbeing and progress. The existence of convinced antisemites among Mosley's inner core would have facilitated this process. In this view, the genesis and extension of antisemitism in the BUF owes more to the party's internal logic than to its external dynamics. Certainly, in the latter half of the 1930s, convinced *racial* antisemites were comfortably entrenched within the BUF's apparatus.

In his speech at the Albert Hall in October 1934, which the BUF itself portrayed as a watershed in terms of the movement identifying and facing up to its principal

enemy, Mosley argued that: "Every great organ for edu-
cating the public mind, for developing the thought of the
future, for moulding the minds and the spirit of coming
generations... is in this alien grip today." The headlines
in *The Blackshirt's* report of this rally denounced "The
Folly of Jewry", and declared: "They have challenged the
spirit of the modern age." According to the paper, this
meeting "marked the commencement of a new battle in
British history in which the forces are arrayed – on the
one hand the cleansing spirit of Fascism, and on the
other, organised Jewry representing an unclean, alien
influence in our national and imperial life."[29]

Mosley himself usually took great care not to descend
to crude racial abuse in his own speeches, preferring to
lambast what he saw as Jewish political and economic
power and influence. But he made no attempts to prevent
the vilest racial slurs being made on BUF platforms and
through the pages of its newspaper and other publications. Another defector from the movement – the former
senior propaganda officer AC Miles who left in early 1936
– has provided evidence that Mosley certainly had the
power to do so.[30]

The whole language of "cleansing" and fighting a "spir-
itual" battle was an invitation to Mosley's supporters to
embrace the racial philosophy of antisemitism and
embark on a total war against everything Jewish. In the
peak period of the BUF's agitation against Jews from
1934-37, its members and supporters reflected the different levels of assent to this worldview. The movement
comfortably embraced those whose antisemitic impulses
were confined to petty economic and political grievances
against certain individual Jews, all the way through to
those who saw themselves in a metaphysical battle for
the destruction of the Jewish spirit and ultimately the
destruction of the Jewish people. As the movement
declined at the end of the decade, its antisemitic influ-
ences at both a philosophical and practical level, however,
found a new lease of life outside the narrow internal

world of the party itself, as Jewish refugees arrived fleeing from Nazism.

The Anti-Alien Campaign

In June 1938, billboards advertising the *Sunday Express*
were adorned with the bald headline, "The Jews", referring to a forthcoming article about the position of the
Jews in Nazi Germany. This article speculated that antisemitism had grown there because German Jews had
become too prosperous, and it generally furnished a sympathetic case towards the anti-Jewish measures that the
Nazis had taken. The focus then shifted back to England
where, it was claimed, "half a million Jews find their
home", adding that, "Just now there is a big influx of foreign Jews into Britain... They are over-running the
country".[31] This was how the "aliens scare" was initiated.

Other local and national newspapers soon followed the
lead taken by the *Sunday Express* in highlighting these
concerns. The *Hampstead Advertiser* claimed that "The
police are becoming more and more concerned about Jews
who are smuggled into the country without passports who
set themselves up in business... from the sale of dope." The
Sunday Pictorial expanded upon this allegation.

In the same issue as the *Evening Standard* reported
with opprobrium an anti-Jewish demonstration in Berlin
against an influx of Austrian Jewish refugees, and their
characterisation in the Nazi press as "drug traffickers,
foreign exchange smugglers, money forgers, gamblers
and similar scoundrels", its respected regular columnist
George Malcolm Thomson wrote: "It is felt by many
people that we hear too much about the troubles of the
Jews in Germany". He described them as "neither quite a
nation nor quite a religion. They are an anomaly... an
undigested particle which causes disorder... they are of
Oriental origin, yet having lived for long in Europe they
claim to be treated as Western people and usually the
claim succeeds."[32]

Thomson went on to assert that: "There is the belief that Jews possess a great and occult power. And certainly the Jews must bear some of the responsibility for keeping this belief alive." He added that they maintain "an international organisation. And they are quick to use their influence over opinion, their power over money to help their fellow Jews". Cutting to the chase on the refugee question, he bemoaned "the stream of Jewish doctors and professional men who pour into Britain", and warned that, "if we get overloaded with Jews there may be a reaction against them."[33]

106

The *Evening Standard* blew hot and cold on this issue. An editorial two weeks later displayed genuine concern for the refugees' plight urging that "Britain must take her share of giving them haven", while simultaneously regretting that, "Alas, already a crowd is gathered there – of our own people, one million seven hundred thousand unemployed. Our first duty must be to our British dispossessed." The following week, though, the former Liberal MP Sir John Hope Simpson was given space by the paper for a feature entitled "Open the Gates" which argued that, "if Great Britain were yet to announce that she were willing to accept one hundred thousand... she would set a worthy example which other nations, including the dominions, could scarcely fail to follow."[34]

However, in many newspapers a malicious press campaign continued over many months. Towards the end of the decade, the dominant theme was employment. Developing another argument popularised by Oswald Mosley, the *Sunday Express* claimed that "aliens who can hardly speak English are now driving London taxicabs and forcing British drivers off the streets". The *Sunday Pictorial* carried a headline that seemed designed to inflame tensions: "Refugees get jobs, Britons get dole."

The impact of the campaign was illustrated in a case involving three "aliens" charged with illegal entry. Magistrate Herbert Metcalfe who, since 1932, had dealt with many cases arising out of disturbances between fascists and Jews, sentenced the three people to six months' hard labour with a recommendation for deportation. He declared, "The way Jews from Germany are pouring in from every port in the country is fast becoming an outrage." His statement was prominently reported in the *Evening Standard*, whose billboards announced: "Alien Jews pouring in – magistrate." Metcalfe later apologised for his remarks. He claimed they were intended as a general statement on aliens, rather than being specifically targeted at Jews – though that hardly makes them more palatable. He added that he believed Jewish refugees should be granted entry, given "proper safeguards and reasonable numbers". The immediate consequence of the campaign, though, was a sharp rise in antisemitic incidents. A Jewish cemetery in Miles Platting in Manchester was desecrated with large chalked slogans: "We will not have Austria's Jews" and "2,000,000 unemployed, 1,000,000 foreign Jews".

The BUF attempted to exploit the "Jew consciousness" that the anti-alien campaign had engendered, but by this time it had significantly declined as an organisation and the fascist aspects of its ideology had been largely discredited. So it was more a case of the media exploiting the arguments made by the BUF rather than vice versa. The BUF's sustained efforts had left a strong imprint of antisemitism. Many charges that the BUF made against Jews were consolidated through this anti-alien campaign. The BUF's persistent allegations of discreditable business practices provided a useful platform on which to build the notion of Jews' involvement in a "racket". Further accusations referred to notions of exclusion and reclamation, which had been prominent in BUF propaganda. When challenged by the *Jewish Chronicle* on the necessity for such extensive and negative coverage of Jewish refugees, the editor of the *Sunday Pictorial* insisted that there was, indeed, a "Jewish question" in Britain. The nature of this question was reduced to the conflict of resources between "Jews" and "Britons" which he clearly saw as exclusive categories. Jews, both alien and resident, were treated as an integral whole that was looked upon with, at best, suspicion and, at worst, open hostility. The organised antisemitic movement suffered setbacks from late 1936 and early 1937 but that did not prevent a populist antisemitism from crystallising.

Notes
[1] *The Blackshirt* 1.4.1933
[2] The friendship between the prominent Jew Lord Melchett and Sir Oswald Mosley continued into the next generation.

Their children, Julian and Nicholas, were close school friends at Eton. Melchett's father, German-born Alfred Mond, was similarly enamoured of the corporate state. He told the *Daily Herald* on 12th May 1928, "I admire fascism because it is successful in bringing about social peace," a statement that he may have regretted had he lived beyond 1930.

3   *The Blackshirt* 16.5.1933
4   *The Blackshirt* 5.8.1933
5   *The Blackshirt* 16.9.1933
6   *The Blackshirt* 30.9.1933
7   ibid
8   ibid
9   At an Albert Hall rally on 22nd March 1936 Mosley proclaimed: "Even Hitler was not antisemitic until he saw a Jew".
10 *The Blackshirt* 18.11.1933
11 *The Blackshirt* 17.8.1934
12 *The Blackshirt* 5.10.1934
13 *The Blackshirt* 18.1.1935
14 *The Blackshirt* 22.3.1935
15 *The Blackshirt* 29.3.1935
16 *The Blackshirt* 24.5.1935
17 *The Blackshirt* 14.6.1935
18 *Jewish Chronicle* 6.7.1936
19 *The British Union and the Jews*, EG Clarke, Abbey, 1937
20 In the "sweated" trades, workers laboured very long hours in poor conditions for low pay. The BUF blamed Jews for introducing sweated trades to East London, despite the fact that these trades had pre-dated mass Jewish immigration to the area.
21 *East London Pioneer* 5.12.1936
22 *Jewish Chronicle* 3.6.1938
23 *Jewish Chronicle* 31.7.1936
24 *Jewish Chronicle* 31.7.1936
25 *Jewish Chronicle*, 6.11.1936
26 See pages 80-81
27 *The BUF by the BUF*, Anchor Press, 1939
28 Nicholson edited the New Party newspaper, *Action*. He abandoned Mosley when the New Party became the British Union of Fascists, and was elected as a Labour MP in 1935.
29 *The Blackshirt* 2.11.1934
30 Miles wrote a pamphlet, *Mosley in Motley*, in which he records how Mosley refused to publish a thoroughly researched article on the multinational Unilever company. Despite the BUF's opposition to "international finance", Mosley told Miles: "We

cannot afford to alienate our friends." Miles claims that every article in *The Blackshirt* was personally approved by two BUF leaders, one of whom was Mosley.

[31] *Jewish Chronicle,* 24.6.1938

[32] This echoed an argument popularised by Mosley in his book, *Tomorrow We Live*, published that same year. He wrote: "the Jew is more remote from British character than any German or Frenchman, for they are Westerners and the Jews are Orientals".

[33] *Evening Standard* 21.6.1938

[34] *Evening Standard* 15.7.1936

5. How Jewish leaders perceived the threat

Antisemitism has not been a constant feature of Jewish history. Jewish life has included many periods of relative calm, peace and creativity. Many different Jewish communities, though, have experienced antisemitism at least as a frequent irritant and at worst a recurring nightmare. It has been composed of many elements and found different forms of expression – political, social, economic, cultural and religious. But in understanding and analysing antisemitism in a particular period and location, it is necessary to focus on how it is reproduced within that specific context. Each of the elements of antisemitism outlined above was undoubtedly present to different degrees in Britain in the 1930s. Britain's Jewish communal leaders initially chose to explain any hostility the community faced primarily in terms of relatively insignificant cultural and religious misunderstandings, but this narrow and complacent approach was challenged as the community became increasingly aware of an intensifying and many-sided threat.

The communal leaders' conceptions of antisemitism were inseparably linked with a set of beliefs about British society, which they felt certain would set firm limits on the potential of antisemitism to take root within the country. For that reason, Jewish leaders labelled the political version of antisemitism that was promoted by a fascist party, Mosley's BUF, as an imported ideology rather than one possessing domestic roots. The BUF failed to win a single parliamentary seat, let alone any greater political power, but its ideas had influence and won enthusiastic backing from very large crowds at indoor and outdoor rallies. It failed, but not because of British society's intolerance of antisemitism.

Nevertheless, Jewish leaders clung doggedly to comforting interpretations that would reinforce their beliefs about British society. Their analysis undoubtedly reflected their generous evaluation of Britain as an overwhelmingly tolerant country that had little time and patience for "extreme" ideologies. It was equally revealing, though, of their own notions about the prescribed position and participation of the Jewish community within British society.

Leaders of Britain's Jews and the mainstream Jewish press generally regarded antisemitism as an alien phenomenon, confined mainly to other European nations. It was rooted, they believed, in historical religious rivalry in Christendom. This view was consistent with a self-image of Jews as a *religiously* defined minority. They recognised that antisemitism could be intensified within a context of economic distress, but did not believe that its origins or prevalence were particularly closely related to economic conflict. When Hitler grabbed political power in Germany on an openly antisemitic platform, it was necessarily viewed as a political phenomenon too, but it was seen as a political instrument in the hands of malign individuals rather than representing a political ideology and philosophy in itself. This dovetailed with Jewish leaders' perceptions about the social roots of antisemitism and the constitution of antisemitic individuals, whom it characterised as ill-balanced, victims of ignorance, or people motivated by irrational hatred. An antisemitic group active in Liverpool in 1933 was typically dismissed by the *Jewish Chronicle* as "amateur Nazis – made in Germany" and "imitators among unstable individuals". The *JC* was not surprised that the "rabid incitements of Nazis... should go to the heads of ill-informed and ill-balanced individuals."[1]

The spread of anti-Jewish hatred was frequently likened to a disease or virus; an analogy that invited scientific enquiry but which ruled out any rigorous social scientific analysis that might locate antisemitism as a phenomenon

rooted in social, political, economic and cultural relationships in the societies in which it was emerging and
growing. An editorial in the *JC* in September 1932
described antisemitism as "a persistent moral and mental
disease", and this portrayal was granted added legitimacy
through similar characterisations by leading clergy and
politicians. The *JC* praised the Bishop of Chichester for
labelling antisemitism "a poison... a contagious disease
spreading to countries where a few years ago it would
never have been dreamt of".

The corollary was that, in the very cases where anti-
Jewish agitation seemed to possess a more "rational"
basis, where conflicts for scarce resources had become
racialised in the minds of those struggling for those
resources, Jewish leaders insisted this had nothing to do
with real antisemitism. For instance, the agitation
against Jewish immigrants in the East End at the turn of
the century, which culminated in the Aliens Act of 1905,
was characterised as "anti-alien" in essence rather than
being specifically antisemitic. Writing in 1939 the leader
of the Board of Deputies, Neville Laski, claimed that,
since 1858, when Jews were finally permitted to stand for
Parliament, there had been no "Jewish problem" in
England: "the great influx of Jews from Russia and
Poland in the last decade of the nineteenth century
caused some outcry and led to certain restrictive legislation. But, strictly speaking, this was an alien and no
Jewish problem. Jews who already possessed civic rights
in this country were not affected", he said.[2]

Consciously or not, he was in denial. Whilst the word
"Jew" was absent from the legislation, Jews formed the
vast bulk of the "aliens" category against whom the legislation was enacted. In 1902, the Bishop of Stepney, Cosmo
Gordon Lang (later Archbishop of York, then of
Canterbury), had accused Jews of "swamping whole areas
once populated by English people".[3] The leading anti-alien
agitator of the time, Arnold White, made no bones about
his social prejudice against Jews. He blamed immigrant

Jews in particular for the "white slave" trade and living off the earnings of prostitutes, as well as harbouring a radical political threat to the realm and endangering its health. White railed against "the colonisation of our great towns by diseased aliens".[4]

The Conservative leader, Arthur James Balfour, revered subsequently by many Jews with pro-Zionist sympathies for his efforts to secure a Jewish homeland in Palestine, steered the Aliens Act through Parliament. His fervent desire for Jews to be securely concentrated in a national state far from Britain's shores was not quite as benevolent as his later admirers imagine. In agitating for immigration controls on Jews coming to Britain, he claimed that Jews were not "to the advantage of the civilisation of this country... they are a people apart and not only had a religion differing from the vast majority of their fellow countrymen but only intermarry amongst themselves".[5]

The Aliens Act drastically reduced the numbers of Jews seeking economic betterment in Britain who were permitted to enter; it also prevented greater numbers of asylum-seekers, escaping harrowing persecution, from finding refuge. In 1906, more than 500 Jewish refugees were granted political asylum. In 1908 the figure had fallen to twenty and by 1910, just five. During the same period, 1,378 Jews, who had been permitted to enter as immigrants but were found to be living on the streets without any visible means of support, had been rounded up and deported back to their country of origin.

The respected political scientist and historian Alfred Zimmern, a contemporary critic of the Act, stated: "it is true that it does not specify Jews by name and that it is claimed that others besides Jews will be affected by the Act, but that is only a pretence".[6] It was the East End, with its overwhelmingly Jewish immigrant areas, that agitators chose for particularly scornful reproach and condemnation. The Aliens Act was followed by further legislation in 1914 and 1919 strengthening and extending

114

its provisions. In the debate on the latter, Sir Ernest Wild, Conservative MP for Upton in West Ham, said: "Anyone who wants to realise what the peril really is has only to walk... in the East End of London. They will find these places literally infested with aliens."[7]

Organised antisemitism in Britain, then, was not a pathological phenomenon but a dynamic political development that built upon and exploited genuine social and economic conflicts and, by the 1930s, a widespread disaffection with the solutions offered by the conventional political parties. The analysis of antisemitism and the accompanying belief in the particularly liberal and tolerant nature of British society, held by Jewish communal leaders, militated against even acknowledging the existence of this development. Antisemitic fascism was considered an imported ideology, and fascism *per se* was seen to have no logical connection with antisemitism, so that if fascist platforms were used for antisemitic propaganda, then "Jewish defence" was conceived as resisting only their antisemitism, not their fascism. Fascism was viewed as a political issue for Jews as individual citizens only, not as Jews.

As the BUF's policy became more overtly antisemitic, Jewish communal leaders and opinion-formers increasingly described it as a force "alien to British politics". At the point when the BUF's elevation of the nation and anti-alienism shifted decisively towards antisemitism, Jewish leaders interpreted this as "a sudden flight to Hitlerism". Reverend Levy, of London's Bayswater Synagogue, commented: "If there was an alien immigrant to be expelled from this country, it was the alien immigrant of antisemitism which came from Germany."

Jewish leaders and spokespersons questioned Mosley's slogan of "Britain First" since, they argued, his movement used "foreign political ideas and methods". Several Jewish commentators claimed that the methods and tactics of the BUF, which marked them off from Britain's conventional political parties, typified the "alien" nature of its movement. The *JC* commented that: "Jews' security and livelihood were threatened by an unscrupulous and ambitious politician working with un-British weapons and drawing ammunition from Nazi arsenals. The present menace has not risen out of the British experience but out of a world situation and a philosophy inspired from without."

The notions perpetuated by the Jewish communal leadership were reinforced by similar characterisations of fascism by influential non-Jews. Just as fascism had used the mystical, unscientific notion of a hidden and sinister, all-pervading, Jewish conspiracy, which, in the British context, was interpreted as a foreign import, opponents of fascism often used a mirror image to characterise this ideology in similar terms. Perhaps Hugh Dalton, MP for Bishop Auckland, was principally attempting to ridicule Mosley's movement in its own language when he described fascism as an "ugly, sinister and international conspiracy" but the conclusion he reached, that "British Jews and Gentiles must stand united against this hateful importation from abroad", suggested that he could not appreciate the possibility of BUF-style antisemitism having any roots in British soil. And if fascist antisemitism was viewed in essence as an artificial European import, then what was at issue was not merely the understanding of fascism but an evaluation of the nature of British society.

Wide sections of the Jewish community believed that the accumulated benign and compassionate cultural and political characteristics of Britain stood as a firm guarantee against antisemitism growing and flourishing on the domestic front. They attributed various characteristics to the British body politic: fair play, love of freedom, tolerance, humanity, common sense, fair-mindedness and a sense of justice. A *JC* article responding to attacks by the BUF on Jewish boxing promoters added still further admirable qualities, saying: "There was no mention of the part played by Jews as competitors, where they have displayed fine examples of British grit, tenacity and courage." The communal leaders believed that, despite the defamation of Jews from some quarters, they had the sympathy of the vast majority of people in the country. The strength with which they held such notions can be illustrated through concrete examples from the community's leading press organ.

In August 1934, the *JC* reported an official visit by the Jewish Historical Society to Lincoln where, 700 years earlier, the accusation of Jewish ritual murder, "the blood libel", had been propagated to explain the death of a young Christian boy.[8] It warmly welcomed the "striking denunciation by the ecclesiastical and civil dignitaries of the foul ritual murder lie", but added, "not that there was much need in this country". Two years later the Imperial Fascist League published the notorious blood libel in its newspaper. During this period the general situation Jews faced in Britain had worsened considerably. Defamation of Jews was increasing, as were demands in the community for stronger defence measures. The IFL leader and publisher were sued for seditious libel, but in acknowledging the incident itself, the *JC* recoiled with shock that the blood libel could possibly surface in this country, declaring: "this, in civilised England".[9]

When Lord Rothermere the owner of the mass circulation newspaper, the *Daily Mail*, gave his powerful backing to the British Union of Fascists in 1934, the *JC* was not unduly concerned, and did not "overestimate the importance" of his adhesion to the fascist cause. Claiming later that he was unwilling to tolerate the BUF's anti-semitism and the brutality of their methods, Rothermere abandoned and denounced the BUF in a well-publicised correspondence with Sir Oswald Mosley. The *JC* did not delve too deeply into how it was that Rothermere allied himself to the fascist cause when Mosley had already given more than enough hints of his party's sense of being at war with the Jews just weeks before the newspaper magnate had signed up as a dedicated supporter. Instead it was satisfied to claim that, "Rothermere's repudiation of antisemitism represents the best and noblest traditions in English life." Whatever Rothermere's initial attraction to the Blackshirts, and indeed to Adolf Hitler, had signified, his disavowal of allegiance to Mosley was, according to the *JC*, derived from the "British instinctive love of fair play and repugnance of injustice".

There are difficulties and contradictions in sustaining this position. When Rothermere was supporting the BUF, both he and Mosley were characterised, and responded to, as British gentlemen, possessed of the various imputed qualities implied by that assignation. They shared similar social backgrounds and were closely identified with British public life: Rothermere through ownership of a daily national newspaper and Mosley through his political career. Early hints of Mosley's antisemitism, following the inception of the BUF, were dismissed by the *JC* with the certainty that "on reflection we are sure Sir Oswald will see the illogicality of his attitude". Nevertheless, when Rothermere expressed his disapproval of antisemitism while Mosley continued to incorporate it, the latter was viewed as placing himself "outside the sentiment of the nation". There had been clear hints of antisemitism in Mosley's speech at the Albert Hall in April 1934, which were remarked upon at the time by the *Manchester Guardian*, though "missed" by other mainstream media. When antisemitism was brought publicly and unmistakably to the fore at a further Albert Hall rally in October 1934 and in a speech at Manchester Free Trade Hall the following month, the *JC* commented:

> *"In attacking the Jews he mistakes the spirit of his fellow countrymen as much as he misjudges the Jews. Britain is not Germany and has no time for garbage rummaged from the dustbins of continental antisemitism."*[10]

It was clear, however, that by 1936 the BUF, whose membership was growing once again at the same time as it was expressing increasingly crude antisemitism, was accurately reflecting the spirit of a substantial section of its fellow countrymen and women. And it was not only in East London that it provided a focal point for their aspirations. However, at the peak of the agitation, the regular *JC* columnist, Watchman, declared that there was:

> *"...no ground for panic... the political instinct, masculine commonsense, to say nothing of the traditional quality of fair play were unlikely to desert the British people at the instance of a second-band Hitler".*[11]

Whilst cautiously welcoming the fact that a parliamentary debate on antisemitism was held in March 1936, the *JC* reflected on how "it must have been painful to British sentiment that a parliamentary debate on Jew-baiting in London was deemed necessary in the public interest". But in opening the debate, the Labour leadership contender and MP for Hackney South, Herbert Morrison, confirmed that there was indeed much to discuss. He referred to questions he and his neighbouring MPs, Ernest Thurtle (Shoreditch), Dan Chater (North East Bethnal Green) and Frederick Watkins (Central Hackney) had put to the Home Secretary about "attacks upon members of the Jewish community in the East End of London by persons who appear to be members or representatives of Fascist organisations". And though the Home Secretary was acknowledged as having been "very helpful" and took "a serious and a firm view of this matter", Morrison and colleagues wanted "to bring certain incidents before the House in a somewhat more extended form, in order that the Home Secretary may realise the gravity of the situation and have an opportunity of making a further and perhaps amplified statement".

They then recounted a shocking collection of incidents involving physical violence necessitating hospital treatment, verbal abuse, murder threats, bricks thrown through the windows of Jewish-owned shops, customers prevented from entering such shops, and people spreading the slogan "Kill the Jews". These were actions, said Morrison, "calculated to cause a breach of the peace and to inflame racial hatred", which were encouraged by inflammatory speeches by BUF propagandists.

Morrison also detailed incidents that revealed police and magistrate courts' responses to be severely lacking. He concluded his speech with a stark warning. "There is a situation in the East End of London which, however, is not so bad as it is and has been in Germany... (but) ...contains the elements of grave potential trouble unless the police and magistrates come down on it firmly and say it is to be stopped."

Ernest Thurtle MP developed the theme of incitement:

"When Fascist speakers in the East End of London denounce Jewish business people, Jewish cinema magnates, or Jewish financiers such as the Rothschilds and the Sassoons, such statements are not calculated to cause a breach of the peace because the Rothschilds and the Sassoons are far away, and there is no immediate danger of a crowd being incited to take action against them. It is a very different matter when speakers talk about shopkeepers who are within... 200 yards, or about Jewish people who are said to have taken jobs... speakers are talking to people who are frightfully discontented and suffering from misfortune, poverty and unemployment, and when these people hear speakers say that they are being robbed and exploited by Jewish shopkeepers, or that jobs which they should have had have been taken by Jewish workpeople, there is a clear danger that language of that kind and in such places is calculated to cause a breach of the peace."

He quoted the words delivered by a fascist speaker in Victoria Park Square, who asked: "When there are any jobs going, who is it that gets the jobs? The Isaacs, the

120

Cohens, the Solomons and the Jacobs. They are robbing the British workers of their daily bread... The Jews among us are the cancer and every foul disease. The situation calls for surgical operation, and we Fascists intend making that operation. We will extirpate them thoroughly from our life."

Thurtle concluded by saying:

> "...if we allow that kind of thing to go on, we may create quite a dangerous situation in the East End of London and other parts of the country. In all of us are latent ignoble tendencies, and those people are appealing to the very basest and lowest prejudices of the people in the East End."[12]

Home Secretary Sir John Simon acknowledged in response that "this preaching of the doctrine of hatred against the Jews, because they are Jews... which is making it its business to encourage our citizens to look on the Jew as an outcast" was creating "a very disquieting movement which potentially is very dangerous". The Home Secretary affirmed that the Jew is:

> "a citizen living: here under the law, like the rest of us, and is entitled to fair and proper treatment like other citizens... I am sure the whole House will agree with me, that in this country we are not prepared to tolerate any form of Jew baiting. We are not in the least disposed to look with an indulgent eye upon any form of persecution. It is, therefore, necessary that public attention should be called to this danger... Therefore, I am glad that the debate has taken place."[13]

But if Morrison's evidence showed how ordinary people were being convinced by fascist propaganda to participate in acts of hate, Sir John Simon still regarded the perpetrators as a marginal and pathological phenomenon. He said of the conflicts that were developing in East London: "it is not a situation which appeals to the instincts of the ordinary Englishman as at all tolerable." By stating that Jews were entitled to "fair and proper treatment", he was merely reiterating a formal guarantee to the Jewish community in the face of a pronounced threat from a vociferous and active organised antisemitic body.

Rather than purely noting this reiteration, the *JC* gratefully and enthusiastically welcomed it. This was, it said, "only what one expects from a British Home Secretary", thus implying a particular set of standards based on imputed national characteristics, whilst simultaneously indicating considerable uncertainty about the prescribed position of the Jewish community. At this stage the *JC* certainly did not take up the more contentious element of Sir John Simon's parliamentary response in which he stated:

> "*I have heard it sometimes suggested or hinted that in dealing with fascist or anti-fascist demonstrations the police discriminate in favour of fascists and that facilities or protection are given to them in contrast to the methods that are adopted with regard to people of the extreme opposite views... it is simply not true that the police in this matter have any bias of a political kind. The only interest of the police and the only interest of the police authorities is to do the best they can in difficult circumstances to keep the peace and to stop people from breaking the peace. It is not true that there has been favouritism*".[14]

On the question of alien refugees, the *JC* conceded the argument that there were perhaps some legitimate feelings against free entry while unemployment was so marked, but concluded that compassionate sentiment based on "the ingrained British spirit of fair play" should and would predominate.

When the newspapers brought the issue of alien refugees to the fore in 1938 and 1939, the *JC* described their panic-mongering as "a deplorable departure from standards that have given the British press its high standing in the journalistic world". After the *Sunday Express* published its article headlined "The Jews", the *JC* asked, "Does it accord with the fine British reputation for fair play and freedom?" For the "British way of life" was perceived as a set of acquired characteristics and qualities which formed an impenetrable barrier against the spread of antisemitism in British society. The *JC* was well aware of a tendency by some to dwell on negative behaviour by certain Jews especially in the area of sharp business practices, but it commented, in 1938, that to "ferret out Jewish wrongdoers then brand them as typical of their race is not only a sin against elementary fact and logic, but cruel, iniquitous and un-English".[15]

It is instructive to record the parallel self-image of the British as perceived by dominant groups in society, and consider the extent to which it was internalised by the Jewish community and served to confirm their beliefs. The Dean of St Paul's stated plainly that "Jew-baiting was not a British sport", and Sir John Simon was convinced that "the commonsense of the British people will prevail... the essence of British social life is tolerance... fascism and communism are utterly un-British in sentiment and purpose". A particularly revealing expression of this self-image, combined with certain perceptions of Jews and antisemitism was contained in a letter to the *JC* from the sales manager of a prominent property company in July 1933. It was headlined "The British attitude to Jew-baiting".

> "*May we... voice our feelings to the authorities concerned in the matter of the persecution in London of individual Jewish men and women. Some while ago unknown and so-called English people attempted in a lesser way to treat a few unfortunate traders after*

*the manner of our late enemies the German nation,
per their accredited leader Hitler. We feel, and we
are sure the vast majority of all decent and law-
abiding members of the British race feel also, that it
is a crying disgrace to our country for it to be possible to bait and menace the Jews, just because of a
few hot-heads who... lack brains enough to estimate
the usefulness of the Jewish community not only in
London, but in all parts of the world. After all, the
Jew makes an excellent and law-abiding citizen. He
works hard at his profession, trade and business.
He quarrels with no one's religion... our experience
is that the Jew is as good as the other man and
sometimes even better.*"[16]

There was no single, simple, dominant "British" attitude
to Jews in this period, but a set of widely differing characterisations. To some in Britain, Jews were an
enrichment to society; to others they were a cancerous
growth to be removed and there were a great many gra-
dations between. These attitudes cut across barriers of
social class and status, and reflected a British reality. If
the leaders of Anglo-Jewry simply dismissed as irrelevant, marginal or anomalous the sentiments that did not
treat Jews with the tolerance they perceived as intrinsic
to British social life, such attitudes nevertheless could
not be ignored but required explanation. Jewish community spokespersons characterised every significant
departure from the expectations placed upon their fellow
countrymen as "un-British" and explained them away as
nefarious influence from abroad. But some influential
writers within the Jewish community sought more satisfactory answers.

The writer, William Zukerman, for example, had initially been shocked by the manner in which fascism
asserted itself in England: "One somehow was accus-
tomed to associate England with good taste. Even if
fascism were to come to England, it would not make its

appearance in the vulgar dress of Nazism." Yet, he continued, "Of all forms of fascism, the one which has descended upon England is the most vulgar and brutal... It took even Germany almost ten years of intense Nazi propaganda before an attempt was made to attack Jews physically." In 1937, though, he argued that "in spite of recent antisemitic events in the East End of London there is no place in Europe (and probably the world) where antisemitism has a less fertile soil at the present moment than in England", but his hopeful assessment rejected any notion of inherent and lasting guarantees based upon imputing "natural" characteristics to the British nation. He believed that culturally acquired attributes might be transformed over time for better or worse. His optimism about Anglo-Jewry's immediate prospects derived from his evaluation of public sentiment in Britain and the "state of mind of the British intelligentsia", which was, he believed, infused in that period "with an intense social idealism, a sense of duty to the poor and oppressed" and a "feeling of high and rare humanitarianism".[17] His case rested not on cast-iron guarantees of a tolerant Britishness but on a contemporary assessment of the balance of social, political and cultural forces. A glance at the Continent would have revealed that similar beliefs were held about German society in the early 1920s. During that period many Polish Jews emigrated to Germany in search of a more sophisticated and tolerant polity. By the early 1930s, though, Germany had begun to demonstrate the limits of that tolerance once a nationwide economic crisis took grip.

The cautious optimism of Zukerman, however, and Jewish communal leaders' attribution of particularly favourable characteristics to British society, often stood in stark contrast to the pessimism and anxieties expressed through the *JC*'s correspondence columns by Jewish residents of the areas in which the antisemitic attacks were most concentrated. This contrast must be seen in the light of an attempt by the community's dominant groups to inte-

125

grate successfully and securely into the "host" society. They developed a set of expectations about that society which were consistent with this ambition. Successful integration, they believed, demanded strong identification with the nation as a unitary whole, and so the community felt compelled to give constant proof of its patriotic pedigree. In April 1939, when the Second World War was looming, a *Jewish Chronicle* editorial expressed this belief succinctly: "The antisemite is an anti-Briton."

The views of British society illustrated through these examples provide the context in which Jewish communal perceptions and reactions to the intensifying antisemitic threat in the period can be understood. Chronologically, they evolved in three phases, reflecting the prominence of particular forms of antisemitism:

- 1st phase: 1932-33, marked by individual antisemitic acts and the incipient growth of the BUF;

- 2nd phase: 1934-37, comprising the peak of public BUF agitation;

- 3rd phase: 1938-39, dominated by the aliens scare and non-systematic popular antisemitism.

In the initial phase communal leaders attempted to deny or, as far as possible, diminish the significance of any antisemitic outbreaks. Early acts of vandalism were regarded as disquieting but not worthy of serious comment. The *JC* said it had "no desire to exaggerate the importance of the incidents". It characterised the perpetrators as ill-informed, unbalanced individuals and irresponsible hooligans. The first major public demonstration by an organised fascist movement, a 2,000-strong Blackshirt march, was seen as "no bad thing" by the *JC*, as, "this noisy movement was exhibited in all its pretentious insignificance". Ironically, it was not until a leading figure of the British establishment, Lord Rothermere, accused Mosley of trading in antisemitism

126

that the *JC* itself was prepared to support such a charge against the leader of the BUF. Although occasionally irritated by Mosley's behaviour, it had, up to that point, been very charitable and understanding towards him. It insisted that Mosley was originally opposed to anti-semitism, but had come under intense pressure from his followers. The *JC* was, by way of contrast, much more forthright about derogatory newspaper articles about Jews that appeared in the Catholic press.

As verbal and physical attacks upon Jews became increasingly frequent and evolved into an organised campaign, the Jewish community began to treat the threat more soberly. As Parliament debated the East End terror, and respected MPs such as Herbert Morrison, and Ernest Thurtle provided detailed and very disturbing revelations of the threats, insults and violence encountered by Jews there, and increasingly anxious letters appeared in the Jewish press from individuals who had experienced or witnessed antisemitic attacks, individual members of the Board of Deputies brought the issues more sharply to the attention of the wider community. Bertram Jacobs (representing Newport Synagogue) spoke of the "communal mind... approaching a state of panic", while Alderman Kershaw, who represented the Association of Jewish Friendly Societies on the Board, described the East End Jews as "trembling with fear." He expressed his frustration that "the vast majority of the Board did not know the East End and what was going on except from what it had read in the press."[18]

The Jewish Chronicle, which had been markedly unwilling to believe the extent of antisemitic activity that was being claimed by grassroots members of the community, embedded a "special correspondent" in East London during the summer of 1936. In a series of reports in July and August 1936, he captured the sense of abandonment and growing alarm that he observed and felt at first hand. Referring to interviews with local Jews, he wrote of their genuine anxiety that, in the

127

heart of London's East End, there was the beginning of what was happening in Germany. He added that the community was not satisfied that all the available means were being employed in its defence, and reflected their growing restlessness at the apparent inactivity of the police.

"No one who witnesses the weekly march of the fascists to their headquarters in Bethnal Green and sees the populace forming into two camps on opposite sides of the road can fail to realise the growing possibility of rioting and violence."[19]

He asserted that antisemitism had always been latent in Bethnal Green and Stepney, explaining it in terms of an "unreasoning dislike of the unlike", but he recognised that a new and menacing ingredient had been added:

"For the first time antisemitism is a plank in the platform of an ambitious political party with a popular... programme, and the Blackshirts are rapidly 'rationalising' this old prejudice against the Jews so that its owners are ready and willing to give it expression in words and deeds."[20]

He followed this assessment with a stark warning:

"...if the Blackshirts are allowed to continue their villainous campaign of lies and incitement, racial riots must not be regarded as an improbable result. This is not scaremongering but a serious and reasoned opinion arrived at quite dispassionately."[21]

The extent of hostility, suspicion and insecurity that had been aroused was illustrated, he argued, in those cases where Jewish victims of physical assault failed to appear as prosecution witnesses for fear of the consequences. Previously sporadic and localised feeling against Jews in the East End had been subject to change within materially altered circumstances, and this, the correspondent argued, demanded a more penetrating analysis. He believed that the organised activities of the BUF had intensified an existing latent antisemitism beyond control. However the Board of Deputies leader Neville Laski claimed that antisemitism was "not rooted in the man in the street but cultivated and cultured by playing on his ignorance". He meant ignorance of Judaism, since he understood antisemitism as being anti-Jewish at a religious level.

The respected local churchman, Father Groser, of Christ Church, Watney Street, who gave practical support to several anti-fascist initiatives, offered another explanation of anti-Jewish activity which challenged the portrayal of anti-Jewish sentiment as simply irrational. He also utilised a concept of ignorance, but in a quite different way to Laski. Addressing a public meeting of the Stepney Council for Peace and Democracy, he argued that the only means by which the BUF could obtain support in the East End was "by bringing in something which cuts across the normal lives lived by the people". He claimed that Jews owned the majority of factories in East London's woodworking trades and fascists could approach workers and say that Jews were responsible for bad conditions. He explained that parallel conditions existed in the Gentile-owned factories in the North and the Midlands but, he argued, "East Enders see little of conditions outside the East End and therefore swallow the propaganda."

Zukerman, writing in 1937, offered a particularly challenging analysis of antisemitism within the context of fascism, which linked directly into Jewish communal responses and the issue of possible alliances. He argued that fascist antisemitism represented a strong class antagonism mixed with an anti-Jewish outburst manipulated by the BUF. Zukerman believed that fascism was essentially a middle-class movement – a view substantiated by a social analysis of its leadership, though contested by later analysts of its urban branches at the grassroots and middle rank levels.[22] Building upon his earlier notion that the East End Jew was no Jewish "type" at all but a variation of the East End labour type, Zukerman argued that, despite their rhetoric, for fascists, Jewish and non-Jewish East End labour equally represented the "alien nation". In Zukerman's view, when the fascists attacked this "alien nation" they revealed themselves as being more imbued with political and economic concerns than national and racist ideology.

> *"To the British fascists and their middle-class sympathisers, the English 'Reds', Labourites and Communists of the 'lower classes' are a true 'alien nation' psychologically as well as socially. They know as little about them as they know about the Jews, and when these 'lower classes' become restive and even threatening, the fascist hostility to them becomes no less bitter and strong than against the Jews. But in these days of nationalism, it is bad form to show hostility to one's own 'alien nation'. The Jew provides a much more convenient outlet for the feeling, particularly if, as in this case, the Jew happens to be so much akin to the object of real antagonism. Fundamentally the British Fascists' outburst against the Jews is an outburst against British Labour, 'Reds', Socialists and Communists. It is more political and economic than national and racial. Its antisemitism is a guise under which its profounder class feeling is hidden."[23]*

This complex and thought-provoking analysis drew a distinction between the surface appearance of fascist antisemitism and its essential logic, and implied that Jewish workers might be better advised to look for class-based rather than communal-based alliances to confront fascism. In contrast, most of the "explanations" debated within the Jewish communal leadership seemed merely to skim the surface.

As 1937 drew to a close, the *JC* uncharacteristically reprinted an item from the Communist Party's *Daily Worker*, which comprised a set of fascist statements made on different occasions to different audiences, illustrating the seemingly contradictory and opportunistic nature of the fascists' antisemitic ideology:

> *"The Jew is a capitalist; the Jew is a communist. The Jew mixes with Christians; the Jew sticks too much to his own race. The Jew desires and foments war; the Jew is a pacifist and refuses to fight. England is the best country in the world; the Jews rule England."[24]*

Both the *JC* and the *Daily Worker* would have felt some inner satisfaction at being able to ridicule the BUF's antisemitic ideology for its apparent irrationality, and no doubt these statements were well used by anti-fascist propagandists. But these contradictions merely illustrated the way in which the BUF could appeal to mutually contradictory elements. In a 1935 pamphlet, *The Blackshirt Racket – Mosley Exposed,* Charles Dolan, a former BUF national propagandist who had defected the previous year, showed how Mosley promised work for the unemployed and "redress for trade unionists betrayed by their leaders", while simultaneously promising the industrialists that they would be represented in a new department of government and that they could be guaranteed "release from the tyranny of trade unions". Another BUF defector, AC Miles notes how Mosley sought support from Irish Catholics against the Jews in the East End but, when he spoke in Protestant areas of Edinburgh, he declared: "The Blackshirt movement comes to free the people from Papal domination". Dolan argued that Mosley's tendency to "promise every faction relief from its opposing faction" was not opportunism but a calculated tactic of "divide and conquer".[25]

Aliens and legitimacy

Towards the end of the 1930s, as the BUF declined, the major threat to the Jewish community was no longer the street-level harassment and violence, and provocative marches, but a growing anti-alien campaign. The *JC* commented in 1938: "Recent exaggerated and misleading articles in the London press have produced an atmosphere little short of dangerous." Despite the weakness of the fascists, growing anti-Jewish feeling in the country was identified. The threat was characterised as "Douglas Reedism" (a reference to the author whose populist brand of antisemitism was discussed earlier).[26] Yet towards the end of the period there was some dismay in official Jewish quarters about the community's alleged "refusal to wake up to the situation". This referred especially to the failure of the wider community to meet the demands of the "Defence Fund" that had been organised. This was accounted for in terms of "fatalism... or the stupid and comfortable theory that 'it cannot happen here'." If such attitudes were present, though, they would have been entirely consistent with many aspects of the communal leadership's analysis that it had hitherto expressed.

There was certainly a contradiction between the community's earlier predisposition to dismiss any possibilities of antisemitism in Britain and its increasingly experienced reality. Attempts to discount the significance of accumulated individual incidents were made redundant through the active existence of a very real antisemitic political party. To a degree, the communal leaders could dismiss this party and its ideology as a foreign import and its supporters as either irrationally prejudiced or ignorant. But given the widespread and enthusiastic support for the BUF in certain areas, such explanations were inadequate, as were very general explanations of antisemitism, that did not account for its particularly charged character during this specific period. Jewish leaders sought explanations that would not undermine an image of British society upon which their attempts to integrate successfully into British life depended, and ultimately there was only one group left to blame. And so it transpired that Anglo-Jewry's leading voices came to place considerable responsibility for antisemitism upon the Jewish community itself. In so doing, they conceded rather than confronted many of the arguments advanced by the antisemites.

Claude Montefiore, president of the West End based Anglo-Jewish Association, had highlighted the need for the community to examine its own behaviour critically before making accusations of antisemitism. At the Association's AGM early in the summer of 1936, even as East End Jews were dodging verbal and physical brickbats, he opined: "Jews can ill afford to give their enemies occasion for reproach. They would do well to remind themselves that they are a minority in a Christian country where tolerance and broad-mindedness existed unexampled elsewhere." East End Jews, however, could surely be forgiven at this time for not recognising such magnanimous attitudes as being dominant among their non-Jewish neighbours.

A constantly recurring theme in self-criticism was the entry of many young Jews into the professions such as law and medicine, with accountancy also rising in popularity. Many concerned Jews argued for a "decentralisation of Jewish economic life" to prevent and eradicate antisemitism. The "rush to the professions" was considered harmful both in terms of "crowding" and in terms of providing a superficial justification for a belief, frequently stated, that Jews were primarily engaged in nonproductive labour.

One correspondent to the *JC*, exemplifying a perspective more widely shared, argued that the issue was not the basic right of Jews to enter any profession they wished to, but the exercising of that right, implying that at that particular time and in that particular atmosphere, it may not be prudent for Jews to do so. The

133

dividing line between this view and one that denied Jews an equal right to choose their occupation was, however, precariously thin. At a conference held on "Jewish Students and the Professions" in April 1938, the keynote speaker, Norman Bentwich, a barrister and legal academic, who had personally taken full advantage of educational opportunities that had been open to Jews of his social background – St Paul's Public School followed by Trinity College Cambridge – argued that the growing "excess" of Jews in certain professions and in the numbers attending university was likely to engender antisemitism, and it was "a matter for all Jewish students to consider seriously whether they are rendering the best service to themselves and their people by thronging certain professions". These widely subscribed views on Jews and the professions conceded the argument that the presence of Jews was a problem and that numbers were its essence. A dissenting view, put by one correspondent to the *JC*, argued pointedly that "antisemites will accuse us whatever our occupations, but it is far better to be accused of being a nation of healers and lawyers than middlemen and money lenders".

The question of "numbers" also featured prominently in arguments raging in the community over whether it was desirable for solid blocks of Jews to congregate in certain districts. One correspondent to the *JC* condemned "excessive clannishness" and argued for the breaking up of "ghettoes". He believed that antisemitism would be more effectively challenged by having "well-behaved, intelligent Jewish families living among Gentile neighbours". Arguments were strongly put against Jews engaging in numbers, or even at all, in any activities that might provide grounds for antisemites to exploit them through adverse propaganda. As the actions of organised antisemites continued to provoke opposition, so this notion was applied to Jewish political activity. The BUF accused Jews of being communists, and certainly many East End Jewish youths participated with communists against fascists on the basis of self-defence, and recognised that the communists were the main organisers of local anti-fascist activities. Many, no doubt, were also impressed by communist-led campaigns to improve the daily lives of poorer working class communities such as theirs, on housing estates and in the workplace, and increasing numbers of Jewish youth joined or supported the Young Communist League. These young people were berated for "playing into the hands of the enemy" by the Oxford-educated Jewish philanthropist Basil Henriques QC, who was instrumental in setting up youth clubs for Jews in deprived areas. In contrast, though, a *JC* editorial of June 1936 argued that:

> "...*communal laxity will drive Jewish youth into the arms of extremist anti-fascists. Don't let our leaders censure these developments if they come. The responsibility will lie at their own doors.*"[27]

Although this comment betrays a biased characterisation of certain kinds of anti-fascists as "extremists", in this instance the sympathies of the *JC* are clearly with the youth rather than with their "elders and betters", who were reprimanding them for working with political forces that members of the Jewish establishment did not feel comfortable with. It recognised that young people's patience had been sorely tested. Underlying the establishment's concern, though, was not merely a question of political tact but a view on the right of Jews to participate as equals in society.

The predominant issue on which some leading groups in Jewry regarded their fellow community members as fostering and encouraging antisemitism was through their social behaviour. Communal leaders condemned Jews who, "by their materialism, vulgarity and ostentation were responsible for antisemitism". Laski denounced "flamboyant behaviour" and the "offences of the social climber". He engaged in stern criticism of "Jews who by their conduct create antisemitism". The Chief Rabbi Dr Joseph Hertz, in a sermon at the consecration of Palmers Green Synagogue in North London in June 1936, denounced Jews engaging in disreputable business practices, saying: "Every Jew who misbehaves is an ally of Hitler and a wicked enemy of his people." A spate of letters appeared in the *JC* in 1937 and 1938 denouncing such actions that might foment antisemitism.

> *"The ever increasing ostentation by a small percentage of the community whose expensive and extravagant apparel and general flaunting of wealth cannot but create disgust and jealousy amongst non-Jews."*[28]
>
> *"The practice of photographing Jewish wedding ceremonies for reproduction in the press is a particularly bad example of the oft-repeated charge of Jewish ostentation which so incenses (and rightly so) both Jews and non-Jews."*[29]

They offered drastic remedies to this perceived problem:

> *"Any synagogue member convicted of a serious crime should be expelled and denied Jewish burial rights."*[30]
>
> *"We should form a disciplinary committee to eliminate from our midst undesirable elements."*[31]

Though a process of stereotyping was recognised, and the *JC* expressed regret that Jews were judged "by their worst rather than their best", the leaders of the community opted to condemn those Jews who, by their behaviour, approximated to generalisations perpetrated by antisemites. It chose this course rather than one challenging the assumptions and motivations that underlie this process. Equally, the *JC* failed to challenge the selective emphasis by which ostentation was considered worse when indulged in by Jews. In this way, the leaders of

Jewry were setting standards for the community that the wider society was not expected to match, and this was promoted as an effective response to antisemitism. The president of the Jewish Board of Guardians, Hannah Cohen, argued that Jews:

"...have been prone to cry out against the injustice of antisemitism and not ready enough to see if by chance there is any shade of excuse for it. It is not enough that the Jew is no worse than his neighbour. He had to be a good deal better as the eyes of the world were upon him."[32]

It was only at the latter end of the 1930s that the more established elements of the Jewish community began to question and counter this stereotyping. In the course of a talk entitled "The Jew and his neighbour", Basil Henriques QC had argued that when he was young there was, as far as he was aware, no antisemitism in Britain and that if a problem had grown, it could be accounted for largely by the religious and social deterioration of the Jew. The regular *JC* writer, Watchman, responded through his column that antisemitism had actually existed for some time, and whilst Jewish error may have fed it, the causes were to be found elsewhere:

"The basis of such a Jewish problem as exists in these islands... outside our own community. Jewish ostentation and wrongdoing may by invoked by our enemies but they can only illustrate the Jew-baiter's creed. They do not create it... Jews are the only community in the country... who are called upon to present a 100 per cent blamelessness of conduct on pain of their being put collectively in the dock."[33]

Similarly, in response to the 1938 newspaper campaign, which suggested that there was an acute "Jewish problem", the *JC's* editorial replied bullishly:

137

"If there is a problem it is a problem of wrongdoers. It is only when on every possible occasion the wrong-doers are labelled Jewish and the whole Jewish people identified with them that a Jewish problem is in danger of developing."[34]

The various ways in which the Jewish community perceived and responded to the antisemitic threat – denial and dismissal, attributing it to malign foreign influence, and ultimately prescribing self-criticism – rested on a questionable set of beliefs about the nature of British society and revealed at every stage uncertainty about the actual position of the Jews within this society. According to Watchman, the community had to address the need to understand itself.

"We are confronted with the need for surveying our entire social position – internal as well as external relationships. We have to look at our social situation, religious position and the organisations we have contrived to carry our community along the dangerous currents of a disturbed age... in nothing have we shown less foresight than in the failure to keep pace with the changes in our social structure."[35]

As far as Jewish community leaders were concerned, Britain's Jews constituted a *religious* group. As such they required *tolerance*. Whilst forcefully defending their rights as a religious group, they were far less prone to argue for their cultural and political rights as accepted equals, integral to the society in which they lived. The attack on the Jewish religion, though, was quite peripheral to the main thrust of anti-Jewish defamation, which actually comprised an all-encompassing attack upon Jewry as an *ethnic* group.

138

Notes

1 *Jewish Chronicle,* 7.7.1933
2 N. Laski, op.cit, pp115-116
3 Recorded by WE Evans-Gordon in *The Alien Immigrant,* Heinemann, 1903. In 1933, Lang, then Archbishop of Canterbury, confided to the High Commissioner for Refugees, James Grover Macdonald, that he believed that German Jews had brought on themselves the hatred of Hitler.
4 B. Gainer, *The Alien Invasion,* p110
5 S. Cohen, *That's Funny, You Don't Look Antisemitic,* p33
6 *Economic Review,* April 1911
7 *Hansard,* 22.10.1919
8 The "blood libel" was an accusation first spread in medieval times, that Jews killed Christian children and used their blood in food prepared for the festival of Passover.
9 *Jewish Chronicle,* 10.7.1936
10 *Jewish Chronicle* 7.12.1934
11 *Jewish Chronicle* 5.6.1936
12 *Hansard* 5.3.1936
13 ibid
14 ibid
15 *Jewish Chronicle* 15.7.1938
16 *Jewish Chronicle* 28.7.1933
17 W. Zukerman, *The Jew in Revolt,* Secker, 1937, pp54-79
18 *Jewish Chronicle* 23.10.1936
19 *Jewish Chronicle* 14.8.1936
20 ibid
21 ibid
22 See, for example, Thomas Linehan's 1996 work, *East London for Mosley: The British Union of Fascists 1933-1940,* Cass.
23 W. Zukerman, op.cit p75
24 *Jewish Chronicle* 31.12.1937
25 *The Blackshirt Racket – Mosley Exposed,* Charles Dolan, 1935
26 See pages 43-44
27 *Jewish Chronicle* 19.6.1936
28 *Jewish Chronicle* 22.4.1938
29 *Jewish Chronicle* 8.7.1938
30 *Jewish Chronicle* 4.11.1938
31 *Jewish Chronicle* 18.11.1938
32 *Jewish Chronicle* 19.3.1937
33 *Jewish Chronicle* 29.4.1938
34 *Jewish Chronicle* 15.7.1938
35 *Jewish Chronicle* 27.11.1936

6. Battle for the East End

The threat posed to Jews in Britain in the 1930s came from many quarters and took many different guises – individuals acting in discriminatory ways; stereotyping and ideological assaults from church pulpits; the musings of prominent cultural figures; and vicious targeting by an ambitious and threatening new political movement. However, if the threat was wide-ranging, the perception and comprehension of its nature by the leaders of the community under attack were narrow, and were considerably distanced from the analysis of those who experienced the threat at the sharp end, especially in London's East End.

By July 1936 the physical danger to Jews, in this district especially, could no longer be played down, and voices among both the leadership and the rank and file of the Jewish community urged that the Board of Deputies and Jewry as a whole face up to the situation. At this stage, "Jewry as a whole" could be enumerated as an uncomplicated statistic, however it constituted a very complex social reality, which may be one reason why the established leadership of the community found itself unable to command unified support behind its programme for combating antisemitism.

A popular organisation called the Jewish People's Council Against Fascism and Antisemitism (JPC) emerged in East London, grounded in an intimate awareness of the threat from antisemitism at grassroots level, and the initiatives that might be required to combat it. Ultimately this body had a profound influence upon how the problem was conceived by prevailing sections of the community and how antisemitism's relationship with fascism as a political ideology was analysed. The extent of the rift preceding the JPC's foundation needs to be understood against the background both of the failure by the leadership to rigorously analyse the form and content of the threat, and the inadequacy of the practical advice it offered the community in terms of required responses. Based upon its limited understanding of what the East End community was actually faced with, advice from the leadership exhibited naivety and complacency.

Between 1932 and 1935, the advice from community leaders was primarily concerned with how Jews should behave in response to the public activities of the BUF, who were holding meetings, demonstrations and newspaper sales, as well as starting to engage in increasing provocation and physical intimidation of Jews. During this period the *Jewish Chronicle's* editorial policy was closely allied with that of the official leadership and other recognised figureheads of Anglo-Jewry, and gave prominence to their statements.

As early as 1933, fights were occurring between fascist newspaper sellers and Jews who were only too aware of what fascism meant for their counterparts in Germany at that time. The *JC*'s "even-handed" policy was that fascists should not sell their newspapers if it was likely to be a provocation, and Jews should act with restraint and dignity. As incidents recurred more frequently, the *JC* seemed to place far more emphasis on demanding that Jews abstain from disorderly behaviour than in exposing the provocation by the fascists. Jews who engaged in physical encounters with fascists were deemed guilty of "stupid and disgraceful behaviour" and their actions characterised as a "rank disservice to the Jewish people". After the disturbances at the Olympia meeting, where BUF stewards had acted with shocking brutality against oppositional forces, the *JC* invoked Jewish theology in condemning *Jews* involved in the disturbances:

"Jews who interfere with the full expression of opinion are false to the Jewish teachings of justice and fair play and are traitors to the vital material interests of the Jewish people."[1]

Leaders of the Jewish community were determined to convey this message principally to the youth, since they were increasingly involved in oppositional activities. Lord Bearsted, an Eton and Oxford educated Jewish philanthropist and art collector, advised members of Stepney Jewish Youth Club in London's East End to be loyal citizens. He told them it was "futile" and "unwise" to join in demonstrations. Fellow philanthropist, Sir Basil Henriques, urged what he termed "a pacific attitude" when he addressed the Association of Jewish Youth. He told young people to send any antisemitic newspaper articles they saw to the Press Committee of the Board of Deputies, and implored them to conduct themselves in a dignified manner. The best answer to antisemitism, he assured them, was simply to be "impeccable and blameless to the outside world".

Leonard Montefiore, a leading figure in the Jewish welfare establishment, preached a similar message at another East End youth club, using a particularly revealing analogy. He argued that the position of Jews in Britain was that of a defendant standing in court before a jury, and to achieve a successful outcome, Jews "must gain the middle class of British opinion". He apparently accepted that Jews stood "accused" and were "on trial", and did not enquire why they had been arrested and charged in the first place and whether that could in any way be justified. He merely urged them to recognise the court and endeavour to exonerate themselves. Even though his own family could be traced back several centuries to the early Sephardic Jewish migration, his view implied that Jews did not form an integral part of British society but were here on sufferance, and were obliged, on demand, to justify their presence.

Montefiore's message illustrated the social divide between the community leaders and those most directly threatened. Jews were advised to stay away from Blackshirt meetings and to challenge Mosley with arguments from a distance, through approved channels, to show fellow citizens that his accusations were false. This generally meant that the community itself was confined to the sidelines whilst its leading lights such as Laski and Melchett disputed Mosley's claims through the press. They challenged him to "name the names". Mosley avoided their challenge and the defamation of Jews and the intimidation and attacks continued.

The two main strands of argument upon which community leaders gave their advice were that fascism, as such, was not an issue for Jews, and that any anxiety provoked by the fascist presence could be dissipated if only people they targeted acted in a dignified manner. This required that ordinary Jews should simply avoid public activities organised by the fascists. Even if there had been a degree of initial ambiguity, by the middle of 1934 it was demonstrably clear that both Jews and communists were the chief targets of the fascists' opposition to sectional interests. The advice proffered by communal leaders exemplified an erroneous belief that the growth and success of antisemitism depended not upon the level of activity of antisemites but upon the behaviour of Jews. The difficulties contained within such a standpoint came to the fore when the BUF announced its intention to hold a major public demonstration at London's Hyde Park in September 1934. Aware that a counter demonstration was being mobilised, and perhaps aware too that the Communist Party in the East End had circulated a leaflet in Yiddish calling people to join the protest, the *JC* declared:

"We urge Jews who feel strongly to have nothing to do with the protests... stay away and refrain from adding to the sufficiently heavy anxieties of the police. Any Jew guilty of lack of restraint is not a good friend of his people or of the principles he professes to hold." [2]

This implicitly recognised that there *was* indeed a case for Jews to feel strongly on this issue, but the *JC* did not wish to grant this feeling any widespread communal legitimacy. The argument of not overburdening the police signified a particularly deferential attitude towards the state authorities, but that was secondary in this case to the major ideological argument about the relationship of antisemitism to fascism, and whether Jews should oppose fascism *per se* as Jews.

In urging Jews to stay away from Hyde Park, however, the *JC* could also claim to stand in line with the demands made by the mainstream Labour and Liberal press outlets such as the *Daily Herald* and the *Manchester Guardian,* as well as trade union leaders who likewise urged anti-fascists to ignore this event and not give Mosley publicity. But the political barometer had changed, and effective leafleting and workplace organising, particularly by rank and file trade unionists and the Communist Party, meant that a staggering crowd of 100,000 workers drowned out fascist speakers trying to address 5,000 Blackshirts, who were assiduously protected by a ring of police. It might reasonably be assumed that the anti-fascist protest included significant numbers of Jews from the East End where the communists were gaining in strength and influence. This would not be the only occasion when East End Jews would ignore the call from their more comfortably ensconced leaders to "stay away".

Mosley's failure to sustain a national challenge after the debacle of Olympia, and the gradual distancing and decline of establishment support for his party, followed by the humiliation of being so heavily outnumbered at Hyde Park, did not herald the demise of his movement. Rather, it entered a new phase – one which impacted ever more heavily on Britain's Jews in the area where they were most heavily concentrated – the East End of London. In October 1934 *The Blackshirt* announced proudly that:

"...the Bow Branch of the British Union of Fascists held an inaugural meeting at Stepney Green on

Thursday October 4th... The Blackshirts marched in procession from Bow Branch premises down the Mile End Road into Stepney Green, where a large crowd of 1,000 or so people had gathered which later increased to well over 1,500. The Blackshirts had a very noisy reception as the larger part of the audience were aliens who resented British people holding a meeting in what they considered to be their own territory... Thursday October 4th will go down in Blackshirt history as a memorable day when the seed of fascism was sown in another East London communist stronghold."[3]

So when Mosley's troops sought to invade the East End on the more commonly recalled 4th October, exactly two years later, they were commemorating not only the national birth of their movement in October 1932, but also a local anniversary – the day when their first branch had come into being in the locality that was to become their most important battleground. By the time of the abortive incursion of October 1936 it is estimated that a very significant proportion, perhaps even half of the entire national membership of the BUF was concentrated within several well-organised and very active East End branches that had formed in Bow, Bethnal Green, Shoreditch and Limehouse. Regular street corner platforms were staffed by speakers such as "Jock" Houston, "Mick" Clarke, Albert Woolnough and Bertram Pile, to spread the fascist message in each of these areas – at Stafford Road in Bow, Victoria Park Square in Bethnal Green, Harman Street near Shoreditch, and in Duckett Street and Salmon Lane in Limehouse.

By identifying and stigmatising this area as simultaneously "alien territory" and a "communist stronghold", Mosley signified that his movement was prepared to raise the stakes and indulge in open and explicit antisemitism. He was also giving further expression to his party's conception of "Jews" and "communists" as a common enemy

145

– an association that became ever stronger in Mosley's mind and in his speeches, and in the rantings of the BUF leaders who surrounded him, until the term "communist" implied Jew. The reverse, though, was not necessarily true: "Jew", in their parlance, could just as easily imply "financier" or "bloated capitalist" as "communist".

Mosley's rhetoric on public platforms and in the press displayed a marked tendency to indulge in hyperbole – a deliberate strategy to increase its dramatic effect and heighten its emotional appeal. Mosley might have preferred the colder, more steely fascism that Mussolini represented over Hitler's more incendiary brand, but he shared Hitler's appreciation of the politics of emotion and its potential to arouse the passions of a mass following.

The communist spectre that Mosley saw as such an impediment to his party's desire to impose its will, especially in this part of London, was much overstated but not entirely without foundation. Phil Piratin, a Jewish East Ender and small businessman who later became the Communist MP for the area, concedes in his book, *Our Flag Stays Red*, that when he joined the Communist Party in June 1934, shortly after the demonstration at Olympia, the Stepney branch of the party consisted of barely more than 100 paid-up members. In contrast, Stepney Labour Party had upwards of 3,000 members. By the end of the decade though, after the Communist Party locally had played a leading role in several bread and butter struggles for better lives, its local branch had grown fivefold – to more than 550 members, supplemented by a growing Young Communist League contingent of more than 250 youth.[4] In the same period the Labour Party locally had grown at a slower rate but in absolute numbers reached more than 6,000 members by 1939. To put these figures in context, though, Stepney's total population was approximately 200,000. Even taking into account an above-average proportion of children – based on the higher birth-rate of a large immigrant population – the vast majority of people in Stepney who were mature enough to become politically involved, resisted the pull of any party political activity.

Nevertheless, whether or not they joined political parties, significant numbers of people of different generations were increasingly politicised through a series of battles around housing, unemployment, and conditions in the workplace. Many were also becoming very concerned by the threat of fascism, both locally and on the international stage, though it was hardly to the extent that Mosley imagined or claimed.

The influence of the Communist Party in the East End was undoubtedly greater than its numerical membership. Its newspaper, the *Daily Worker*, launched in 1930, had a readership, especially among trade unionists, that considerably exceeded party membership. Through its work in many local arenas, the Communist Party won at least passive support and admiration, if not the membership dues, of a broader stratum of Stepney's residents, especially among Jews seeking a militant response to the fascist threat. Despite its relatively low actual membership – considering the breadth and volume of its activities – the Communist Party won a number of council seats in Stepney in the local elections of 1937, and the new councillors included several Jews, among them Piratin himself. In 1945, communists in Stepney nominated Piratin for the parliamentary seat of Stepney, Mile End, which he won by a majority of 11.4% in a surprise victory over the sitting Labour MP, Dan Frankel.[5]

At the turn of the 20th century, when the precursors of Mosley's movement were organising through the British Brothers League, there had been a vibrant revolutionary element among the first generation of Jewish immigrants to the East End. This was exemplified in the drive for unionising sweatshop workers and agitation on wider issues, promoted by dedicated, ideologically-driven anarchists through the *Arbeter Fraynd* (Workers' Friend) Yiddish newspaper and through self-organised trade union-based bodies such as the *Arbeter Ring* (Workers'

Circle). The broader Jewish population of the area, though, was not drawn to revolution. It satisfied its political desires through participation in the political mainstream. East End Jews who enjoyed the franchise overwhelmingly voted Liberal, though a significant number, deterred by the cost of the naturalisation process, remained disenfranchised until they had completed this process.

When the Labour Party established itself more securely in London after the First World War, it might have been anticipated that this would provide a more natural home for the Jews of Stepney, who were still overwhelmingly confined to poor housing, and low-waged work. Stepney Council was dominated by the Labour Party and its councillors comprised roughly equal numbers of councillors of English, Irish and Jewish descent. The Stepney Labour Party had some high-ranking Jewish officials, such as Morry Davis;[6] it supported a Jewish MP, Dan Frankel, and had a number of grassroots Jewish members, but it was largely controlled by a clique of Irish Catholic descent. This clique was regarded as being largely unsupportive or antithetical to the local Jewish community and its interests and concerns.

East End Jews were increasingly drawn towards more radical political solutions to their everyday concerns. Many of them were more attracted to the Communist Party than the Labour Party especially in a period of economic depression and high unemployment, exacerbated by the activities of Mosley's Blackshirts, who were particularly targeting East London. This was reflected in the high proportion of Jewish members and officers in local Communist Party branches.

The rift between Catholic and Jewish concerns locally was well illustrated by responses to the Spanish Civil War, which erupted in July 1936 when General Franco led a military revolt against the democratically elected Republican government. With Franco enjoying backing from Mussolini and Hitler, East End Jews, who already felt themselves to be standing in the front line against the fascists who were organising on their doorsteps, intuitively supported the Republicans and contributed enthusiastically to the "Aid Spain" movement of this period. The Labour Party nationally took a position of neutrality on the conflict in Spain, which many grassroots members contested. But in Stepney several Labour councillors of Irish descent openly sided with Franco, arguing that the Republican movement that opposed him was anti-Catholic.

The Communist Party's Stepney branch, increasingly influential within the wider Jewish East End population, played a major role in publicising the Spanish Republican cause, and recruited many local activists to the International Brigades. Information from MI5 files recently released by the National Archive suggest that as many as 4000 individuals went from Britain to fight against Franco in Spain; the two largest contingents were from Glasgow and the East End of London. Jews were recruited in numbers that greatly exceeded their percentage in the population. Several testimonies of Jewish members of the International Brigades identify their involvement in anti-fascist activities in the East End and their experience on the day of the Battle of Cable Street (discussed in detail on pages 203-208) in particular, as the trigger for their decision to join the Brigades.[7] By contrast, in Ireland itself, though there were indeed a number of *brigadistas* who went to aid the Republican cause, Eoin O'Duffy was busy recruiting 700 "Blueshirts" for an Irish Brigade that would fight *for* General Franco.

Sir Oswald Mosley's casual coupling of "alien territory" and "communist stronghold" expressed his growing willingness to indulge in conspiratorial and racialised fantasies, but he barely knew the East End. If he had acquired a deeper knowledge and understanding of the area, he would have recognised that it was actually the combination of material realities, localised political factors and international issues, which brought increasingly significant elements of the local Jewish population and

149

the organisational structures of the Communist Party closer together in the East End of the 1930s.

When the Mosleyites' campaign of agitation and intimidation ceased making its unpleasant statements from the distance of their headquarters in central London but operated much more openly in the East End itself, Jews locally were instinctively drawn towards an active response. But they were not the only ones, and their responses were necessarily merged with those of other elements in the East End who were increasingly concerned about and committed to confronting the fascist threat. In developing these shared responses, many Jews moved beyond the traditional route of mobilising solely through Jewish organisations, and were increasingly to be found as members, fellow travellers and followers of radical political organisations locally. These included not just the Communist Party but also the Independent Labour Party and the Labour League of Youth.[8] The same material realities that brought Jews closer to the communist movement, also impacted on the non-Jews in the surrounding area, whom Mosley wanted to recruit to his antisemitic crusade. They were largely working class and impoverished, and this meant that if the BUF wanted to compete for their allegiance, it had to offer something tangible to them.

Many scholars identify fascism as a movement that focuses especially on harnessing the active support of a resentful lower middle class, squeezed by more powerful capitalist economic interests and simultaneously threatened with descent back into the ranks of the impoverished lower classes from which many of them thought they had escaped. When Mosley the aristocrat shifted the agitational base of the BUF towards the East End, he was compelled to highlight his appeal to ordinary working men and women. While in some parts of Bethnal Green he was able to win members among the self-employed and small shopkeepers, elsewhere in Bethnal Green, and especially in Shoreditch and

Limehouse, the BUF's constituency was solidly working class and engaged in a wide range of typically working class occupations. In Thomas Linehan's study *East London for Mosley* (1996), based on interviews and surveys of many former BUF members in East London and South West Essex, he shows that these included skilled workers (for example, tailors, bricklayers, cabinet makers, electricians, welders, lock-makers, sheet metal workers, and stonemasons) as well as many semi-skilled and unskilled workers (such as labourers, factory workers, wood machinists, dockers, railway workers and shop assistants).

Not surprisingly, the BUF focused on the two key issues of jobs and housing in these constituencies. Unemployment was rife in the borough, reaching an official figure of 13.5 per cent in 1933, and a real figure that was probably considerably higher, masked by the fact that many local workers subsisted in insecure, casual or seasonal employment. Given these economic circumstances, and the constant presence of a reserve army of labour, jobs in the East End were invariably poorly paid. In notes accompanying an invitation to a conference on "Unemployment in the East End" held in the same month that the BUF was born, the prominent local church leader, Reverend St John B Groser, graphically identified the ways in which the experience of long periods without work affected those trapped in unemployment: "In addition to physical depression and ill health," he wrote, "there is clear evidence of the frustration of personality, the loss of proper self-respect and the creation of an embittered and hopeless section of the community." These powerful personal factors left them ripe for recruitment by the fascists, who promised to restore their dignity and to empower them with a renewed sense of identity and purpose – but at the expense of others in their neighbourhoods.

In a speech in November 1934, which has enjoyed more recent echoes, William Joyce declared that:

151

"...the interests of the British people and nation must receive the first consideration... British work should be given to British people, so that our workpeople should not be driven out of house and home by aliens coming to invest money in our great cities... it is only until we can solve our own unemployment problem that we can make a home for those people who desire to make a living out of this country."[9]

The BUF may have accused conventional trade unions of being under communist influence and subservience to Moscow, but it recognised the real issues that the unions addressed. The fascists consistently highlighted the plight of the unemployed locally and nationally. They demanded a productive, high-wage economy that could rebuild the home market through ensuring that there would be increased purchasing power in the hands of workers. The economic arguments in Mosley's speech at Olympia in 1934 have been somewhat sidelined and overlooked due to the more pronounced emphasis among historians and contemporary commentators on the violence that was meted out to opponents that evening, but in that speech Mosley declared that fascism was "a creed which comes to abolish poverty in an age of plenty", pointing out that:

"...if we compare the present boom with the last... there are 1,000,000 more unemployed in 1934 than in 1929... we have had an immense swing-over from the industries that produce the goods which meet the needs of the population into distributive and luxury industries... wages in the same period went down by £10 million... we must raise wages and salaries systematically over the whole field of industry to provide a home market which industry at present lacks... we must set about a systematic building of our home market and the creation of a

*new industrial system to take the place of the indus-
trial system that is falling before our very eyes."*[10]

In September that year, an editorial in *The Blackshirt*,
headed "The Right to Combine", recalled the pioneering
efforts of the Tolpuddle Martyrs in the 1830s – whose
struggles to this day are commemorated above all by the
trade union movement – as a battle against selfishness
and individualism:

> *"These men, living poor miserable lives, were early
> heroes in the struggle against a harsh individual-
> ism. They desired nothing more than the right to
> combine and to protect each other against a
> common enemy... The fundamental new faith of
> these men was that unity was strength, a faith that
> is identical with that of the British Union of
> Fascists... The opponents to the Tolpuddle Martyrs
> were inspired by selfish greed."*[11]

But when it came to the matter of applying that other
basic trade union principle of solidarity – in this case
across ethnic or national boundaries – the BUF preferred
to practise narrow protectionism. Its appeal to East
London's non-Jewish workers was characterised by scapegoating. It attributed Gentile workers' experience of
unemployment to the preponderance of Jewish immigrants and aliens, who supposedly encountered no
difficulties finding work. In fact, many Jews were unemployed too and those in employment still largely worked for
Jewish employers – a hangover partly from the patterns
established in the East End when immigrant Jewish workers had to find employment in establishments where they
shared the Yiddish mother-tongue of their bosses. But this
wasn't the only reason for such segregation in the local
labour market. It was also a direct result of many Gentile
employers continuing to practise discrimination. The
BUF's spin on these factors, however, managed to make

the argument that the Jews had "stolen" Gentile jobs, and were in league with richer Jews, sound plausible to many unemployed non-Jews.

At a meeting in Stratford, East London, in July 1935, Mosley claimed: "...the little Jew sweats you in Whitechapel; the big Jew puts you out of employment by the million to maintain his system of usury". He characterised "little Jews" as puppets of big Jewish interests, who, he insisted, were his real target: "A movement has arisen," Mosley declared in the same speech in East London, "...determined not to relax in this bitter fight until it has overthrown the power of Jewish finance."[12]

Later that month *The Blackshirt* railed against what it saw as an attempt to prevent fascists meeting in Bethnal Green. It also claimed that "East End Jews and communists" were seeking signatories to petitions to evict local Blackshirt families. The BUF consciously sought to mobilise its East End supporters to "reclaim territory", which it argued had been usurped by "alien forces". In shifting its national emphasis to this localised district, the BUF propagandist Clement Bruning attempted to theorise for the party's own followers why this area held such promise for them. A year to the day after the BUF's first East London branch had held its inaugural public activity, he wrote:

"The most surprising phenomenon in the growth of British fascism is the great popular support we have gained in East London... It would be superficial merely to attribute our East End strength to the natural and healthy antisemitism which is always to be found in areas thickly populated by Jews... the cause is to be found deep in the character and history of East London. The people there, not so well fed or well housed as are the inhabitants of more prosperous London, have yet a deeper patriotism, deeper loyalty to tradition than is to be found in the suburbs where the sickly enervating propaganda of

154

so-called modern thought has softened the fibre of British youth... Fascism appeals to the sturdy East Ender because it recognises the value and dignity of labour... We are winning wholehearted adherence because we have preached a cause and a system bringing hope and sunlight into lives darkened by long years of hunger, squalor and despair, because we have shown them a way to cast off the foreign yoke of a domineering, all pervading Yiddish culture, which strives to make East London take on the character of Odessa or Warsaw."[13]

The fascists took up the theme of overcrowding, squalor and despair especially in relation to housing. Population density in Stepney was 127 persons per acre compared with 58 per acre across London as a whole. However, their profound concern was evidently limited to those they considered "British" victims of these plagues. Nevertheless, many of their descriptions were accurate and sharply expressed, such as this portrayal of Bethnal Green by Anne Cutmore, a frequent contributor to BUF publications, and drama critic of its monthly journal, *Action*:

"The narrow streets of Bethnal Green straggle across East London, hidden like a shameful secret behind the city's facade of wealth. The tiny box-like houses were hastily put up years ago, without thought, without plan, without consideration to beauty or regard to health, to accommodate the unhappy population which manufactures the city's goods... they are oppressed by poverty and deprivation... Humiliated from their birth by the condition in which they live".[14]

Her points were amplified in *East London Pioneer*, a BUF newspaper specifically targeted at the East End's working classes. In January 1937, it described a home where

18 people lived, sharing one outside toilet and one water tap, both of which were infested with cockroaches. The paper declared that:

> *"The men who are fit to produce Britain's wealth and are fit to fight to protect that wealth are entitled to live as human beings and not as companions of every type of vermin that gather where filth and squalor are rampant."*[15]

Jewish migrants to the East End at the end of the 19th century concentrated in those areas which had previously consisted mainly of Irish migrants. As streets around Spitalfields and Whitechapel became more Jewish, the Irish-Catholic communities that had settled there earlier tended to shift to the east and south of the district. By the 1930s this had resulted in a large number of segregated estates, some almost wholly Jewish, others populated by those of predominantly Irish Catholic descent, and fewer with a more balanced mixture of these two communities that formed the largest of the East End's minorities. These demographic realities were ripe for fascists to exploit through false propaganda. Solly Kaye, who became drawn to anti-fascist initiatives and served later as a Communist councillor locally, recalls the Mosleyites' propaganda of the 1930s:

> *"The fascists had their strongholds in places... which were on the edge of Stepney where the large Jewish population lived... they could involve people on the basis of envy, fear... by saying 'over there the Jews, they've got your houses, over there the Jews, they've got your jobs.' Even though we were living in bloody poverty with bugs crawling all over us in the night."*[16]

The BUF highlighted and exploited the fact that many landlords were Jews. In that period the East End of

London had very little social housing, and while philanthropic trusts managed a certain amount of housing stock, most tenants were at the mercy of private slum landlords whose sole interest was to obtain a regular return on their investment. Families who fell behind in rent payments were summarily evicted without sentiment. There was nothing intrinsically "Jewish" about this behaviour – it was in the nature of slum landlordism. But Jews owned enough of the properties for the Blackshirts to promote the narrative that "decent British East Londoners" had become "victims of alien exploiters".

In its agitational work, the Communist Party produced special "speakers' notes" for activists on platforms in the Irish areas of the East End, such as Shadwell and Wapping, to counter arguments over jobs and housing based on crude scapegoating and lies. Platform orators would remind their audience how their grandparents were called "job snatchers" and accused of "ruining conditions in this country... The Jewish worker is a victim of unemployment equally with non-Jewish workers. In Liverpool, Glasgow and Belfast this old racial incitement is still being used against Irish communities." The speakers' notes provided statistical estimates of the size of Jewish communities in several towns and cities, and compared these figures with the number of unemployed in those cities. Their examples included Liverpool, home to 7,000 Jews and 92,000 unemployed workers; Blackburn with 200 Jews but 16,000 unemployed; and Hartlepool with just 60 Jews but 9,000 people out of work. Anti-fascist arguments directed towards the Irish community were also found in the *Irish Front* – a radical London-based newspaper of the Irish diaspora of this period, edited by the young poets and writers – Charles Donnelly from Co Tyrone and Lesley Daiken from Dublin – of Catholic and Jewish Irish backgrounds respectively.[17]

Mainstream Jewish organisations concentrated their energies in anti-defamation propaganda. Through the written word and ultimately through street-corner speakers, they tried to disprove the lies, misrepresentations and stereotypes that the fascists perpetuated, but the Communist Party particularly through its work within the more broadly-based Stepney Tenants' Defence League (STDL), seemed to possess a deeper and more effective grassroots strategy which did not operate purely at the abstract level of ideas. It was a strategy that could directly challenge the assumptions of those tempted by the fascists' lies, while simultaneously bringing about concrete and lasting changes to families' real lives that undermined the appeal of fascism to these tenants as an answer to their misery and frustrations.

The architect of this strategy was Phil Piratin, whose direct experience of clandestinely observing a local event at first hand, strengthened his resolve to promote this approach:

"One evening Mosley held a meeting in Salmon Lane, Limehouse, Stepney... I went along to the meeting, made myself inconspicuous, and watched to see the support which Mosley had. When the meeting ended there was to be a march... The fascist band moved off, and behind them about 50 thugs in blackshirt uniform. Then came the people. About 1,500 men, women (some with babies in their arms), and youngsters marched behind Mosley's banner. I knew some of these people, some of the men wore trade union badges. This had a terrific effect on my attitude to the problem... while we would fight Mosley's thugs, where did you get by fighting the people?... Mosley's appeal struck a chord. There were certain latent antisemitic prejudices, it is true, but above all these people, like most in East London, were living miserable, squalid lives. Their homes were slums, many were unemployed. Those at work were often in low-paid jobs. Therefore we urged that the Communist Party should help the people to

improve their conditions of life, in the course of which we could show them who was really responsible for their conditions, and get them organised to fight against their real exploiters."[18]

The Communist Party recognised that the anti-fascist element of this strategy for making real improvements to ordinary people's lives would work best in mixed estates, where Jews and non-Jews encountered each other frequently, faced common difficulties and could be engaged in joint campaigns to deal with their common problems. Typically tenants would fight for demands such as getting repairs and decorations done, replacing old lavatory seats and scullery sinks, repairing drains and defects in drinking water supplies, replacing old refuse chutes, tackling vermin, improving lighting, demanding rent controls and seeking to get rents lowered. Through these joint campaigning activities, not only would economically disadvantaged non-Jews understand that their Jewish neighbours faced similar problems, and vice versa, but joint campaigning against bad landlords, whether Jewish or not, emphasised the point to the tenants – especially those of Irish Catholic descent whom Mosley felt would warm to his antisemitic themes – that it was the practices of bad landlordism, not the ethnic origins or religious beliefs of the landlord, that were most significant. And when East End Catholics saw their Jewish neighbours going on rent strikes against Jewish landlords it directly challenged Mosley's false propaganda which characterised the "little Jew" as a mere "puppet" of larger Jewish interests. If the strategy were successful, it would cut away the base that the fascists were building.

The Communist Party, which, in its national form, had tended to operate in a top-down, bureaucratic and centralist manner,[19] recognised locally how important it was in the context of East End housing struggles that the tenants themselves felt they were in charge of the campaign. The party therefore encouraged its activists to help form a Tenants' Defence League as a federation of tenants' defence committees which would be democratically elected at public meetings held on various estates. The Stepney Tenants' Defence League had no formal political affiliation – its president was Reverend St John B Groser, the vicar of Christ Church in Stepney, and a Labour Party member – though it was undoubtedly very much influenced by the Communist Party. And the party provided key activists to do practical tasks. Through the STDL, tenants learnt how to organise, how to determine their legal rights, and how to fight landlords in a collective, disciplined way. The STDL's full time organisers were the Communist Party members Tubby Rosen, Harry Konn and Ella Donovan – between them combining Jewish and Irish affiliations. This was significant because most of the Roman Catholic Church hierarchy in the East End had set their faces against the STDL, and indeed the STDL's attempts to organise in the Irish heartlands of Shadwell and Wapping met with much less success.

In 1938 tenants of two large East End estates – Brady Street Mansions and Langdale Street Mansions[20] – held bitter rent strikes simultaneously, which lasted several months. The significance of this action lay in the fact that, whilst the tenants of Brady Street Mansions were almost entirely Jewish, Langdale Street Mansions, situated on the border of "Irish" and "Jewish" streets, had a very mixed population of Jews and non-Jews. The actions were coordinated because the same company – clothing manufacturers in North-West London rejoicing in the names Craps and Gold – owned both estates. Piratin wrote movingly of the cross-communal unity that was established, especially among the women on picket-line duty against the landlords and bailiffs:

"In Langdale Street Mansions there are many Jewish and non-Jewish families living together. Many of the Jewish housewives would only buy

160

kosher meat. Arrangements were made that the shopping for those on the picket line should be done by other women... Then this question arose of the buying of kosher meat, and conversely, of the orthodox Jewish women buying ordinary meat. Without any hesitation... Mrs Smith would go to the Jewish butcher shop to buy meat for Mrs Cohen on the picket line and the next day Mrs Cohen (who would never have thought of doing it in all her life) would go to buy meat at the local general butchers for Mrs Smith."[21]

The STDL was capable of organising huge rallies of local residents in support of their demands. A demonstration of 15,000 people, including rabbis, church dignitaries and the Mayor of Stepney, was held in support of the rent strike at Langdale Street, and by the end of the decade an STDL official claimed the organisation had a membership of 11,000 tenants.

The most significant single event that exemplified how the strategy could succeed occurred at Paragon Mansions near Stepney Green in June 1937, where evictions of two families in rent arrears – one with five children, the other with six – were imminent. This was an estate that had experienced sporadic rent strikes since 1935, and Tenants' Defence League activists geared themselves up for a further battle. In this instance, though, the families that were directly affected stayed aloof from the tenants' committee and did not want their assistance. When Piratin heard about this, he was puzzled, and went to meet the families. It transpired that they were members of the British Union of Fascists. Piratin records:

"One family would have nothing to do with us whatsoever that evening. The other was prepared to listen. The only way to stop the eviction was to fight. The BUF was not prepared to do anything to help their own members, despite their 'radical' rhetoric."

161

Whatever the feelings of anger and resentment any Jewish members of the STDL may have had against families attached to a political party trading in vicious antisemitism, there was no real dilemma about what the next steps should be. Piratin continues:

"A defence was organised, and after a battle with the bailiffs and the police the notice to quit was withdrawn. It was a small victory, but it showed what could be done. The lessons did not require to be pressed home. BUF membership cards were destroyed voluntarily and in disgust."[22]

These methods of attempting to neutralise support for the BUF among its most promising base – angry, frustrated, impoverished and powerless people who felt disenfranchised, who felt that nobody listened to their concerns or cared for them – did not occur only within the housing sphere. They were practised too within boxing clubs, which were frequented by many young men on either side of the local political divide. Astute anti-fascist strategists encouraged young and enthusiastic adherents to join the same boxing clubs and physical training institutes as the young fascists, not for the opportunity to deal them a painful physical blow, which they may have felt was no more than deserved, but to mingle with them, befriend them and engage them in conversations, asking apparently naïve questions in order to ascertain precisely which issues were driving these young men into supporting fascism. On this neutral territory the anti-fascists could challenge their new acquaintances' assumptions and seek gradually to turn young fascist adherents away from Mosley's ideas, and even win them over as partisans against fascism. Piratin records in particular how a number of young anti-fascists from Blakesley LCC Physical Training Institute, were persuaded to transfer their membership to Ocean Street LCC Institute for this purpose. He writes:

"They were warned that there was to be no 'politics' when they were having a couple of rounds on the mat with the fascists. These lads did excellent work in neutralising and winning over these young fascists. On one occasion in the course of a spar, one of our lads knocked a fascist unconscious. When he was called to account for this, he was apologetic, but explained that it was due to the other man hitting too hard for a friendly spar."[23]

Piratin's version of these struggles, which claimed the backing of the Communist Party nationally for the strategies it developed in East London, has been partially challenged in a fascinating memoir by another local Jewish communist activist, Joe Jacobs, who had a more troubled relationship with the party hierarchy and was expelled twice from the organisation.[24] Jacobs acknowledges Piratin's organisational skills but claims that local anti-fascist initiatives owed more to the sustained, independent efforts of the grassroots fighting for a unified approach in the local branches and local trade unions initially, then wrenching support from the London District Committee and the party nationally, which he felt had seriously under-estimated how problematic and urgent the situation had become in East London. Jacobs also argues that the party's involvement in tenants' campaigns began much later than Piratin claims and that the party did not pay enough attention to organising among the unemployed who might be drawn to fascism, preferring to concentrate on trade union work amongst those who remained in employment.

Neither Piratin nor Jacobs can participate directly any more in resolving the struggle between them for a better past. Both of them clearly played key roles in mobilising many others around them and strengthening a victorious anti-fascist majority in the East End. But the key point that emerged from the activity of the local communists, however much they were or were not supported by the party hierarchy, is that the successful battle for hearts and minds in the East End rested on a firm belief that fascism was not in the interests of most of those it had drawn into its ranks; and that the ideology and practices of fascism, rather than those individuals temporarily attracted to its flag, were the enemy.

Notes

[1] *Jewish Chronicle* 15.6.1934

[2] *Jewish Chronicle* 7.9.1934

[3] *The Blackshirt* 19.10.1934

[4] During this same period the national membership levels of the Communist Party in Britain doubled, so the growth rate among Stepney's membership was much higher than the national rate.

[5] From information about numbers of votes cast in particular wards, and estimates of their ethnic composition, analysts such as Geoffrey Alderman and Henry Srebrnik believe that the local Jewish population's votes contributed very significantly to Piratin's 1945 victory. See Geoffrey Alderman, *The Jewish Community in British Politics*, OUP, 1983, and Henry Srebrnik, *London Jews and British Communism* 1935-1945, Vallentine Mitchell, 1995

[6] Morry Davis was President of the Federation of Synagogues from 1928-44, and Labour leader of Stepney Borough Council from 1935-44. In 1944 he was imprisoned for fraud.

[7] Approximately 35,000 individuals from 53 countries joined the International Brigades that fought in Spain between 1936-39. Though Jews comprised fewer than 1 per cent of most contributing countries, the percentage of Jewish *brigadistas* is estimated at between 15-20 per cent. The Workers' Circle focused its "Aid Spain" efforts on supporting the mainly Jewish Naftali Botwin battalion from Poland, which published a Yiddish newspaper in Spain.

[8] The Labour League of Youth was a radical youth section of the Labour Party, with about 150 branches nationally. It was at odds with the more moderate national Labour leadership on several issues.

[9] *The Blackshirt* 30.11.1934

[10] *The Blackshirt* 15.6.1934

[11] *The Blackshirt* 7.9.1934

[12] *The Blackshirt* 2.8.1935

[13] *The Blackshirt* 4.10.1935 Curiously, Bruning was killed by the Nazis as a civilian prisoner of war in Krakow on 17th

August 1942.

14 *Action* 11.6.1936

15 *East London Pioneer*, January 1937

16 Interview with Solly Kaye, www.csb-berlin.com/.../battle_of-cable-street.interview.htm

17 Donnelly joined the International Brigade and died at the age of 22 in the Battle of Jarama on 22nd February 1937.

18 P. Piratin, *Our Flag Stays Red*, p18

19 Many contended this was true also at an international level with the British Communist Party loyally following decisions made by the Comintern, the international organisation of the Communist movement dominated by Soviet leaders. However, the British party seemed to show more independence from the mid-1930s.

20 Where Mosley's former Jewish bodyguard, Gershon Mendeloff, grew up.

21 P. Piratin op.cit, p47

22 ibid pp28-29

23 ibid pp27-28

24 See *Out of the Ghetto: My youth in the East End – communism and fascism 1913-1939*, by Joe Jacobs (originally self-published, 1978 later Phoenix Press, 1991).

7. Divided on defence: the grassroots rebellion

Most scholars of British fascism agree that Mosley turned towards explicit antisemitism in autumn 1934, though he had dropped heavy hints of this trajectory much earlier. And yet as late as June 1936, the Council of Manchester and Salford Jews was being reminded by one of its most respected leaders, Nathan Laski JP, father of the President of the Board of Deputies, Neville Laski, that, "as long as the Jewish community are not attacked by fascists, the Jewish people have nothing to complain of". He typified a stubborn reluctance by a section of the more economically comfortable members of the Jewish community to acknowledge the threat posed to the wider society by fascism or to understand the link between fascism and antisemitism. The *Jewish Chronicle*, which itself had been indisposed to make that link explicitly until the later years of the decade, noted that some "leading figures" in the Jewish community "were not convinced that, apart from antisemitism, fascism was a deadly political error".[1] This comment referred in particular to Board of Deputies Vice President, Robert Waley-Cohen, who had made remarks indicating that he was personally attracted to aspects of fascist ideology, in a speech to the Jewish Ex-Serviceman's Legion. (He had not been aware that a *Jewish Chronicle* reporter was present.)[2]

Such leading figures frequently referred to Mussolini's fascist regime in Italy, which included many Jews among its members, with warmth and sympathy. They were at pains to show that Italy's 40,000 Jews (among a population of 43 million) were prospering under Mussolini's rule. They highlighted the fact that many Jewish individuals had achieved positions of prominence within the ruling fascist party and in Italian society at large. In 1936

Mussolini personally appointed a Jew, Olivetti, as president of the Italian Cotton Corporation. It is estimated that 230 Italian Jews participated in the March on Rome in 1922 that had installed Mussolini in power, and several historians claim that approximately one third of Italian Jewish adults were paid-up members of the Italian Fascist Party in the 1930s.[3]

At the same time, though, Jewish individuals were prominent in anti-fascist activities as leading members of oppositional forces. These included the eminent Socialist Party figures Claudio Treves and Renato Modigliani, Communist leader Umberto Terracini, and prominent activists within *Giustizia e Liberta* (Justice and Liberty) such as Carlo Levi, Leone Ginzburg and Vittoria Foa, the latter of whom argued that there existed a "certain link between the Jews' affinity for anti-fascism and their democratic roots" since "they were liberated by the process of democracy".[4] So any sense that Italy's Jews as a corporate whole were satisfied with life under fascism was certainly inaccurate. And, although it is routinely stated that antisemitism, as an official policy of Italy's fascist government, was inaugurated in September 1938 when it adopted racist legislation against Jews, enhanced by further laws in November that same year, the association with antisemitism began much earlier. Two prominent fascist newspapers – *Regime Fascista* and *Gazeta del Popolo* published overtly antisemitic articles in 1936. The former was edited by Roberto Farinacci, an ardent pro-Nazi, and the latter frequently attacked "Jewish communism".[5]

In Britain, the Jewish Economic Forum, an organisation based in the City of London, displayed a firm desire to defend the British version of fascism from any criticism or attack by fellow Jews. When Mosley published an article in 1933 entitled "Fascism is not Antisemitic" the Forum reprinted it in leaflet form, declaring that it wished to ensure "that this declaration receives all the publicity which it is in our power to give".

167

Those who had more direct and intimate knowledge of Mosley's movement, however, were convinced otherwise. The defector Charles Dolan, a former national propagandist of the BUF, wrote in 1935, "Sir Oswald Mosley, for political reasons only, often declares that he is not anti-Jewish, but I know that 90 per cent of the movement is definitely antisemitic in feeling... I have myself seen officers of high rank in Mosley's headquarters, leave headquarters with their friends specially bent on Jew-baiting expeditions."[6]

After Mosley started to reveal his attitudes about Jews more explicitly, in autumn 1934, the Jewish Labour Council, a trade union-based organisation in East London, circulated 50,000 copies of a four-page leaflet entitled *Sir Oswald Mosley and the Jews*, specifically aimed at non-Jewish workers. It accused Mosley's movement of using scare tactics about Jews, who barely constituted 0.7 per cent of Britain's population, to drive people "into the fold of fascism... (and) ...convince the British public that Jews are responsible for all the evils of the present day". The leaflet explained how fascism uses antisemitism in a period of economic turmoil and uncertainty:

"The antisemites in this country are treading in Hitler's path. At present the country is still in the grip of a crisis. Millions of men, unemployed and only partly employed are contemplating the future with abject despair. When they are tramping the streets in search of work most of them do not think of the basic social causes of their poverty and hopeless position... In many countries Jew-baiting has been the means through which past reactionaries and modern fascists have wormed themselves into the confidence of masses of people only to plunge them into more abject slavery."

In 1936 a deputation of Jewish small businessmen who were actively anti-fascist, and seeking endorsements

168

from luminaries for broadening such activity in the Jewish community, sought an interview with Lionel de Rothschild, a former Conservative MP, scion of the Rothschild banking family, prominent zoologist and leading exponent of Zionism. His private secretary responded to the group, explaining that Rothschild was "merely watching events" and he was not prepared "to make any statement of opposition to fascism".

However, the escalating antisemitic attacks in 1936 in the name of fascism had prompted a shift in the *Jewish Chronicle's* editorial line on fascism *per se*. Its regular columnist, Watchman, who often tended towards provocative or contrarian positions, had originally concurred that there was no necessary ideological connection between fascism and antisemitism, but as early as 1934 he issued a prescient warning that:

> *"Fascism practised on purely political lines may pose a question for the Jew as Jew, for it involves the suppression of political minorities, and when it comes to suppressing the political opinion of minorities, there is no way of saying in what other ways these groups might suffer. The whole system breathes a spirit of intolerance and it may bode ill not only for the Jew but... for others similarly circumstanced".*[7]

When he revisited these arguments in 1936, at a time when Britain's fascists were more clearly focused on intimidating Jewish communities, he found his editor had become more receptive. The *JC's* conviction that both the fascists and their Jewish opponents were answerable in equal measure for an escalation of physical confrontations, and that responsibility for defusing the situation lay principally with the conduct of Jews, gradually gave way to a more considered analysis which sought to isolate symptoms from causes. Whilst it still admonished physical reactions by Jews to fascist intimidation as "counter-productive", the *JC* became much more inclined to blame the fascists for provoking confrontations in the first place. And it ventured to the authorities that rather than waiting for public incitement to result in physical assaults, it would be wiser to look for legal remedies to prevent people parading the streets and shouting abuse at Jews. It reasoned that this "would strike at the cause rather than the consequences". This shift in perspective did not mean that the prevailing advice to Jews would alter but it indicated that such advice was now bound more by political tact than by ideological preference.

The insights offered by the *JC*'s reporters and columnists certainly facilitated this ideological shift and led to a better appreciation of the nature and extent of the antisemitic threat. But another factor probably had greater influence. The defiant voices of ordinary Jews who were victims of antisemitic abuse and assault were starting to be heard through the *JC*'s letters pages and, as a result, the temperature of the debate was rising rapidly. In its editorial of 3rd July 1936, the paper commented that: "The Jewish community has awakened with a bolt to the need for Jewish defence and letters on the subject continue to pour into this office from all parts." The editor assured readers that, as far as space permitted, he would print "a representative sample". And indeed, many different standpoints and interests in the community from a variety of postal areas were represented in this debate. The majority of published letters subscribed to three common points:

- there was a need for the Jewish community to create an independent defence organisation;

- this need was absolutely urgent;

- this organisation should co-operate with other anti-fascist bodies.

This set of demands was underpinned by an assumption that antisemitism and fascism were inextricably linked, and must be tackled together. A smaller number of letters lent general support to these points but remained more cautious about alliances. Some suggested that religious harmony could provide the best common platform. A further minority view, peripheral to the major practical debate, was put by Zionists, who dismissed conventional counter-measures to antisemitism and seemed to internalise and adopt the narrow nationalist values of Jewry's defamers. They argued that the best answer to the defamation of Jews in Britain was an assertion of Jews' constructive achievements in Palestine. One Zionist correspondent expressed concern that pro-Jewish propaganda could have a reverse effect, because he believed that antisemitism was, "a virus... a pathological complex that cannot be cured by rationality", whilst another argued that Jews in England suffered from an inferiority complex and that "Englishmen will only respect the Jew who has the courage to link his identity with the future of the whole Jewish nation". Another nationalist-inclined correspondent sought to dispute the patriotic claims of the BUF whilst proclaiming the true adherence of Jews in Britain to these values. He proposed forming a "British League of Jews", which would adopt as its symbol a Union Jack with a Star of David superimposed.

This highly charged public debate generally focused less upon matters of underlying philosophy than on practical suggestions. It posed a direct challenge to many of the assumptions and methods on which the communal leaders based their responses, and pointed up the dramatically widening gap within a community increasingly experiencing a crisis of identity internally at the same time as it faced hostility and aggression from the fascists externally. The policy of "dignified apathy", proposed by several Jewish establishment figures, was strongly attacked. One correspondent even suggested that the "inertia and over-caution of our so-called leaders" had "contributed directly to the fascist menace against the Jews". This drew a sharp rejoinder from Mr N Lazarus, a member of the Board of Deputies representing New Road

Synagogue in East London. He argued that "to create a belief that antisemitism is growing because of the Board's inactivity is to mislead the Jewish people". He located the source of antisemitism in economic depression and national political setbacks, which were providing a context for "anti-alienism" to take root. But he also derided the efforts of Jewish leaders as insufficient and called for attacks upon Jews to be answered more vigorously through protest activities. Lazarus was particularly disparaging about the stock of officially sanctioned pro-Jewish literature, which he felt was not fit for the purpose of challenging antisemitism. It was, he said, "good reading for our friends and those uninclined to harm us... it arms our friends" but it "does not disarm our enemies."

The strongest recurrent theme in the debate was the gulf between those who directly experienced the threat and those who sanctioned responses to it. The notion that Jews should ignore Mosley and trust in the "merits and innate decency of their fellow Englishmen... is defensive and humiliating", argued one correspondent, who contrasted the feelings of security of communal leaders such as Melchett and Laski, derived from their social and economic position, with that of the average Jewish worker. Another correspondent recounted how he had written to the Board of Deputies about Mosley's antisemitism three years earlier, but the Board had replied that it did not consider it serious and no action was necessary. His subsequent letter published in the *JC* stated:

> *"The position has now definitely reached a stage when action must be taken. I wonder how many of our leaders have ever been to a Blackshirt meeting or have read* Blackshirt *or* Action".[8]

There was growing consensus that the seriousness of the situation required responses that went beyond simply countering and denying antisemitic accusations. Many voices argued that it was time to expose and combat the *propagators* of defamation. It was becoming widely acknowledged that the process by which a political party subscribing to fascist ideology came to use antisemitism was not random but based on logical and comprehensible factors. Correspondents argued, therefore, not only that the Jewish community should go on the offensive, but that, in doing so, it must also cooperate with other explicitly anti-fascist bodies. As the debate continued to rage, and the communal leadership deliberated ponderously, independent initiatives arose that were intrinsic and extrinsic to the Jewish community, aimed at challenging the twin related threats of antisemitism and fascism. These included the British Union of Democrats, The Portsmouth Jewish Truth Society, The New World Fellowship and the grandly named World Alliance for Combating Antisemitism.

The bitter tensions stoked up by fascist activities, and the desire to be part of bold activities to counter their menace, were felt and expressed especially by young people. In the East End of the 1930s there were many Jewish youth clubs, established mainly by wealthy Jewish philanthropists with a barely concealed "civilising mission" among young Jews from impoverished families, though they preferred to characterise their efforts as securing a greater sense of "self-worth" and "self-confidence" among members of their clubs. These philanthropists feared that young Jews were in grave danger of being tempted into underworld activities as a means of supplementing the meagre incomes of their families, or alternatively of being drawn into the orbit of political radicals – a scenario they seemed to regard with even greater alarm.

Joyce Goodman, who grew up in Brady Street Mansions in the highly charged atmosphere of rent strikes and street corner political meetings, recalls the day she was thrown out of her local Jewish youth club for attempting to sell *Challenge*, the overtly anti-fascist newspaper of the Young Communist League, at the club:

"The club leader was Miriam Moses [a local Liberal politician and the first female Mayor of Stepney]. She called me in and told me that... I wasn't allowed to sell Challenge *in the club. 'It was not a political club,' she said. I said it wasn't true that it was a non-political club because you have the* Evening Standard *and you had all the other papers. 'It's OK to sell Conservative papers but not Communist ones.' She decided I was 'incorrigible' and so I was expelled."*[9]

Lady Rose Henriques, who managed the Oxford and St Georges Youth Club with her husband Basil Henriques, was disturbed enough by falling attendance of club members in the autumn of 1936 to write to parents warning them that, unbeknown to them, their children may be involved in communist and anti-fascist activity: "I would strongly advise you in the interests of your daughter, to satisfy yourself as to where she is spending those evenings in which she is not in this club," she wrote to them.[10]

Several individuals who became actively engaged in anti-fascist activities in their late teens and early twenties refer, in their reflections on that period, to the clash of political perspectives that emerged between users and providers within the arena of youth clubs, and to inter-generational conflicts. Parents and grandparents, quite a few of whom were themselves immigrants, shared the young people's sense of outrage at antisemitic accusations and assaults but were constrained by a dominant mindset of gratitude that they were living in a free and democratic society, such a far cry from the Czarist Empire from which they had fled. They were understandably less forthright about advancing their rights through militant political protests or by engaging in activities that might have brought them into conflict with the authorities. Their British children, though, had a much less clouded sense of their rights as free citizens born in Britain. And, if the older generation could not identify as strongly with what they characterised as the "hot-headedness" of the youth, many among them, nevertheless, also felt a sense of abandonment by the Jewish political establishment.

A *JC* editorial early in January 1936, headed "A Question of Self-Protection", acknowledged how dissatisfied and anxious many Jews were feeling about the Board of Deputies' failure to provide adequate leadership on the defence question. It reminded them that: "the defence of the community can no longer be played with. The Board was made for the community, not the community for the Board". A further editorial in May, headed "The Reply to Calumny", referred specifically to two letters the newspaper had received, from London and Leeds respectively, calling for vigorous action against antisemitism. The *JC* categorically declared its lack of faith in the present defence structure: "We have a Lecture Committee and a Press and Information Committee but nobody believes this penny-whistle piping is an effective response to antisemitic blasts."[11]

The Board had promised the community that a new defence scheme would be formed, but its appearance was continually delayed as meetings were adjourned with few advances. Robert Waley-Cohen, who was responsible for preparing the scheme, appealed for "patience and restraint", but the *JC* warned that "patience should not be stretched to breaking point". The elements of the community that had been consistently stressing how urgent the situation had become, clearly believed that, with sufficient willpower, effective machinery could be assembled swiftly and without difficulty. The patience demanded by Waley-Cohen, though, was not simply, as the Board's detractors accused, indicative of lethargy. It reflected a different conception of the nature of the defence machinery to be established and the basis upon which it would operate. Waley-Cohen justified his plea for patience by saying it was necessary "to ensure that the defence of Jewry in this country shall be worthy of its unique traditions... and so ordered as not to forfeit the smallest fraction of the good opinion of our friends and all of the best elements in the civilised world".[12]

Watchman had ratcheted up the pressure in an article on 5th June 1936 entitled "The Question of Self-Defence", which provided a powerful indictment of the contemporary theory, practice and advice of the communal leadership, and called for firm action. It lambasted the "public silence and private manoeuvring" that had typified its responses, preferring indirect pressure on government departments to any publicly-based campaign. The leadership feared that too much visibility might lend credence to the notion of a Jewish problem. The paradox, said Watchman, was that an invisible community was difficult to unify when the situation demanded a closing of ranks. Private activities had included leading Deputies requesting the *JC* to refrain from giving antisemites publicity, holding that they would regard any such publicity as positive propaganda. The *JC* had supposedly rejected this demand, although Watchman confirmed that for a long time the newspaper had indeed "refrained from noticing fascist carryings on". He believed that "this quietism did not appease the enemy and was only met with increased anti-Jewish activities". He spoke for many in the community who were growing impatient at the lack of action being taken by those who regarded themselves as its official leadership, when he wrote: "the most decisive act of our leaders has been the resolve to do nothing".

In his column of 17th July, headed "The Problem of Defence", Watchman vehemently denied and ridiculed the utility of the repeated advice to those who complained of intimidation by fascists, to "stay away". He quoted (anonymously) a powerful remark made by Willie Gallagher, Communist MP for West Fife, in the House of Commons debate on antisemitism a week earlier, which asked how it might be humanly possible "to stay away from the chalking of offensive remarks on the pavement and walls of houses, the placards stuck on doors and people who go into shops and intimidate Jewish shopkeepers. Jewish pedestrians set upon by gangs of thugs would be only too glad to stay away".[13]

Such criticism of the leadership found echoes among many of the Board's "backbenchers" on the floor of its monthly meetings, the most outspoken being Bertram Jacobs (Newport) and M Turner-Samuels (Newcastle). Representatives of the areas in which attacks on the Jews had been most concentrated gave considerable support to these critics. The pressure was sustained and, as the Deputies prepared for their July meeting, the *JC* justifiably claimed that there were strong grounds for believing that the Jewish leadership had been stirred by public opinion as expressed through its own columns.

On 24th July 1936, in a tone that betrayed relief as much as expectation, the *JC* enthusiastically declared: "Forward to Defence". It reported that the Board had just taken a major step in setting up the machinery through which it could more adequately respond to antisemitism in Britain. It had created a Coordinating Committee to unify and direct its defence work, expanded the brief of its Press Committee and appointed a full-time executive officer to direct operations. The sole purpose of the body was anti-defamation. The circumstances within which this development occurred were considerably influenced not merely by continuing debate about possible initiatives but by a specific combination of factors, a central feature of which was a break in the consensus between the Board and the *JC*. Though they had earlier been united in a cautious and careful approach, the *JC* increasingly came to articulate and advance the urgent demands of its readers as expressed so trenchantly through its correspondence columns. Within long-established, top-down communal structures, which were not over-accustomed to responding to proceedings in democratic arenas, the Board was ultimately compelled to show much greater sensitivity to grassroots opinion on the Jewish street.

When the new defence structures were finally established, the *JC* offered the community four points of advice and warning: firstly, as defence was now committed to the hands of a responsible body, any unauthorised individual and group action should be abandoned; secondly, now that the individuals had grasped the helm, the time for bringing up their past unsatisfactory record had gone; thirdly – aimed specifically at the Deputies – if they were to receive the confidence of the community, they must deserve it: "Let the Deputies not fail and the community will not fail the Deputies"; and fourthly, it issued a plea to the community which had "cried aloud for defence against its detractors": it was now promised satisfaction, but, the JC reminded its readers, the Defence Committee required the community's financial support.

The combination of a rapidly intensifying antisemitic threat, the strident demands among wide sections of the community for more adequate defence measures, the tentative growth of independent initiatives, and the growing dissent within its own ranks, had compelled the Board to revise its defence policy and structure. The *JC* emerged as a significant catalyst in the process, channelling the urgent demands of the community towards definable policy steps, but it, too, was tarred with being slow to recognise the seriousness of the situation until it had become blindingly obvious. No sooner had the Board established its independent Co-ordinating Committee, though, than it was faced with a major rival representative organisation, rooted in the East End community that was suffering most from the attention of Mosley's fascists. Its very name – the Jewish People's Council Against Fascism and Antisemitism (JPC) – indicated its grassroots origin and orientation, and it was in terms of the contrasting analyses and responses developed by the JPC and the Board's Coordinating Committee that the debate about Jewish communal responses to antisemitism and fascism continued to be fought out.

The Jewish People's Council Against Fascism and Antisemitism

While the wheels of the Board of Deputies were grinding slowly towards the moment of decision, those at the grass-roots of the community felt they had already waited long enough. They decided to take matters into their own hands. The Jewish Labour Council, comprising trade unionists, particularly in the clothing and furniture industries, which had published and distributed the leaflet about "Mosley and the Jews", invited organisations to a delegate conference at ABSA House on Commercial Road, in the heart of London's East End Jewish community, on 26th July 1936, to discuss how to develop an organised response to the threat from fascism and antisemitism. [14] The response was overwhelming: 179 delegates attended, representing 87 organisations including Workers' Circle branches, trade unions, political organisations, friendly societies, synagogues, Zionist bodies, youth organisations and ex-servicemen's organisations.

The conference confirmed that there was indeed a shared conviction that a strong, popular and participatory Jewish anti-fascist body was urgently needed which would be capable of taking the necessary steps for Jewish defence. Participants acknowledged that the established leadership of the community was in the process of assembling fresh defence structures, but they were not willing to place their faith in the efficacy of these moves, not only because community leaders were taking so long to put these structures in place but also because they did not believe that the Board of Deputies represented, in any meaningful sense, the breadth of the community. A 26-member delegate council emerged from the conference, and this was later formally constituted as the Jewish People's Council Against Fascism and Antisemitism.

The chair of the Jewish Labour Council, the Latvian-born Aaron Rapoport Rollin, made the keynote speech at the conference. He was a highly regarded and longstanding Jewish trade union leader in the garment industry. He told the conference:

> "There may be some delegates amongst you who might say that when the Board of Deputies have taken the matter in hand there is no need for further conferences and action against fascism and anti-semitism by other Jewish bodies... (but) ...the Board of Deputies, constituted as it is on an obsolete and often farcical basis of representation, does not represent the widest elements of the Jewish people in this country... the mass of the Jewish people are not at all yet convinced that a complete and sincere change of heart and mind has taken place in the leadership of the Board. There must therefore be in existence a strong and virile popular Jewish body to act as a driving force in our fight against the dangers confronting us. We shall welcome and cooperate in all efforts undertaken by the Board in that direction."[15]

The central tenet of the JPC's analysis, which clearly distinguished it from the Board, was its contention that, in contrast with episodes of antisemitism in previous decades, antisemitism in Britain at this time had to be understood in terms of its political necessity to the fascist movement. The JPC characterised antisemitism as "both a rallying cry and a smokescreen, thus hiding from the British people as a whole the true purpose of fascism". It argued that antisemitism was a weapon of fascism and although antisemitism primarily impacted on Jews, *fascism* was a threat to the democratic liberties of all. The JPC saw antisemitism primarily as a political instrument, but with an appeal rooted in economic conflict within the society in which it arose. While recognising that its proponents were influenced by political developments and philosophies expounded abroad, its ability to gain some degree of mass support in Britain indicated that it had home-grown roots. This characterisation of antisemitism had implications for the kinds of responses and working alliances that would be developed to counter it. The JPC argued that:

"The struggle against antisemitism is as much a task for the British people as a whole as for the Jews; and the struggle against fascism is a task for Jews as much as for the British people as a whole."[16]

The JPC declared that it was impossible to combat antisemitism purely through anti-defamation work, as this would be merely attacking the symptoms. It organised a campaign of public protest meetings, often open-air, both within the Jewish community, where it was seeking to mobilise people into practical activity, and in the streets where the fascists were strong, often close to BUF platforms, where it directly challenged the arguments put by fascists to their audiences. It made appeals to Parliament, particularly on the question of political uniforms and racial incitement. The JPC sent speakers to Jewish and non-Jewish organisations, and cooperated with other anti-fascist groups. It established a particularly strong cooperative relationship with the National Council for Civil Liberties (NCCL) – today known as Liberty – which itself was a relative newcomer to the British democratic scene, having been established by the radical bookshop proprietor Ronald Kidd in 1934. The NCCL conceived its role as the defence of individuals and minority groups, having been alarmed in particular about invidious police actions against hunger marches of unemployed workers in the early 1930s. The JPC and NCCL organised joint conferences, and NCCL speakers regularly appeared on JPC platforms.

The intense flurry of activity which had been set in motion prompted the formation of numerous other groups, each one genuinely wishing to take practical steps in defence of the Jewish community. The

Association of Friendly Societies organised speakers' classes with a view to holding open-air meetings in the areas where the fascists were mobilising support. An Ex-Servicemen's Movement against Fascism was founded at a rally held at Circle House, home of the Workers' Circle, and within six weeks of its formation claimed 1,000 members including 700 Jews. In North West London a rapidly growing Jewish Council of Action had been inaugurated, which took as its charter Watchman's article in the *JC* on "The Question of Self-Defence". This group later merged with the JPC. These independent initiatives represented a wide range of approaches to Jewish defence, derived not only from diverse interests expressed in a wider collective framework, but also from strongly held analyses that represented some degree of incompatibility between different approaches.

The enthusiasm for activity brought both opportunities and dangers. The *JC* expressed a legitimate concern that such a multiplicity of bodies "does not make for strength unless there is a clear understanding of the functions of each and harmonious cooperation". It called for unity to avoid "a squandering and misdirection of energies". Alignments and cooperative working arrangements were made, but they did not result in one unified defence body. Instead, the defence of British Jewry between 1936 and 1939 was led principally by two different Jewish organisations, both claiming in their own way to be "representative". One was the Coordinating Committee, established mainly from above by the Board, and the other, the JPC, established from below. They had a different analysis of the problem the community faced and developed contrasting strategies.

The Board was concerned solely with countering antisemitic defamation and would not embroil itself with the issue of fascism as such. This was, firstly, because, in the face of a great deal of evidence, it believed that fascism did not have any special relationship to antisemitism, and secondly, the Board claimed that if it adopted a position on fascism, it would be involving itself in partisan politics. In this latter stance they were generally supported by the *JC*, which, although it gradually conceded the philosophical connection between fascism and antisemitism, argued that it was dangerous for Jews to take a single collective attitude towards a legal political party since "no other religious section takes up such a position towards a political party".

The Board's favoured method of countering antisemitic calumny at ground level was through distributing leaflets and pamphlets and organising public meetings, many of which were outdoors. Its leaflets and pamphlets, such as *The Jews of Britain*, *Bolshevism is not Jewish*, and *What the Jews of Britain did in the Great War*, concentrated on facts and figures, and extracts were periodically featured in display form in the *JC*.

One such extract asked: "Do the Jews control British finance?" It then stated that there was not a single Jewish director of the Bank of England, that only three out of 150 directors of the "Big Five" banks were Jewish, and there were no Jews among the 70-80 directors of the other major clearing banks. This exemplified both the utility and weaknesses of the anti-defamation approach. Its utility lay in its unambiguous refutation of distorted or invented claims; but, by accepting that the argument may be reduced to numbers, it conceded the principle contained within the underlying argument, and itself delegitimised the role of Jews in Britain as equal citizens. For what if there *were* Jewish directors of the Bank of England? Would that have justified antisemitic calumny? Facts in themselves did not create antipathy towards Jews. This depended on individuals or collective political bodies convincing people to attribute relevance to real or exaggerated facts. Anti-defamation work blunted the antisemitic attack, but it did not challenge its fundamental principles.

More than 1,500 people attended the Board's inaugural open-air meeting at Hyde Park. Following its success, meetings were regularly held at recognised "street corner" venues. These were organised in close cooperation with the more locally-based Association of Jewish Friendly Societies (AJFS) and the Ex-Servicemen's Movement Against Fascism. Before embarking on its campaign of open-air meetings, the AJFS discussed principles with the Board and submitted itself completely to the Board's authority. Eventually the Board's campaign and that of the Friendly Societies were further coordinated under the auspices of the London Area Council (LAC), which set up an office in Whitechapel Road, East London. The Friendly Societies, whose platforms were non-political, were crucial to the Board's campaign because they were drawn from the wider elements of the community and, in that sense, made its implementation more representative. But they shared

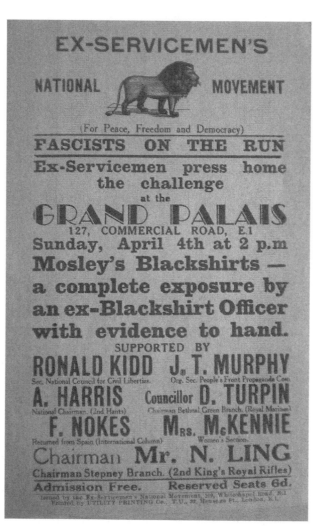

EX-SERVICEMEN'S

NATIONAL **MOVEMENT**

(For Peace, Freedom and Democracy)

FASCISTS ON THE RUN

Ex-Servicemen press home the challenge

at the

GRAND PALAIS

127, COMMERCIAL ROAD, E.1

Sunday, April 4th at 2 p.m

Mosley's Blackshirts — a complete exposure by an ex-Blackshirt Officer with evidence to hand.

SUPPORTED BY

RONALD KIDD **J. T. MURPHY**

Sec. National Council for Civil Liberties.   Org. Sec. People's Front Propaganda Com.

A. HARRIS Councillor **D. TURPIN**

National Chairman. (2nd Hants)   Chairman Bethnal Green Branch. (Royal Marines)

F. NOKES Mrs. **McKENNIE**

Returned from Spain (International Column)   Women's Section.

Chairman Mr. **N. LING**

Chairman Stepney Branch. (2nd King's Royal Rifles)

Admission Free.   Reserved Seats 6d.

Issued by the Ex-Servicemen's National Movement, 308, Whitechapel Road, E.1
Printed by UTILITY PRINTING Co., T.U., 22, Hanbury St., London, E.1

the Board's narrow, apolitical analysis of antisemitism and its tendency to take arguments at face value rather than question the motivations of those advancing antisemitic propaganda. This is illustrated in the arguments on street platforms made by the LAC's principal speaker, Frank Renton:

"Jew-baiting is a contradiction of everything which Christianity has stood for. Jews are trustworthy... they have rendered illustrious service to Britain and the Empire. The overwhelming majority of Jews in Britain are sober, hardworking and with a social and moral standard as high as that of any other denomination."[17]

The Board and the AJFS published a series of pamphlets providing "speakers' notes" on more than twenty different topics. These were later compiled into a handbook, which also gave wise practical advice on effective styles of public speaking. It urged speakers to non-Jewish audiences not to refer to their audience as "non-Jews", "Christians" or "Gentiles" but to address them as "fellow citizens". Several of the speakers' pamphlets they produced contained very useful arguments for tackling misinformation and misunderstandings. For example, challenging the accusation that Jews owned and controlled the press, they pointed out that of seventeen national Sunday papers, only one, the *Sunday Referee*, was owned by a Jew, and of 116 daily newspapers in Britain only the *Daily Herald*, published by Oldham's Press was associated with a Jew – Lord Southwood of Fernhurst who grew up as Julius Elias in an impoverished East End family.[18] Notes to counter the claim that the Jew was not patriotic, but internationalist, highlighted the loyalty shown through military service by both German and British Jews respectively who were decorated with honours by their countries during the First World War. The claim that Bolshevism was Jewish was answered with the argument that the inspiration for Bolshevism – the German Jew Karl Marx – was negative about Jewishness, while another German Jew, Frederic Julius Stahl, had founded Germany's Conservative Party. The boycott of German goods encouraged by several Jewish organisations had been frequently condemned in Oswald Mosley's speeches as ruining English traders but the AJFS notes argued that the boycott had strengthened British industry. It claimed that there were 160 classes of goods that were previously made only on a very small scale in Britain, as many of them were largely imported, but since the boycott they were now recognised as British industries.

The speakers' notes were less convincing against some charges, for example, the claim that Jews were dispro-portionately involved in criminal activity. The figures it provided, that 455 Jews were among the 46,699 inmates of Britain's prisons in 1935, indicated that the Jewish prison population was actually a little higher than their proportion in the society at large. The notes did point out, however, that 165 of these were first time offenders and that many offences related to debt, but didn't acknowl-edge explicitly the simple point that most Jews were poor, and poor people disproportionately engaged in criminal activities to mitigate their situation.

The notes to counter the accusation that Jews were averse to sporting activities were met with the retort: "While we cannot claim that Jewry has attained pre-eminence in sport generally in the country... there is hardly any branch of sport which is without Jewish play-ers of outstanding ability." It furnished much evidence of Jewish involvement in boxing, where Jews displayed their "prowess, courage and endurance", but struggled to match these claims for football, quoting the involvement of just two professional players – Levine who played for Tottenham Hotspur and Charlton Athletic, and Mosson who played for Grimsby Town and Swindon Town!

The Jews of Britain was a publication aimed at a gen-eral readership, bearing the imprint of the Woburn Press identified with the Board of Deputies. It provided a great deal of ammunition for the campaign by street-corner speakers, especially on Jewish contributions to Britain's economy. It described the Jews as:

> "...*a refugee population who brought new ideas, established industries and created wealth and*

created employment for hundreds and thousands of people of all religions... In recent times many productive industries have been created and expanded by Jews on which the livelihoods of so many workers depend."[19]

Such arguments were used to challenge those promoting an "aliens scare" about Jewish refugees from Germany and Austria, in the summer of 1938. The authors of this handy publication urged their readers to "judge the Jews by facts not fables".

Whilst the public activities of the Board brought it closer to the reality of those Jews most exposed to attack, it did not alter its basic advice. It maintained that Jews should abstain from challenging Blackshirt meetings and demonstrations, and that their behaviour should be impeccable, blameless and devoid of vulgarity and ostentation. If "volatile Jewish youth" stayed away, argued the Board's president, Neville Laski, "the charge that Jews are communists would soon be proved baseless".

The JPC concentrated its efforts more selectively, combining general anti-defamation work with meetings for particular audiences such as trades councils, trade union branches, political organisations and small shopkeepers. Armed with an alternative analysis, its message contrasted considerably with that of the Board. The JPC's exposure of antisemitic calumny was placed within a framework directed towards unmasking the methods and motives of its propagators. Whilst the Board reproached Jews with the antisemites' accusations that they were sweating employers, bad landlords and price-cutters undermining other local businesses, the JPC rejected the notion that these were particularly Jewish characteristics. Its practical advice to Jewry similarly contrasted with that of the Board; it printed and distributed thousands of leaflets urging Jews to join public demonstrations against fascism, and the JPC participated fully in the events of 4th October 1936, which subsequently became known as the Battle of Cable Street.

The clash of perspectives between Jewish opponents of antisemitism was given an opportunity for a formal airing on neutral territory in 1938 at a debate in Whitechapel Art Gallery, organised under the auspices of the Harcourt Club. Frank Renton, the foremost speaker of the London Area Council, spoke in a personal capacity but faithfully represented the perspectives that were shared by this Council, which was backed by the Board of Deputies. His opponent was Julius Jacobs, representing the Jewish People's Council. Jacobs was also a prominent member of the Communist Party.

Renton stressed how important it was that the fight against antisemitism remained aloof from politics and did not embroil itself with the question of fascism as such. He argued that, in any case, the enemy that Jews faced in areas like Bethnal Green, Shoreditch and Limehouse was not "highly intelligent fascism but the same old anti-semitism that existed 30 years ago, filthy, wicked and vitriolic". He praised the achievements of the London Area Council, stating that during the previous two years it had held 1,400 meetings in the heartlands of the East End's fascists. He accused the Jewish People's Council of holding its meetings at "Brick Lane or Bloom's corner" in the heartlands of the Jewish community, instead of con-fronting antisemites with arguments in the streets where they congregate. He dismissed the JPC's emphasis on speaking to trade union branches as meetings "where you talk to the converted". In a thinly veiled swipe at the Communist Party, he said that the fight against anti-semitism must avoid "involving the Jewish community in becoming a branch of a political organisation in this coun-try which is suspected of disloyalty by the overwhelming millions of British people".

Jacobs did not rise to the insinuations about the Communist Party, but simply pointed out that the JPC had received active support from across the political spec-trum, which was reflected by their platform speakers at many of its events. He disputed the charge that the JPC only held its open-air meetings in safe Jewish areas, and stressed that the JPC deliberately chose to hold many open-air meetings in precisely those areas where fascists had put candidates up for the local elections. On the more theoretical questions, Jacobs rejected the view that anti-semitism could be fought purely through anti-defamation. He said: "The Jews are being attacked by fascists. They are not being attacked by defamation. We cannot get the whole of Jewry to unite to fight the lies that are being told without telling them who are the liars." He directly challenged Renton's understanding of the antisemitic threat by arguing that the antisemitism that Renton referred to thirty years ago *was* different from the antisemitism that was faced today because it had a completely different function. He said that antisemitism then, "was not an attack on democracy", whereas the antisemitism they currently faced was, and it was "being bred and spread by *fascists*". That was why the JPC believed that Jews needed to link up with the democratic forces in this country who were also threatened by fascism. He argued that Renton's approach – that antisemitism was only a threat to Jews and could only be combated by Jews – isolated the Jews instead of providing opportunities to find allies. The JPC could point to the successes it had enjoyed through joint activity with other democratic forces, not least at the Battle of Cable Street in 1936.

Notes

[1] *Jewish Chronicle* 27.11.1936

[2] Waley-Cohen expressed embarrassment and annoyance about the remark, which he felt the *JC* had taken out of context. The paper stood by its reporter's interpretation of what was said.

[3] Jews in Italy suffered many barriers to acceptance and equality before 1870, but after their liberation individual Jews rose to high office among educational, scientific, political and military elites. In 1910 a Venetian Jew, Luigi Luzzatti, became Prime Minister.

4   In 1935 Foa was sentenced to 15 years imprisonment for anti-fascist activities.
5   *Jewish Chronicle* 29.7.1938
6   C. Dolan, *The Blackshirt Racket Exposed*, 1935
7   *Jewish Chronicle* 16.2.1934
8   *Jewish Chronicle* 10.7.1936
9   Interview of Joyce Goodman on tape at Imperial War Museum
10 Quoted by Nadia Valman in "Jewish Girls and the Battle of Cable Street" in *Remembering Cable Street*, Tony Kushner and Nadia Valman (ed), Vallentine Mitchell, 1999.
11 *Jewish Chronicle* 15.5.1936
12 *Jewish Chronicle* 26.6.1936
13 *Jewish Chronicle* 17.7.1936
14 The Jewish Labour Council was formed in 1934 from a convention of the Workers' Circle Friendly Society, with the aim of defending and advancing the interests of Jewish workers, especially in the workplace itself.
15 Rollin Papers held at the Modern Records Centre, Warwick University
16 *Jewish Chronicle* 28.5.1937
17 *Jewish Chronicle* 23.10.1936
18 Lord Southwood is also remembered as a dynamic Chair of the Great Ormond Street Hospital for Children from 1937-1946.
19 *The Jews of Britain*, Woburn Press, 1938

8. Rally to Aldgate and Cable Street

The awakening of the Jewish community to the truly serious nature of the threat posed by organised antisemitism, and the widening gap between differing perceptions and understandings of this problem, were graphically illustrated by the events that took place in the East End on 4th October 1936, and the subsequent interpretations of these events.

In *The Blackshirt* of 26th September 1936, the British Union of Fascists announced plans to celebrate the fourth anniversary of the birth of its movement through a "Great Anniversary Demonstration on Sunday October 4th",

192

which would culminate in "four great London meetings" each to be addressed by the leader, Sir Oswald Mosley. It advised members to "report to their District Officers as soon as possible for details". Over the following week, posters advertised the venues for these meetings, which were all in East London: at Aske Street, Shoreditch; Salmon Lane, Limehouse; Stafford Road, Bow; and Victoria Park Square, Bethnal Green. Mosley would be joined on these platforms by other leading ideologues, William Joyce, John Beckett, Alexander Raven-Thomson and Thomas Moran. Most significantly for London's largest and most concentrated Jewish community, the meetings would be preceded by a parade of "four marching columns" of fascists starting at Royal Mint Street in the City.

The marchers were due to set off in the middle of the afternoon, after they had been inspected by the Leader, and the meetings would begin between 5pm and 6.30pm. Unless they were planning a long horseshoe-shaped route to tiptoe round the outskirts of the East End, the implication was clear: the BUF were intending to march right through the heart of the East End in which 60,000 Jews were struggling against great economic difficulties to make a living while simultaneously fending off growing acts of hostility and violence from the very organisation that was now making preparations to invade their streets.

In the days before the intended march, anonymous slogans appeared on the walls of East London streets urging the locals to "Kill the Jews". According to the *New Statesman*, an invasion had already effectively been taking place for several months:

> *"Fascist meetings organised from its headquarters have been more frequent and speakers with their bodyguards of uniformed stewards brought down in vans. Their speeches have been increasingly violent and threatening to the Jewish population. Determined efforts are also made to establish local organisations in the heart of most Jewish districts*

and outrages on individual Jews have grown more frequent and brutal."[1]

The national offices of the British Union of Fascists at this time were in Westminster, far from the East End of London. Before that they had operated from the "Black House" barracks in Chelsea. If Mosley wanted to celebrate his party's fourth birthday, he could have chosen to hold a celebration event at or near his national headquarters or perhaps hired a boat to take his supporters along the Thames between Westminster and the party's first location in Chelsea. The decision to mark the occasion with an incursion into the East End was undoubtedly intended as a provocation. One local resident told a *Daily Worker* reporter: "Mosley is not coming here to convince Jewish people that fascism is good for them!"

In the week immediately preceding the demonstration, the Jewish People's Council collected nearly 100,000 signatures from local Jewish and non-Jewish residents for the following petition, urging the Home Secretary to ban the march.

"We the undersigned Citizens of London view with grave concern the proposed march of the BUF upon East London. The avowed objective of the fascist movement in Great Britain is incitement to malice and hatred against a section of the population. It aims to destroy the friendship and goodwill that has existed for centuries among the East London population irrespective of differences in race and belief. We consider such incitement by a movement which employs flagrant distortion of truth and calumny and vilification as a direct and deliberate provocation. We make an earnest appeal to HM Secretary of State to prohibit this march and thus retain peaceful and amicable relations between all sections of the East London population."

On Thursday 1st October, five East London mayors, led by Helena Roberts, the Mayor of Stepney, met with Home Office officials for an hour to express their fear of the consequences of allowing Mosley's march to proceed. The following day a further delegation, which included James Hall, MP for Stepney, Whitechapel and St Georges, AM Wall, secretary of London Trades Council, Reverend Father Groser, of Christ Church Stepney and JPC officers delivered the mass petition to the Home office. The JPC's secretary, Jack Pearce, recalled the response: "Our deputation was received courteously by a highly placed official of the Home Office but we were informed that the Home Office could not, or would not, intervene... it was decided (not without some opposition within the Executive) to appeal to the people to bar the road to fascism." The JPC distributed a further leaflet thanking "Citizens of London" for their "energy and work". It asked that they "continue to support us in the campaign we have initiated against fascism and antisemitism" by enforcing the demand that "this march must not take place". He continued:

> *"A public appeal was issued to the authorities. We declared that there would be disorder, that clashes would occur between people and police, and that many would be hurt, that the responsibility rested with the authorities to end the provocation against East London citizens, Jews and non-Jews alike, whose hatred of fascism was well known to the authorities."*[2]

The authorities knew this assessment was accurate and mobilised 7,000 police from all over London to seek to ensure that order was maintained. Their instructions, though, were to clear a path for Mosley's troops to march. The democratic demands of the local populace to be spared this act of gross provocation were ignored as the Home Office decided, in the name of protecting freedom of speech, to enshrine the BUF's right to insult, intimidate and terrorise the local community.

The mood of militancy on the Jewish street that the JPC accurately gauged, but which seemed to take Jewish establishment bodies completely by surprise, was described by its Secretary, Jack Pearce:

> *"...within a few days the build-up of opposition to the proposed march became increasingly evident. The streets of East London were a ferment of discussion and agitation. The JPC issued dozens of leaflets... in lots of about 20,000... street corner meetings were organised by the score, and we were able to call upon the support of hundreds of unknown young men and women who willingly undertook all the jobs that had to be done – leaflet distribution, whitewashing slogans, carrying platforms to street corners, collecting funds."*[3]

On the Thursday evening, three days before the demonstration, the Independent Labour Party hired loudspeakers and toured a van through the streets of East London calling people to come in their thousands to block all entry points to the East End on Sunday from the city streets where Mosley's troops would be gathering. Its appeal was reported as a front page item in the *Evening Standard*, a London-based newspaper that had not previously shown a great deal of sympathy with those determinedly combating Mosley's ideas. The *Standard* unwittingly aided the anti-fascists' mobilisation by publishing "Big ILP counter rally" on its hoardings throughout the London area. On the Friday night the ILP held a large indoor anti-fascist rally in the neighbouring district of Hackney, supporting the fight against fascism in Spain and in London, in which it passed a resolution calling on people to block Mosley's proposed march on the Sunday.

On that same day, the *Jewish Chronicle* published an "urgent warning" advising Jews to "keep away from the

Citizens of London.

THE Jewish People's Council has presented a petition with nearly 100,000 signatures to the Home Office requesting that the provocative Fascist march on Sunday, October 4th through East London should not take place.

You have done your duty by signing and helping us to present this petition. We thank you for your energy and work, and ask you to continue to support us in the campaign which we have initiated against Fascism and anti-semitism.

The Jewish People's Council wishes to make clear to the people of London that in no way does it depart from its original contention. This march aims to promote ends which seek to destroy the harmony and goodwill which existed for generations among East London's population, irrespective of difference in race and creed.

The banning of the proposed march does not conflict with the principle of free speech and assembly, for its special provocative character affords a sufficient basis for discrimination and exclusion.

This March Must Not Take Place !

Issued by the Jewish People's Council,
Against Fascism and Anti-semitism.
164, Commercial Road, E.1   Tel. Stepney Green 3906

route of the Blackshirt march and from their meetings". It wrote: "Jews who, however innocently, become involved in any possible disorders, will be actively helping antisemitism and Jew-baiting. Unless you want to help the Jew-baiters, keep away." The Board of Deputies likewise used its influence through synagogues to appeal to Jews to stay away. The *Daily Herald*, *News Chronicle* and other Labour and Liberal press organs appealed to their readers to steer clear of the event. But their advice was to be roundly ignored.

The depth of anger and frustration felt by the Jews of the East End manifested itself even within the political party that had taken a decisive lead in confronting fascism. By selecting 4th October as the date for his East End foray, Mosley may also have been consciously playing a spoiler aimed at the Communist Party, who had already declared their backing for an "Aid Spain" rally in Trafalgar Square that same day, fronted by their youth section, the Young Communist League. From the moment in July 1936 that Franco's revolt began against the democratically elected Republican government of Spain, events there regularly commandeered the front page of the *Daily Worker*, which, under more normal conditions gave highest prominence to domestic news and campaigns. The Communist Party, aware of the support Franco had from Hitler and Mussolini, threw itself into the fray on behalf of the Spanish Republic, arguing that a victory for Franco's right-wing ultra-nationalists could only herald further triumphs for fascism on the world stage.

Mosley's movement, by contrast, was initially very reluctant to pronounce so clearly on Spain, barely giving more than a short paragraph of news copy to a rebellion initiated by what it termed "Monarchist Centre Catholics". A week after the revolt started, the BUF's Director of Propaganda, William Joyce, insisted on calling Franco's troops "rebels not fascists", whilst a *Blackshirt* editorial of 8th August described the escalating civil war in Spain as a battle between "the ill-treated, ignorant and starving peasantry" fighting "desperately for Moscow, while Moors, foreign Legionaries and half-disciplined troops fought for the aristocrats at the bidding of a few military adventurers."[4] Unconvinced by General Francisco Franco's credentials as a fascist leader on a par with its own unassailable leader, Sir Oswald Mosley, the BUF nevertheless engendered support for Franco's forces, through publishing over-whelmingly negative propaganda against the Spanish Republicans. The BUF repeatedly accused them of carrying out anti-religious atrocities against Christian institutions and individuals.

In contrast the Communist Party in Britain was thoroughly convinced of Franco's dedication to the fascist cause. Furthermore, it regarded Franco's attempted coup as the most urgent political issue of the moment, with major international implications dwarfing other concerns and controversies. For that reason it decided to prioritise the fight against the advance of actual armed fascism and reaction in Spain over the provocations, pretensions and bluster of a would-be-dictator here in Britain. So when local East End activists asked the Communist Party's London District Committee to reconsider its plans for 4th October, the committee initially declared that the Trafalgar Square rally had to remain the party's main priority, but it would encourage the demonstrators there to march to the East End afterwards to show that they opposed Mosley's domestic fascism as well. The party had also organised a rally at Shoreditch Town Hall for the evening of 4th October combining both local and international anti-fascist agendas, under the heading "Unity Against Fascism and in Defence of Spain", which would be addressed by the veteran trade unionist, Tom Mann, a founder of the Spanish Medical Aid Committee, Isabel Brown, and leading Communist Party official, Dave Springhall, who later went to Spain as part of the International Brigade. With so many key activists already committed to being present in Trafalgar Square that afternoon, the Communist Party did not feel that, at such short notice, it would be able to mount a powerful enough demonstration to oppose Mosley effectively in the East End at the same time. If it changed tack at this late stage, the party feared losing out on two counts; it would have abandoned the rally for Spain and been outflanked by Mosley in the East End.

This response, though, was not the answer that the Party's overwhelmingly Jewish East End branches wanted to hear. They had much more confidence that the mood of the people of the East End, who had been enduring a reign of terror from fascist thugs for several weeks, would ensure an exceptional turnout. And confidence that the diverse communities of the East End could unite had been strengthened by locals physically driving off Blackshirts who had arrived in vans with loudspeaker equipment on two successive weekends at the corner of Dellow Street and Cable Street, just east of St Georges Town Hall, where Jewish and Irish communities lived in close proximity. A militant docker, Ernie Leek, led this localised anti-fascist resistance to the Blackshirts, while respected local churchmen, Father Groser and Reverend Jack Boggis, played prominent roles also in mobilising the community.

The argument within the Communist Party continued in the days leading up to the fascist march. In his exhilarating and at times painful memoir, troubled local activist Joe Jacobs argued that the reticence among the party hierarchy for direct confrontation with Mosley's fascists reflected a political strategy by a section of the party at odds with the instincts of many grassroots members.[5] His book includes a photographic reproduction of the handwritten advice given to local activists on 29th September 1936 by the East London organiser, Frank Lefitte, representing the London District Committee hierarchy. The note instructed local branches to hold mass anti-fascist meetings at either end of the Mosley March but "avoid clashes" and not allow the Government to say that the Communist Party "like the BUF are hooligans...Time is too short to get a 'they shall not pass' policy across. It would only be a harmful stunt."[6]

Late on Wednesday evening the London District Committee relented, and on the Thursday morning it relayed an urgent bulletin to its local organisers informing them that:

200

"The District Secretariat decided at its meeting this morning to cancel the all-London youth demonstration to Trafalgar Square this Sunday and instead to organise a tremendous all-London mobilisation of protest against Mosley's Blackshirt march into East London."

It added: "We must get the whole Party machinery working during the next 72 hours at top rate in order to be able to succeed in mobilising scores of thousands of London workers into the East End." The District Committee announced plans for the party's newspaper, the *Daily Worker*, to have a special London four-page anti-fascist supplement on the Saturday, 24 hours before the counter-demonstration. The committee appealed to its local organisers: "Let us have London white with chalked and whitewashed slogans – utilise every method of producing and distributing leaflets and rousing the workers to join in this big anti-fascist action. The agitation is being conducted under the following slogans:

'Mosley is provoking civil war in East London'
'Protest against Mosley's military operations'
'We want no Hitler torture or Franco brutality here'
'End fascist hooliganism in East London'."

Thousands of leaflets that had already been prepared to mobilise people to Trafalgar Square were printed over with "ALTERATION: RALLY TO ALDGATE 2pm".

This notice was followed by intense activity round the clock to encourage as many people and organisations as possible to commit themselves to blocking Mosley's path. On the Friday evening the Party led an anti-fascist march, 4,000 strong, from Tower Hill, through the East End, right into the fascist strongholds of Bethnal Green. The *Daily Worker's* Saturday supplement urged locals to mass in their tens of thousands at Gardiners Corner,

201

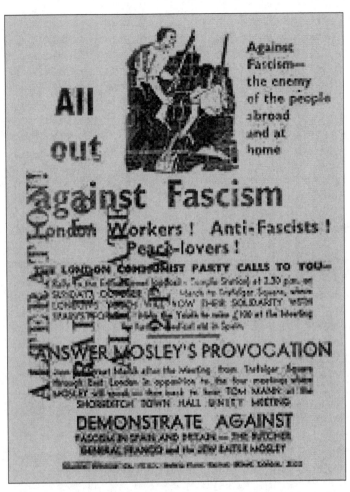

Leman Street, Cable Street and St Georges Street. The
Ex-Serviceman's Movement Against Fascism, largely
based in the Jewish community, called on its members to
march through the East End on the morning of the same
day as Mosley's intended march, both to show its own
opposition to Mosley's plans, and to encourage people to
mobilise against Mosley's forces in the afternoon. The
reaction of the police to this march provided a foretaste of

what might occur later. At 11.30am, as the ex-servicemen marched along Whitechapel Road towards Gardiners Corner, wearing war medals and decorations and hoisting the British Legion standard, they were met by a police cordon and told they could go no further. They vociferously demanded their right and freedom to march on the streets of their own borough – the same right that the Home Secretary had without any hesitation granted the fascists descending on the area from outside to intimidate the local population – but they were attacked by mounted police. In the skirmishes that followed the police captured the British Legion standard, tore it to shreds and smashed the pole to pieces.

By 1.30pm the junction of Whitechapel High Street and Commercial Street at Aldgate was completely blocked by a wall of people who showed themselves to be courageously resistant to police batons and a series of charges by police horses; the human wall was supplemented by trams driven down Commercial Road then strategically abandoned at Gardiners Corner by anti-fascist tram-drivers. The scene there was graphically described in the *Daily Herald*.

> *"Bursts of shouting, cheering and booing mingled with the sound of police whistles, the galloping horses of mounted police, the clanging of ambulance bells and the roar of buses racing extra police to the scene...all the time the crowd was shouting in unison 'They Shall Not Pass'."*[7]

Thousands of workers also massed at Royal Mint Street where a column of three thousand uniformed fascists with emblems and banners had assembled, "stretching for half a mile with two hundred black bloused women in the centre... (and) ...with men in peaked caps and jack-boots at the head of each detachment."[8] They were waiting firstly to be inspected by Mosley and secondly, for the signal from the police that their march could begin.

203

"The police struggled to prevent fighting between the demonstrators and the Blackshirts at this location. The latter were chanting 'The yids, the yids, we are going to get rid of the yids' and 'M-O-S-L-E-Y we want Mosley'. To which the crowd shouted back, 'so do we dead or alive'."[9]

With Aldgate remaining solidly blocked, despite several mounted police charges, the Police Commissioner turned his attention to an alternative and much narrower route into the East End via Cable Street. According to the locals, this road was so narrow that, "you could lean out of one side of the street and shake hands with someone on the other side of the street." It was populated largely by Jewish families occupying crowded tenements above shops at the end where it met the City, opposite Royal Mint Street; But as Cable Street stretched to the east, the milliners, bootmakers, haberdashers, capmakers, bakeries and kosher butchers, adorned with recognisably Jewish names such as Abrahams, Goldstein, Klyman, Markovitch and Rodinsky, gave way to groceries, ship's chandlers, tobacconists and pubs bearing names such as Higgins, Kelly, O'Brien, Reilly and Sullivan, whose tenements above mainly housed dockers' families of Catholic Irish descent.

The Communist Party had wrestled with the fascists for support from the dockers, but on this day it was clear that the Communists had the upper hand. The East London docker, Jack Dash, who became a prominent figure in post-war dock strikes, recalls the activity that took place the night before the fascist march:

"Throughout the night the Stepney folk, Jew and Gentile from all walks of life – dockers, stevedores, tailors, engineers, ship repairers, council workers, busmen, railwaymen... with their wives and kids were busy lugging and hauling old furniture, bed springs, tables and chests of drawers out on to the

streets building barricades. They used anything they could lay their hands on, packing cases, old fish boxes, which found their way from nearby Billingsgate fish market... when Sunday dawned, Stepney was ready to prevent the fascist march".[10]

As Jewish and non-Jewish anti-fascists were completing the erection of barricades and fighting police charges, they were reinforced by dockers marching to their aid from the "Irish" end of Cable Street, some among them armed with pick-axe handles for lifting paving stones to bolster the improvised barriers blocking the road.[11]

Aubrey Morris, a Jewish member of the Labour League of Youth, whose family ran a bakery at 86 Cable Street, and who helped build the barricades, recalls the scene:

"We 'borrowed' a flatbed truck sufficiently long to close off the street... When the first wave of mounted police arrived to clear the way they were pelted from ground level with broken paving and cobble stones and from every window with missiles ranging from filled piss-pots to lumps of wood, rotten fruit and old bedding, all sorts of items rained down on them. There were hand to hand skirmishes...The timely arrival of a large number of dockworkers from the surrounding areas reinforced and helped sustain the resistance."[12]

Phil Piratin confirmed in his memoir of the period, *Our Flag Stays Red*, that the "wrong" lorry had been used. Three points had been identified for the barricades: "The first was near a yard where there was all kinds of timber... and also an old lorry. An arrangement had been made with the owner that this old lorry could be used in a barricade." When the instruction went out to get the lorry, it hadn't been fully explained that it was parked in a nearby yard, "some of the lads, looking up the street, saw a stationary lorry 200 yards away. They... brought it

Paving stones torn up for use as barricades

back and pushed it over on its side before anyone even discovered that it was not the lorry meant to be used."[13]

A young Jewish tailor called Charlie Goodman acted that day as one of the "runners" between Gardiners Corner and Cable Street, helping to direct the demonstrators to strategic points. At Cable Street he helped assemble the barricades. Beneath some of the tenement buildings were "sheds with old carts and barrows... we opened the doors and pulled them out and built three barricades... at 100 yard intervals."

He later witnessed and participated in extraordinary scenes:

> "...the police charged and they were driven back
> and women in the tenement buildings picked up
> everything they could lay hands on and threw

them at the police... the police ran into the sheds
and the women came down from the tenements
and bashed the doors in and police came out with
their hands up. We took their helmets and told
them to shove off."[14]

Goodman was arrested on his way back to Gardiners Corner: "I got taken to the police station. They lifted me up like a battering ram and opened the charge room door with my head. They knocked me down and started bashing me with truncheons, shouting, 'yellow bastard. Jew bastard'."[15]

Fellow activist Jackie Shuckman received similar treatment: "I was brought to the police station and slung on the floor. There were all these young police in plain clothes saying, 'You don't like Mosley? You Jew bastard.' And they beat the lights out of me."[16]

Women as well as men were among the 79 anti-fascists arrested that day. Just five fascists were arrested. Shuckman recalls a young woman being dragged into the station by a huge policeman. The policeman ripped off her blouse and held his truncheon as if to strike her in the face. He remembers: "She stared straight at him and said: 'I am not afraid of you.' As the room went quiet the policeman called her a Jewish bitch and put her in a cell."[17]

Back on the streets many protesters took the blows of truncheons on their heads, arms and legs. With support from anti-fascist medical staff who normally worked at London Hospital in Whitechapel, the Communist Party set up a number of ad hoc first aid units in local cafés to treat the wounded. The party feared that if protesters were treated in the hospital itself, they risked being arrested at their hospital beds.

Shortly after 3pm, Fenner Brockway, Secretary of the Independent Labour Party and former MP for Leyton in East London, contacted the Home Office from a telephone box on Whitechapel Road. The Home Secretary was unavailable but the official he spoke to assured Brockway that his message would be passed on. In his message Brockway said:

> "*There are a quarter of a million people here. They are peaceful and unarmed but they are determined that Mosley's provocative march shall not pass. If you permit it yours will be the responsibility for the serious consequences.*"[18]

By late afternoon the Commissioner of Police, Sir Philip Game, assessing the highly charged situation and lacking any further guidance from the Home Office, took the decision himself to inform Mosley that he would not be permitted to march through the East End but instead must turn back towards the West End and disperse his troops on the Embankment. In denying East Enders' vociferous demands for Mosley's march to be banned, which had been expressed through the Jewish People's Council's petition with nearly 100,000 signatures, the Home Secretary, Sir John Simon, in fact, granted the locals the opportunity for an even greater victory of "people's power" over Mosley's fascists. The *New Statesman* commented:

> "*It was not Sir Philip Game who banned the parade: the common people banned it by filling the streets that even police charges could not clear the way for Sir Oswald's army... His march did not take place because the people, Jews and Gentiles alike, would not have it.*"[19]

Loyal fascists, in their Bethnal Green heartland, waited for their leader and his triumphant columns of Blackshirts to appear at the platform they were guarding in Victoria Park Square. Instead they had to give way to a victory march by thousands of anti-fascists. And *The Times* reported that the meeting the Communist Party held that evening in Shoreditch Town Hall was so oversubscribed that loudspeakers had to be erected across the road in Hoxton Square to convey the speeches to an overflow crowd that had gathered there. The paper's editorial, though, maintained its characteristically centrist view that "the activities of both fascists and communists in this country seem to most people to be a tedious and rather pitiable burlesque."[20]

Mick Mindel, a young trade union leader among the tailors and garment workers, had been busily organising his members in workshops and factories within his industry to combat Mosley, and he had encouraged fellow union leaders to do the same. He recalls:

"It was a marvellous day. There was such a feeling of achievement, of working class unity... I was so elated, running all over the place – the sheer excitement of it all. I saw it through the eyes of a trade unionist – appealing to workers to come out. I can't tell you how many of our members were there but the following day everybody was talking about it and you would think that everybody organised it!"[21]

Phil Piratin had long urged his party members to conduct the task of exposing fascism to its own supporters in the belief that they could turn a significant number of them away from Mosley's party, and even persuade them to fight against fascism. On that day the BUF's followers, who had shown undying faith in their leader and believed in both the righteousness of their cause and the invincibility of their movement, received a blow they hadn't anticipated. They were compelled to acknowledge how relatively isolated they actually were in an area where the poor and downtrodden had more reason than most to look for radical and vibrant political alternatives to improve their squalid lives. For several years Mosley had depicted the physical opponents of fascism as small gaggles of crafty, underhand, violent razor-gangs from the Jewish ghettoes. His fellow ideologue, William Joyce, had claimed that in the East End, "Ambush, injury, beating and slashing was the fate of any fascist who walked the streets alone at night." But it was plain to any fascist foot-soldier who had eyes to see, that, on that day, they faced a massive turnout of ordinary men and women of all ages, determined through collective action, solidarity and sheer force of numbers rather than random acts of thuggery to defend their area from incursion and intimidation.

Scotland Yard, which might have been expected to utilise stock phrases blaming "red mobs" and "paid agitators" creating "violent disorder" avoided such falsehoods and tried to account for the numbers involved in the demonstration in depoliticised terms. In its statement a few hours after Mosley was advised to march his troops back in the direction they had come from, the Yard blamed the weather for encouraging such a huge turnout on the East London streets, saying: "...owing to one of the finest days of the year many people were attracted to it, including a large number of women and children". It was the kind of language it might have used to describe a circus parade, rather than a determined community response to sustained fascist hostility and the threat of an invasion by thousands of fascists in four jackbooted and uniformed marching columns.

Mosley was enraged but complied with the Police Commissioner's order. He had always advised his members never to confront the police but to be seen as supportive of "law and order". For personal reasons, too, he did not want to risk any confrontation that might have resulted in his arrest on that day.[22] He later issued a statement in which he accused the government of "surrendering to red violence and Jewish corruption", and described the events that day as a "riot" for which "the British people of East London were in no way responsible". Then, in a reversal of his standard conspiracy theory, Mosley claimed: "An alien mob from all over the country was imported by socialists and communists to turn... peaceful streets into a battleground." Perhaps the shock defeat had temporarily dazed him. The next issue of *The Blackshirt* returned the conspiracy theory back to its default setting. Any doubts about whom it should really be blaming were eliminated:

> *"Jewry had humiliated Britain for a few short hours but in doing so, had showed her the way to future greatness... free from Red violence, from Jewish arrogance and Government cowardice... a country for British people, ruled by British people, without the unclean influence of alien contamination."*[23]

The Jewish People's Council arranged free legal support at the Workers' Circle premises for anti-fascists arrested on 4th October, many of whom were treated severely by the courts, heavily fined, and in some cases given custodial sentences. Two brothers Sam and Jack Jacobs were both fined forty shillings. Sam Jacobs' claims that the police had beaten him were met by the magistrate declaring, "I don't believe a word you say." His brother Jack had been arrested as he was trying to liberate others whom the police had apprehended. The magistrate told him: "I do not understand you people. You expect the police to protect you from your enemies – the fascists – but when the police are endeavouring to keep order you do your best to create a disturbance and riot."

Charlie Goodman and Jackie Shuckman, who both received custodial sentences, were bitter about the attitudes of Jewish establishment figures to their situation. Shuckman, who was convicted on evidence from a Jewish doctor that he had struck a police officer with a brick he was alleged to have hurled, which he absolutely denied, said,

> "...while I was in Wormwood Scrubs there was a Blackshirt there who had thrown a Jewish kid through a window and he got six weeks. The visiting magistrate, Basil Henriques [a prominent Jewish philanthropist], came to see me and others. He said: 'This is a free country. You should have let Mosley march. You're a hooligan. This isn't a Jewish attitude.' I more or less told him to piss off and the next day he had me transferred to Bristol prison, so my parents couldn't visit."[24]

Goodman and fellow prisoners received an unexpected guest:

> "I was visited by a Mr Prince from the Jewish Discharged Prisoners Aid Society, which was an arm of the Board of Deputies. They called all the Jewish prisoners together and asked, 'What are you here for?' And one chap said 'Well I've been out of work, things have been bad... I went and did a bust.' Prince replied, 'Oh don't worry, we will look after you.' The next five or six received the same response and then he came to me. 'What are you here for?' he asked. 'Fighting fascism,' I said. 'You!' said Prince, 'you are the kind of Jew who gives us a bad name... it is people like you that are causing all the aggravation to the Jewish people."[25]

THEY DID NOT PASS!

UNITED ACTION

defeated Mosley and won an inspiring victory for Democracy last Sunday.

Mosley's aim was not as he suggests merely to "lay his case" before the public but to terrorise and intimidate East London people, Jew and Gentile alike.

London people were not and will not be intimidated.

The great strength of the Workers defeated Mosley.

UNITED ACTION

can force the National Government to

Sack Simon! Dissolve Mosley's Army! Supply Arms to the Spanish People!

UNITED ACTION

Must be maintained and carried forward to the L.C.C. Elections to defeat all Fascist and Reactionary Candidates and return a sweeping Labour majority.

JOIN GREAT UNITED VICTORY MARCH AGAINST FASCISM ORGANISED BY THE LONDON COMMUNIST PARTY ON SUNDAY,

OCTOBER 11

from **Tower Hill**, 2.30

to **Victoria Park**, 4p.m.

Fascism shall never pass

Issued by L.D.C., Communist Party, 133 East Rd., N.1. and printed by Marston Printing Company (T.U.), Nelson Place, E.C.1

Goodman promised Mr Prince that after he was released from prison he would do a speaking tour of the East End of London and other Jewish areas, adding, "I am sure I can convey the sentiments of the Board of Deputies to them." But his planned speaking tour was shelved by more pressing priorities as Goodman continued his practical work against fascism by joining an International Brigade battalion in Spain in early 1937. Shuckman also managed to join Republican forces fighting in Spain by obtaining a job as a ship's hand on a Spain-bound vessel and then absconding. After six months, though, he was returned to Britain when his Brigade superiors found out he was only seventeen years old.[26]

For the local Jewish community, the battle for the East End highlighted the extent of the gulf between the consciousness of the population on the ground and its West End-based Jewish communal leadership. Jewish East Enders had shown themselves to be very responsive to the lead given by local independent grassroots Jewish organisations, such as the Workers' Circle, and the bodies that united under the umbrella of the Jewish People's Council, as well as the local branches of political organisations including the Communist Party, the Independent Labour Party and the Labour League of Youth, who had called on them to take part in collective direct action to confront fascist provocation. They rejected the calls of the rabbis, Jewish community leaders, national politicians and the establishment press to give the event a wide berth.

On the day of Mosley's invasion of the East End on 4th October 1936, Jewish youth clubs arranged extra football matches in a transparent attempt to divert young people away from involving themselves in a demonstration that looked likely to result in disorder. But the young people, with their eyes fixed firmly on their political and social goals, abandoned the football pitches to tackle fascism. The *Jewish Chronicle's* advice in its issue of 2nd October had been roundly ignored, but in the following week's issue, the *JC* maintained that its position was completely vindicated. It stated:

> *"Much as we detest the campaign waged by the Fascists, we cannot pretend to any satisfaction with*

214

the result... The chief effect is to enable Mosley to pose as a martyr to the cause of civil liberty and... win new recruits... The stopping of meetings and marches is a matter for the constitutional authorities... On the long view we believe the action to be profoundly mistaken."[27]

Having primarily attacked the local population's active response to the fascists, the editorial then changed tack and argued that the fascist cry of free speech was "bogus", because it amounted to a licence to single out Jewish areas, in which:

"Humble traders are abused and assaulted, little children taught to lisp 'Down with the Jews', Jewish residents afraid to leave their homes at night and as the Mayor of Bethnal Green has stated, it is impossible to walk the streets without fear of insult."[28]

Elsewhere, though, in the very same issue of the *JC*, could be found a very different account of the day and its implications. The special correspondent's report was euphorically headlined: "The People Said 'NO!' – He Shall Not Pass – East End Answers Mosley".[29] His report claimed that:

"On Sunday, Fascism received the greatest blow that it has had yet in this country... As the crowning stroke of Fascist impudence Sir Oswald Mosley proclaimed his intent of personally invading the East End on Sunday last, at the head of columns of his blackshirts and of marching to four open-air meetings where he would deliver speeches... but neither the march nor the meetings took place. They were stopped by the people of East London, hundreds of thousands of ratepayers thronged the streets and chanted 'He shall not pass!'... Popular

feeling was too great... Cable Street, Leman Street and the Minories were a seething mass of indignant eastenders... A most amazing thing was the great spirit of solidarity that was shown on the streets – solidarity between Jew and non-Jew... When the march was called off in the East End, scenes occurred almost as amazing as those that had preceded the decision. Suddenly the tension was lifted. The police strolled casually away from the crowds they had been holding back. As casually the crowds followed them. In a moment there was just a sea of friendly humanity."[30]

Just as the mass counter-demonstration on 4th October enormously boosted the self-confidence of the East End's beleaguered communities, it was an immense psychological blow to the fascists. And although police intelligence reports show that the BUF enrolled some 2,000 new members in the two months following the Battle of Cable Street, these were largely young thugs motivated more by the opportunity to engage in physical confrontations than by any deep ideological commitment to the corporate state, the "Greater Britain", or fascist theories of "authoritative government", and their involvement proved ephemeral. Most significant was the loss of faith in the leader by key party ideologues, which resulted in resignations, sackings and splits in the months to follow. Mussolini decided that the recipients of his substantial investments for several years might not be quite as powerful or politically promising as they had portrayed themselves to him. After the Battle of Cable Street the funding from Italy began to dry up. Earlier that year, while some Jewish businessmen were shortening their names to anglicise them and help them move onwards and upwards, the BUF was lengthening its name. By labelling itself the "British Union of Fascists and National Socialists", Mosley's party was indicating its desire to become more closely identified with the Hitlerite brand of the "modern movement". And as Mussolini started to withdraw financial support, that process intensified.

The search for unity

The defiant attitude towards the authorities that the Jewish People's Council demonstrated stood in stark contrast to the deferential attitude displayed by more long-established, mainstream Jewish bodies. This was an indication of the JPC's socio-cultural significance as well as its political positioning. It represented what several commentators had termed the "new community" – the children of the immigrants who had grown up on British soil, fully aware of their absolute rights to equality. The new community would not tolerate any attitudes from without, or indeed from within, that treated them as second-class citizens. Zukerman noted what he termed the "curious effect" of the advance of fascism in relation to Anglo-Jewry. Instead of heralding greater unity and a closing of ranks in a critical period, it gave rise to a new division – between the Board of Deputies and the Jewish People's Council – which, in his view, threatened to become "a wide and dangerous schism". He located the source of that division in the social composition of the JPC, arguing that it represented precisely those elements of the community that had no possibility of being represented on or by the Board.

This underlying problem that gave birth to two competing Jewish defence blocs, was only superficially addressed by the *Jewish Chronicle*, which concentrated on pragmatic and one-sided calls for unity in a community under attack. It condemned the "rival pretensions" of the JPC, claiming that the latter's very title was "misleading". In its eyes, the Board was the "sole legitimate and authoritative representative body" of Britain's Jews. The newspaper reiterated that it was not the task of the

Jewish community to attack fascism as a political movement, only its antisemitic manifestations. The activities of the JPC were depicted by the *JC* as undermining the Board and thereby weakening the community's hand. It was urged to "loyally come into line with the recognised Anglo-Jewish authority".

The JPC rebutted the charges that had been thrown at it, and went on the counter-attack. It claimed that the Board, which excluded from representation important sections of the community, did nothing in the face of the fascists' onslaught except censure and criticise those who did. From its perspective, the JPC claimed that the boot was firmly on the other foot; it was the Board that had stubbornly rejected a productive unity that could have been forged on a principled basis. The JPC would not budge from to its central political argument, that antisemitism could *not* be divorced from the party that propagated it.

Any possibility of both bodies combining their talents and operating symbiotically according to their differing approaches was thrown into jeopardy just a few weeks after the Battle of Cable Street when the JPC called a conference of Jewish organisations for Sunday 15th November 1936. Despite deep misgivings about the Board's approach to combating antisemitism, the JPC extended its invitation to the Board of Deputies and the Coordinating Committee it had established. At this conference these bodies would have had ample opportunity to argue for their strategies, though perhaps among a more sceptical Jewish audience than they customarily faced. On most matters affecting the community the Board assumed that there was just one, unified, commonsense, communal standpoint for Jews to support. If it felt uneasy about bringing conflicting perspectives into the open, it could have decided to stay away from the conference and convey its apologies. In the event the Board went much further by not only snubbing the JPC's convention but also organising its own high-profile event about combating antisemitism, to be addressed by the Board's president Neville Laski, on the very same day. It circulated a letter to Jewish organisations urging them to attend its own event and boycott the conference organised by the "self-appointed" JPC, a body whose actions the Board condemned as "independent and sporadic and undisciplined".

Until this point had been reached, the JPC had studiously tried to avoid any public conflict with the Board of Deputies. It concentrated instead on what it saw as the job in hand – uniting as many Jews as possible with non-Jews to combat fascism and antisemitism. But in the face of such an overt attack the JPC felt compelled to reply and it published a leaflet entitled "The Jewish People's Council Against Fascism and Antisemitism and the Board of Deputies". The leaflet pointed out that the Board's own decision to finally create a Coordinating Committee had only taken place well after invitations had already been distributed for the conference that founded the JPC. Discussion about creating such a committee had been going on for much longer but there was little sign that it would actually bear any fruit. The JPC countered the charge of being "self-appointed" by demonstrating that its officers were democratically elected at a conference attended by delegates from 87 Jewish organisations.

Annoyed and provoked by the Board's open act of hostility, the JPC made public, through its leaflet, the details of earlier behind the scenes attempts at unity, which, it believed, the Board had deliberately scuppered. It described a meeting that took place soon after the JPC had been formed, between JPC representatives and John Dight, Chair of the Association of Jewish Friendly Societies (the body fronting the public work of the Coordinating Committee). This meeting had been amicable and productive, and Dight offered to arrange a further face-to-face meeting, this time between the JPC and the Board of Deputies. Dight was present at the subsequent meeting alongside leading deputies such as Laski, Brotman, Janner, Bernal and Saloman. The leaflet recounted that at this meeting the JPC actually offered to place itself under the control of the Coordinating Committee but this was rejected on the ground that the Board could not accept any organisation committed to "fighting fascism" rather than simply combating anti-semitism. The leaflet reported that a second proposal to exchange speakers and organise meetings in such a way as to avoid clashes of venues and dates was also declined. Nevertheless the meeting ended with Laski saying: "We part friends, you going your way, we going ours," and Saloman held out the prospect of assisting the JPC with information where possible.

But after the crude attempt to sabotage the JPC's November conference the JPC's intense irritation at the Board's response to Mosley's plan to march through the East End on 4th October, which it had hitherto suppressed publicly, was now expressed very clearly:

"On October 4th Mosley challenged Jewry, announcing his intentions to march uniformed columns through the Jewish quarters of Stepney... the Board instead of meeting this challenge, retreated from it!... The Board argues that to expose the lies and defamation is sufficient to safeguard Jewry. Antisemitism is a part of fascism. Only the defeat of fascism will remove organised antisemitism. Can the Jews alone defeat fascism, the breeder of antisemitism? No! Jewry alone cannot.... Who are our possible allies? Only the democratic forces also threatened by fascism. Can we say to them 'Help us in our fight against antisemitism, but we will not fight with you against fascism?'... In essence the line of the Board of Deputies is – here is a struggle to be waged by the Jews against their defamers, the fascists, but not against fascism! It makes the issue a Jewish one, which is precisely the impression that Mosley tries to

create. To the extent that we make it a Jewish ques-
tion, to that extent do we isolate ourselves from the
people of this country – and thereby strengthen anti-
semitism. The issue is not the Jews versus their
defamers but fascism against the whole people, with
antisemitism its main weapon."

It quoted an interview with Sidney Saloman, Secretary of
the Coordinating Committee, published in the *Evening
Standard,* in which he said:

"...when the original Blackshirt march was
announced we distributed numerous bills and had
messages read in every synagogue, urging Jews to
keep off the streets on that Sunday. What more can
we do?... We admit there is some ground for com-
plaint against certain Jewish employers and
landlords in the East End."[61]

The JPC commented: "These statements received the
widest publicity. This is how the Co-ordinating
Committee fights antisemitism... today they are engaged
in fighting not fascism but the Jewish People's Council
against Fascism and Antisemitism." The leaflet concluded sardonically: "It took the Board years to make up
their minds about opposing antisemitism, but days in
which to try and disrupt the Jewish People's Council
Against Fascism and Antisemitism." Nevertheless the
JPC assured its supporters that it did not wish to dissi-
pate its energies in an intra-communal struggle. It
pledged that it would continue the struggle against fascism and antisemitism and "will mention the Board only
in so far as it hinders us in our work".

Through its practical day-to-day work within the community, the JPC continued to make deeper inroads into
the communal consciousness and its understanding of
antisemitism, and gradually the criticisms of it from
Jewish establishment sources began to diminish both in

severity and quantity. It attracted the support of influential individuals within and external to Jewry, with leading churchmen, local politicians and respected rabbis regularly speaking from its platforms. The Jewish student movement gave the JPC considerable support, with individual Jewish student societies and their representative body, the Inter-University Jewish Federation, passing resolutions expressing indignation at the hostile attitude to the JPC displayed by the Board of Deputies, and offering assistance to the JPC's campaigns. The JPC's popularity within the East End community was confirmed during the course of a fundraising bazaar that it held in December 1937, which attracted 3,360 people over eight evenings. Jewish bakers provided food – their trade union was affiliated to the JPC and members were levied for support – and local Jewish businesses donated goods for stalls.

While the JPC was winning support and adherents through its own extensive efforts, its arguments concerning the relationship between antisemitism and fascism were increasingly confirmed by international events such as the Spanish Civil War, the intensifying antisemitic terror in Nazi Germany and the increasing incidence of antisemitism in Italy, which moved to the legislative level in 1938. Evidence of the latter undermined the distinction that many Jewish communal leaders had previously upheld between the brands of fascism propagated by Mussolini and Hitler respectively.

In late 1938 and early 1939, as the threat of war loomed in Britain, the political articulation of a struggle between democracy and fascism gained more widespread acceptance in society at large, and within the Jewish community too. The acute danger posed by international fascism undermined the communal leaders' assertion that the security of Jews in Britain could be guaranteed by simply refuting antisemitic calumnies, an approach that the JPC's Secretary, Jack Pearce, had characterised as "tackling the symptoms without touching the disease."

As the JPC's thesis became more widely agreed, the *Jewish Chronicle* ventured the suggestion that the London Area Council, associated with the Board of Deputies, "should not adopt too stiff and standoffish an approach to bodies doing similar work not represented on the Council". As analyses began to converge, the JPC again offered to dissolve if agreement on its central argument could be reached. Such agreement ultimately proved elusive, but a degree of informal cooperation was reached, which included exchanges of speakers. JPC representatives were invited to a dinner and ball held in recognition of Jewish defence workers, at which the Board of Deputies president, Neville Laski, stressed: "We must emphasise that we are citizens on equal terms with citizens of other faiths in this country." This was a significant reappraisal of the position of Jews, for it demanded not *tolerance* but *acceptance*. The same sentiment was apparent in a full-page advertisement in the *JC* from the Coordinating Committee, listing a set of meetings to counter the menace of antisemitism, which stated: "Remember it is your natural rights as Man and Citizen that are being assailed."

In the interpretation of antisemitism and responses to it, some common ground was eventually found among the community's most diverse elements. In the process, the established leadership conceded to several aspects of the JPC's analysis, while the JPC stood firmly on its basic ideological foundations. But it was only towards the end of the decade, by which time the forces of organised political antisemitism were largely in decline, that this understanding was achieved. For most of the period in which Jewish communities, especially in East London, Manchester, and Leeds, were subjected to sustained attack, the responses of communal leaders were confined to combating the defamation of Jewry without undertaking a thoroughgoing analysis of the roots of antisemitism in Britain, and how and why it was reproduced within the British body politic. Their previously held notion that antisemitism was not a serious threat had been confounded by the outcry that emanated principally from members of the community most directly suffering its consequences. The responses they offered reflected a static and seemingly naive set of beliefs about the nature of British society. They took it for granted, or perhaps wanted to believe, that Britain was necessarily composed of tolerant people fundamentally sympathetic to Jews, save a small minority who were ignorant of Judaism or vulnerable to believing antisemitic calumnies when they were initially presented.

Jewish leaders simply did not countenance the notion that such prejudices might be deeply ingrained and powerfully reinforced rather than superficial, which is perhaps why they believed that simply providing accurate information would be sufficient to undermine and eradicate them. The anti-defamation campaign rested on the assumption that, if a reputable body presented the public with facts, the case would be discredited and die. Its architects discounted the possibility that there were material social forces at work which could reproduce and intensify the basis on which an underlying ideology supporting such defamation might flourish and create new adherents for the politics of hostility and hatred. However, if the leaders of Anglo-Jewry had given full and public recognition to the nature of the political phenomenon with which they were confronted, they might have been placing serious obstacles in the way of their efforts to secure the form of integration they sought within British society. They were seeking an uncritical integration, which preferred not to interrogate too closely the values held within the British establishment.

Notes

1 *New Statesman* 10.10.1936
2 *The Circle*, Workers' Circle, September 1942
3 ibid
4 *The Blackshirt* 8.8.1936

5. The "Popular Front" approach, dominant among the Communist Party leadership in this period enjoined party members to minimise confrontation with the Labour Party as it sought affiliation and unity. The Labour leadership had advised workers to ignore Mosley's provocation.

6. Joe Jacobs, *Out of the Ghetto*, pp238-240

7. *Daily Herald* 5.10.1936

8. ibid

9. ibid

10. Jack Dash, *Good Morning, Brothers*, p39

11. There had been a long history of solidarity at trade union level between Irish dockers and Jewish tailors, who had supported each other in very practical ways during major strikes in 1889 and 1912. This is discussed in WJ Fishman's *East End Jewish Radicals 1875-1914,* Duckworth, 1975.

12. Aubrey Morris, *Unfinished Journey*, pp52-53

13. Piratin, op.cit, p23

14. Interview of Charlie Goodman held on tape at Imperial War Museum

15. ibid

16. Interview of Jack Shuckman held on tape at Imperial War Museum

17. *Searchlight*, October 1996

18. *They Did Not Pass: 300,000 workers say no to Mosley*, ILP, 1936

19. *New Statesman,* 10.10.1936

20. *The Times*, 5.10.1936

21. Mick Mindel, "Socialist Eastenders", *Jewish Socialist,* No 6, 1986

22. He was due to get remarried (to Diana Mitford) in Goebbels' house in Germany two days later in a ceremony attended by Hitler.

23. *The Blackshirt*, 10.10.1936

24. Interview with Jack Shuckman held on tape at Imperial War Museum

25. Charlie Goodman, "The East End battles on", *Jewish Socialist,* No 1, 1985

26. The Brigade's minimum recruitment age was 21.

27. *Jewish Chronicle* 9.10.1936

28. ibid

29. The same headline "The People Said NO!" also appeared in the Communist Party's *Daily Worker* that week.

30. *Jewish Chronicle* 9.10.1936

31. *Evening Standard* 4.11.1936

9. Antisemitism, fascism and the state

Antisemitism in 1930s Britain presented itself as a different order of problem from a decade or two earlier. In the years following the First World War it was mostly experienced as a latent prejudice which intermittently gave rise to ostentatious individual outbursts, but rarely engaged the attention of the state authorities. By the mid-1930s, however, antisemitism was disseminated to large audiences by an organised movement which revelled in provocative processions, held meetings and rallies in public venues, and sold its literature and staged aggressive street corner meetings on public highways. As this movement matured, it seemed to pay less attention to its internal development and more to its external display as it thrust itself on the public and sought the widest possible adherence to its message and its goals. In the face of this formidable and wide-ranging onslaught, the Jewish community, after much initial hesitation, felt compelled to respond in an equally public manner. The issue of antisemitic defamation increasingly acquired the character of a public confrontation and, as such, became a law and order issue for the wider society. It demanded the involvement of the state authorities, particularly when the responses of the Jewish community became linked to demands upon these authorities to guarantee the protection of Jewish people.

Antisemitism in Britain became a concern for Parliament, the police and the law courts, especially in 1936. In that year the Attorney General initiated proceedings against Arnold Leese, a veterinary surgeon and acclaimed expert on camels. More significantly, he was the leader of the Imperial Fascist League, which surpassed Mosley's movement by far in its open espousal of crude Hitlerite antisemitism. Indeed, Leese had written in February 1935 that, "the most certain and permanent way of disposing of the Jews would be to exterminate them by some humane method such as the lethal chamber".[1] He was brought to court after he republished the classic antisemitic "blood libel" accusation of Jewish ritual murder. The court prosecuted him on four counts of seditious libel and two counts of public mischief. He was acquitted on the former but convicted for the latter, and fined. When Leese refused to pay the fine he was sentenced to six months in prison. In the meantime, the Metropolitan Police largely provided the front rank, authoritative presence between the public propagators and victims of antisemitism, and Parliament discussed the steps it deemed necessary to contain and remedy an increasingly critical situation.

The response by the leaders of Britain's Jewish community to the threat of antisemitism in Britain in the 1930s reflected their particular understanding of its nature, bound up with a set of expectations about British society and the prescribed position of the Jews within it. The manner in which the state authorities treated the issue of antisemitism directly tested these expectations. Although the activities of organised antisemites had been a factor since the British Union of Fascists' inception in 1932, and had certainly become more directly threatening to Jews and active opponents of fascism from 1934, it was not until 1936 that Jewish community leaders acknowledged the gravity of the circumstances and began to assemble what they considered the appropriate machinery to enable the community to respond, and engage in more public contact with the state authorities. Previously, they had been happy to entrust the authorities with the task of ensuring the safety of the community as they saw fit, but, from 1936, Jewish leaders increasingly placed specific demands upon them. These leaders' earlier analysis of antisemitism was such that, whilst they found individual incidents troubling, they were not unduly concerned, and they presumed that British institutions of justice, in which they placed great faith, would not disappoint them. Nevertheless, in the period before 1936, the attitude towards Jews expressed by the state authorities when they dealt with antisemitic incidents, or court cases involving Jews, had occasionally caused disquiet.

In 1932, the *Jewish Chronicle* expressed its concern that in several court cases the Jewish origins of those accused were emphasised. A recorder in Leeds, for example, told a defendant, "I have to deal with you as a Jewish receiver of stolen property".[2] As the activities of the BUF intensified, so the law courts increasingly presided over cases arising out of confrontations between Jews and fascists. The *JC* drew attention to a case in September 1935 in which a self-confessed fascist had been charged with unlawfully and maliciously inflicting grievous bodily harm with an iron bar upon a Jew. He was found guilty of common assault but merely bound over. The paper commented: "The courts must act with greater sternness and efficiency... this case is not an isolated one." From 1933, the police received many complaints from Jews of insults and assaults. It was felt that such incidents were not receiving the attention they merited.

More specifically, from 1935, the police were increasingly accused of partiality between fascists and antifascists – and this latter category included growing numbers of Jews. Often, the police on the ground, presumably guided by orders from their superiors, ensured that fascist speakers using threatening and insulting language about Jews were given a free rein, while they acted to remove hecklers. However the general view, expressed by the Jewish communal leaders, was that, despite instances in which the police or law courts may have shown leniency or partiality towards fascists, the community could nevertheless rest assured that it would be adequately protected. The serious escalation of BUF actions, and events connected with the subsequent counter-demonstrations they provoked, undermined confidence in these assurances. As the matter was raised in Parliament more frequently, local East London MPs played a prominent part in demanding stronger measures from the Home Secretary to protect Jews. It was in the period from 1936-1938 that the issue of the state's reactions to antisemitism came to the fore most frequently.

The House of Commons held a debate on antisemitic terror in March 1936 in which a range of incidents were described that shocked many members. Herbert Morrison, MP for Hackney South, and a challenger for the Labour leadership, described the verbal intimidation, the bricks and stones thrown through windows of Jewish-owned shops by gangs of Blackshirts, and the death threats and actual physical violence that Jews were enduring, especially in Shoreditch and Hoxton but also in Stoke Newington. He concluded his speech:

"There is a case of a man living in Stoke Newington who was attacked by a gang of Blackshirts in December last while walking along Hackney Downs at 11.45pm, and a friend was so badly knocked about that he was obliged to receive hospital treatment for two weeks. These people are spreading the slogans, 'Kill the Jews' and 'Dirty Jews', and so on in the neighbourhood, and are actually affixing to various places... a gummed slip with 'Jew' on it, and other slips with the Hitler trademark, the Swastika, in the middle and the words 'Perish Judah'. That is obviously action which is stimulating a breach of the peace and is endangering the security of His Majesty's subjects... it is obvious that action of that kind is calculated to... inflame racial hatred in a district where, clearly, it is particularly undesirable that that should be done... we simply cannot tolerate a situation in which these people are taking the law into their own hands and making the Jews feel, when they go on to the King's highway, that they are not safe from molestation."[3]

The Home Secretary acknowledged that this was "an issue which must be regarded as of first-rate importance by everybody who is concerned with civil rights and human liberty." But he added that he did not think "there is any widespread feeling of hostility towards Jews in this country, though it is undoubtedly the case in certain areas."[4]

He assured the House that "in this country we will not tolerate Jew-baiting", and spoke of the need to strengthen the hands of the police, but regretted that it was often difficult to obtain hard evidence. This related directly to the issue of police partiality, which was a widely expressed allegation in East London, and appeared regularly in the accounts of meetings reported by the *JC*'s special correspondent. The latter had frequently described meetings where the language of incitement and slander had been used whilst the police effectively acted as stewards for the British Union of Fascists rather than as law officers determined to prevent such incitement. At one open-air meeting, with police present, the speaker declared: "Blackshirts – at the Yids. Let us fight the dirty Yids and not let them get the upper hand." At another, with a police note-taker on hand, the speaker declared: "Jews are venereal-ridden vagrants who spread disease to every corner of the Earth." Local councillors and clergy in Bethnal Green supported claims of police partiality towards fascists made by Jewish victims, and reports in local newspapers gave further substance to these claims.

The question of police attitudes was raised in Parliament by the MPs for Hackney Central and Stepney. The Hackney Central MP, Frederick Watkins, suggested that existing police actions had failed to prevent the growth of Jew-baiting, and he alleged that police were showing political sympathy towards the fascists. But the Home Secretary continued to deny that there was any police favouritism towards the fascists.

"I have taken personally the greatest care to inform myself and I am completely convinced that there is no truth at all in that suggestion... it is simply not true that the police in this matter have any bias of a political kind... the only interest of the police authorities is to do the best they can in difficult circumstances... to stop people from breaking the peace."[5]

The *JC* felt that Parliament had taken serious note of the issue, but was conscious that increasing numbers of MPs were questioning whether the Home Secretary was acting firmly enough on the fascists. Following a large demonstration and counter demonstration in Finsbury Park, North London, in June 1936, Sir John Simon commented: "We have to take the difficulties of this being a free country into consideration and the best thing we can do is appeal to everybody on all sides to behave reasonably."

This applied a notion of symmetry that did not meet the case, but it reflected the dominant government position, which understood the issue primarily as a question of public order, and this dictated the limits of its responses. Reports of police protection of Blackshirts accumulated, and the severity of the situation compelled leading elements in the Jewish community to reappraise their attitude towards open political expression. The *JC*, having adopted a liberal position of absolute commitment to free speech, had forcefully defended this view when it condemned the activities of Jews in opposition to fascists in the early 1930s. The newspaper repeatedly emphasised that it considered any interference at all with free speech as ultimately more damaging to Jews' vital interests than the insults and abuse of their detractors. But as time wore on, it adopted a more selective attitude. It urged the banning of fascist meetings in Jewish areas, and drew a distinction "between liberty and licence". In September 1936, local police decided to divert a planned march by Mosley's Blackshirts away from the largest

Jewish districts of Leeds. The stark failure to adopt a similar policy in London a few weeks later led to the disorder at Cable Street.

In July 1936, a more comprehensive parliamentary debate took place on the mounting terror in East London. Lasting five hours, it was filled with detailed reports of the physical, verbal and written attacks against Jews, the latter of which had included the blood libel published by the Imperial Fascist League. The paramilitary nature of the BUF was detailed and MPs raised questions about the wearing of political uniforms. Several MPs alleged that the police were failing in their duties to the victims of antisemitism. Denis Pritt, MP for Hammersmith, gave examples from different parts of the capital city. Having described police standing idly by while fascists beat up their political opponents, he also described instances of police inaction, "while fascists utter statements that are obviously criminal in their incitement".

Pritt read from testimony he had received from a member of the Bar holding "a minor but important government position", who attended an open-air meeting at Hampstead Heath and heard a fascist speaker say: "Whatever has been done to the Jews in Germany is nothing to what we are going to do to them here when we get into power." He recorded that the speaker turned to one of the people in the audience and said: "And that is meant for you in particular." Meanwhile, Pritt's informant wrote: "A couple of policemen, grinning fatuously, stood by."

Pritt offered further examples from Stepney in East London where,

> "...in the presence of the police... a speaker threatened the hecklers that he would have them removed by the police if they objected to what he was saying, and what he was saying was: 'Rats and vermin from the gutters of Whitechapel. Jews are the biggest owners of prostitutes in the West

End.' And think of this, to people in a poor and crowded neighbourhood: 'Jews stole your jobs and houses while you were fighting in the war.' He referred to 'dirty Jews'."[6]

He added that, "The police were there in large numbers, mounted and unmounted", but took no action. Pritt claimed that "the laxity of the police has led the fascists on", giving them the courage to make wild antisemitic accusations. He described reading the "blood libel" in a recent edition of a fascist newspaper – "that old, that brutal, that cruel accusation (that) preceded every pogrom in Russia, every pogrom in Poland". He warned that if the government did not act soon "it will precede pogroms in this country".

Reginald Sorenson, MP for the East London constituency of Leyton West, described several incidents where police had acted only against hecklers at meetings where speakers were indulging "in language which even the Home Secretary admits would be likely to cause a breach of the peace", which was "fouling of the liberty-loving air of this country". He cited a meeting where the speaker referred to:

"...by name a number of well-known Jewish persons, including possibly some who sit on the other side of the House... (saying) ...they were a lot of hook-nosed, yellow-skinned, dirty Jewish swine. I am sure the Home Secretary will agree that if a crowd gathers and listens to such statements they are almost entitled to interject... (and) ...If they do interject, surely if there be any exercise of power on the part of the police, it should be rather to pull up the speaker than to pull out the interrupter."

He suggested, "If the Home Secretary were to disguise himself and go to one of these meetings and were to hear himself being denounced in violent language, he would be inclined to interject."[7]

233

Local East End MP, George Lansbury, who first represented a constituency in the district in 1910, added his
personal observations:

> *"There is, I believe, in nearly every East End dis-
> trict, east of Aldgate, real terror among the Jewish
> population... the sellers of (fascist) literature go into
> a market-place full of Jewish traders and use the
> most foul language to them... it goes on at regular
> weekly intervals. These men go down the street
> offering their paper and at the same time use most
> cruel language about the Jews, and occasionally the
> Jews retaliate... It is not merely that the Fascists
> are insulting the Jews... but they are inciting others
> to attack them, and to visit their horror and spleen
> upon these unfortunate people. I am a firm believer
> in free speech and a free press... but that right... to
> speak must be circumscribed by the fact that I must
> not be allowed to blackguard those with whom I dis-
> agree in such a manner as to incite people to treat
> them as the Jews are being treated today, and to
> lead to a condition of affairs where Jews, as in
> Germany, Poland and elsewhere, are not allowed to
> live and are treated as people outside the pale...
> unless this thing is put an end to – I have known
> East London all my life – there will one of these
> days be such an outburst as few of us would care to
> contemplate... I do not want to stop the Fascists
> from preaching their theories, I do not want to pre-
> vent anybody from preaching their theories of
> government, but I do want to stop this terrible
> incitement and intimidation."*[8]

Hackney Central MP, Frederick Watkins, supported
Lansbury's warnings:

> *"All this anti-Jewish activity is inspired by one org-
> anisation. I cannot see why some action cannot be*

234

taken to stop the propaganda that goes on day by day in the East End of London. There is nothing too foul or bestial for a human tongue to speak that does not come from Fascist platforms when they are being used. All the old prejudices are being aroused, and my fear is that unless very strong action is taken rioting will occur in the East End."[9]

He described how he had struggled with great difficulty to dissuade a large group of Jewish ex-servicemen from a plan to rush a fascist platform and physically break up a meeting:

"I said that the obligation is on the police to prevent statements being made which will incite to disorder, and that we must leave the police to do their own job of keeping the peace. But I am being met in the East End… with the statement that the police are no longer impartial. I have fought against that idea; I do not want to believe it. I want to believe that the police will treat all classes and all political opinions with equal impartiality. When I attempt to put that point of view before Jews and workers who have suffered, before Gentiles as well as Jews, they ask me why it is that there is no prosecution of Fascist speakers who make these terrible utterances in public."[10]

He concluded with two practical suggestions: the banning of uniforms for political purposes, and prohibiting the holding of provocative meetings in areas where there is a large Jewish population.

Sir John Simon admitted that it would be "a very cheap thing to say to people who are being exposed to this abuse in the East End of London that they should show more courage", but he reiterated that "the best advice in many cases is to stay away". To the extent that Sir John acknowledged that the fascists were "a terrible nuisance" – it was with regard to the police! Again he defended the police against charges of partiality, and cited a discussion he had held with the president and vice president of the Board of Deputies repudiating any such allegations. However, in an indication of the widening rift in Jewish establishment circles, the *JC* commented that they found the Home Secretary's reply far from reassuring. And on 24th July 1936, much to the annoyance of the Board's leaders, the *JC* published an extract from a memorandum to the Home Secretary, which it acknowledged had come into its possession under "conditions of secrecy". It had been prepared by other leading figures in Anglo-Jewry such as Sir Max Bonn, Basil Henriques and Miriam Moses – under the auspices of the normally very conservative Association of Jewish Youth (AJY). It described the strongly held feeling by the local Jewish population that they were not getting the protection to which they were entitled from the forces of law and order.

Board president Laski and his vice presidents Cohen and Waley-Cohen sent a stern letter to the *JC* simultaneously claiming involvement with the AJY memorandum while pouring scorn on its conclusions:

> *"The memorandum was a confidential document prepared at our request and submitted to the Home Secretary in confidence. We assume that you were unaware of the confidential nature of the document when you published the extract... the article contains a serious reflection on the Home Secretary and the police and we think it right to state publicly that at our interview with Sir John Simon... we made it quite clear that, as far as we were concerned, we made no allegation against the police of any prejudice or bias. Moreover we desire to add that we are still of the opinion that this allegation is entirely unfounded."*[11]

Ironically, this angry missive from the leaders of the Board of Deputies was published on Friday 2nd October

1936. That was the same week that the Home Secretary ignored nearly 100,000 signatories of a petition initiated by the Jewish People's Council demanding that Sir Oswald Mosley be prevented from sending his marching columns of uniformed fascists through streets inhabited by the beleaguered Jewish communities of East London. He chose instead to mobilise 7,000 police, including the whole of London's mounted police regiment, to try to ensure that this provocative march would be permitted to proceed without hindrance. It confirmed just how far removed the community's leaders were from the feelings at the grassroots and how desperate they were to avoid being seen to be critical of the state authorities.

Two days later, the BUF's attempted invasion of the area was blocked at Gardiners Corner in Aldgate and at Cable Street. In the wake of the violent confrontation between police and an incensed local population at the "Battle of Cable Street", the Government decided to act. The major areas on which public opinion had crystallised were the desirability of banning provocative marches, measures to deal with racial incitement, and the banning of political uniforms. Deputations comprising London MPs, mayors and other local authority officials reiterated the need for such situations to be handled more resolutely. Within three weeks a Public Order Bill was prepared. Nevertheless there were doubts about the rationale upon which the government was preparing its counter-measures, and the *JC* reprinted a warning from the left-leaning *New Statesman* which cautioned: "Government spokesmen have told us that the conflict in the East End is between two bands of equally responsible extremists. We hope the government will not use the pretext for general restrictions on civil liberties." The Jewish People's Council echoed this argument within the Jewish community. While this fear was acknowledged in its reporting, it was not fully shared by the *JC's* editor, who wrote:

"The government has been as good as its word and the Public Order Bill... should at the very least impose a halt upon the subversive movement which has threatened the peace of the neighbourhoods and of Jews in particular."[12]

He warned however that the efficacy of the Bill "will depend in the last resort upon the determination and resolution with which its provisions are enforced".

Sir Philip Game, the Police Commissioner, had urged the Home Secretary to outlaw political antisemitism and ban the fascist movement, as had several Labour Party and trade union leaders. No direct reference to antisemitism appeared in the Public Order Bill, but Jewish leaders believed that this would be adequately covered in the clause relating to threatening and insulting behaviour. Organisations that had been in the forefront of grassroots opposition to the BUF expressed their concern about the degree to which the Bill might generally impinge upon civil liberties. On a Jewish People's Council platform, Ronald Kidd of the NCCL argued that the Bill was not actually the government's answer to the state of crisis which Mosley had created, but reflected instead its broader public order agenda, which had implications for democratic rights to protest for all citizens. The Jewish People's Council distributed a leaflet which argued that the passing of the Public Order Bill:

"...has aroused a false sense of security. The banning of fascist uniforms does not prevent attacks on the Jewish community and on the liberties of people... Fascism and antisemitism are not yet defeated... the fascist uniform is the outward symbol of provocation. The main provocation is the use of racial incitement and Jew-baiting for the purpose of dividing Jews and non-Jews."

In addition to demanding that the government ban political uniforms and provocative armbands, the JPC demanded "an Act of Parliament against racial incitement". The *Jewish Chronicle*, whilst warning against the illusion that the Public Order Bill would signal the end of the Jewish community's worries, was, in contrast, willing to grant the government the benefit of the doubt on the issue of civil liberties.

Reviewing the (Jewish calendar) year to September 1937, the *JC* drew attention to "many acts of violence not always suppressed with the vigour which the victims have a right to expect from the police, whose apathy more than once gave rise to the suspicion that their traditional impartiality could not be relied upon". The Public Order Act came into force on 1st January 1937. It banned political uniforms, gave extended powers to the police to restrict processions and considerably increased the maximum penalty for offence to the peace arising out of threatening, insulting or abusive behaviour. From 40 shillings (£2), the maximum penalty was raised to £50 and three months imprisonment. Under the 1936 Public Order Act, speakers could be arrested not just for intent to provoke a breach of the peace, but also if "a breach of the peace [was] likely to be occasioned".

Neville Laski welcomed the Act on behalf of the Board of Deputies, describing it as "magnificent as a gesture of the almost united opinion of the British public that Mosley and his followers merely had nuisance value". He did not appear unduly concerned that the Act might be used to curtail civil liberties more widely. However, in the weeks during which the Bill was passing though its committee stages, the East End community's confidence in the police waned further. The *JC*'s special correspondent identified "a rising tide of East End suspicion". Jews, he said, were "beginning to feel that they had no one on whom they could rely".

In November 1936, Dan Frankel, the MP for Mile End, one of the few constituencies in the country with a very high proportion of Jewish voters, and one truly in the eye of the storm, felt compelled to speak out:

"During the time that I have been a Member of the House, I have scrupulously, I might even say religiously, kept out of discussions with regard to fascism and with regard to the Jewish people. I was not elected a Member of this House as a Jew... and I am glad to say that I number among my supporters thousands of people who are not of the same race as myself. I have not thought it specially to be my job to come here as a partisan representative of one creed or one race, but I am afraid that a stage has now been reached at which, in order properly to represent the people in my constituency, I must voice the opinions which many of them hold, and must let the House know the real position as I see it in that district."

He described how the problems had magnified over a period of a few weeks while he was absent visiting America. He said he had "known for some considerable time that things in that district were boiling up to such an extent that one was afraid of what might happen any day; but I did not dream on 16th September, when I left, that within a few short weeks such an enormous and important change could take place." Reflecting on the advice he had given his constituents before his departure, to be patient and stay calm, he remarked:

"I have asked them to be quiet; I have appealed to them as far as possible to do nothing which might provoke any retaliation or attack on the part of the fascists. On the whole, that has been obeyed, but on my return I have found in my constituency, and all over the East End, a real, living fear. I have found on the part of the ordinary men and women in my constituency – not only those of the Jewish race, but all decent people in the area – a feeling that we are living in bad times... that, unless something really important is done, nobody knows what will occur in

*that district during the next few months or even in
the next few weeks... It has been said... that perhaps the Jewish people in the East End and
elsewhere are hysterical and excitable. Perhaps they
are exaggerating... but where fear exists one must
expect people to be disturbed... They know what has
occurred to their race in Germany, and they know
that the fascist movement there started more or less
as it started in this country. It is no use saying it
can never happen in England. You cannot say that
to people whose relatives and those near to them
have been tortured and persecuted as they have been
and are still being in Germany."*

He reminded the House how the Jews in the East End of
London were only one generation removed from those
who were persecuted in Russia, Hungary and Poland. He
concluded:

*"For the whole of my life I have stood for the maxi-
mum of freedom as far as public speech is concerned,
but freedom must not be translated into licence or into
an expression of hatred or of arousing the worst
desires in people, not against political opponents but
against the whole of the members of one race... (and)
...it is very disturbing to note that little children are
now being brought up in the creed of antisemitism...
Children are being used every day to distribute fascist
literature. They are being taught antisemitic phrases
by heart, and they shout them at every opportunity...
from the experience of the last few years, it is no
longer any use trusting to what we all thought was
the common sense of the English people and their
spirit of fair play, which we know exists as much in
the poorer areas as anywhere else."*[13]

As 1936 drew to a close, the *Jewish Chronicle's* special
correspondent claimed that the police had consciously or

unconsciously supported the fascists. As a result of their failure to check slanderous and inflammatory statements, it was, he concluded, "safer to be fascist than anti-fascist". The brutality of the stewards towards any expression of opposition at a BUF meeting in Hornsey, North London, in January 1937, compelled Jewish communal leaders to take a more sober view of the Bill. The incidents were of such severity that comparisons were made with the notorious Olympia rally of 1934, but the Jewish community was most discomfited by the apparent indifference of the police. The *JC* editorial ventured "to direct the Home Secretary's attention to our correspondent's statements", and added: "We do so in no irresponsible spirit and in no hostility to the police force."

The Hornsey episode was followed by a series of open-air meetings where vituperative language, rather than being diminished by the strengthened clauses relating to insulting and threatening behaviour, increased even in the presence of official police note-takers. The principles of English justice upon which the Jewish community had placed its faith were, the correspondent noted, being flagrantly disregarded. He asserted that "the conduct of the police in Bethnal Green had every appearance of being pro-fascist and anti-Jew".

The behaviour of the police in relation to antisemitic incitement raised acute problems for the Jewish leadership, who had attempted, in the face of overwhelming evidence to the contrary, to claim that there was no foundation to persistent allegations of police partiality. Its analysis, which rested initially on denying the existence of antisemitism and later on dismissing it as a foreign import, was grounded in a firm belief in the tolerant and just nature of British society and its institutions. It could explain the behaviour of local police partly in terms of their "infection" by the "disease" of antisemitism which was being so assiduously spread, but this was tempered by recognition that the police were not acting autonomously, but were presumably following the orders of superiors whom Jewish leaders regarded as immune from antisemitism. When Sir Philip Game, the Commissioner of the Metropolitan Police, published his report for the year 1936 in which he claimed, "numerous complaints were received from Jews of insults and assaults upon them but the great majority were unsubstantiated by any evidence upon which action could be taken", the sympathetic and charitable attitude of Jewish communal leaders towards the police was further undermined. A trenchant *JC* editorial recorded how it had,

> "...*never underrated the difficulty and the delicacy of the task with which the police were entrusted of maintaining order in the East End in the face of fascist Jew-baiting... nor have we been anxious to attribute to the police partiality towards the fascists even though the evidence is to the contrary... but we are compelled to ask whether his statement of lack of evidence still holds good.*"[14]

Citing the Hornsey meeting as a clear example, it concluded by enquiring whether the Public Order Act was "a working reality" or whether it might turn out to be "a pathetic illusion".

In the meantime, the courts were busy handling many cases arising out of continuing confrontations, especially from street meetings, and several antisemitic orators were eventually charged under the new Public Order Act. However, there was little consistency in the authorities' actions, and whilst relatively mild speeches may have been prosecuted, speeches of greater verbal virulence were frequently unheeded. Alexander Raven-Thomson, who had been prominent in the BUF since its inception as one of its leading ideologues, was charged in one such case. His numerous speeches in this period utilised all the stock phrases of antisemitic slander and incitement but the particular incident on which he faced a charge was dismissed because of "no evidence of general insults to

Jews". In July 1938 the *JC*'s special correspondent wrote: "Jewish people are beginning to feel that the forces of law and order are against them."

The demands made by the Jewish community for stronger action against the propagators of hatred were in part realised through quite extensive use of powers of diverting or banning political processions. As a party that stressed the politics of emotion and pride in identity, which sought to stir people to action at street level and revelled in defending what it saw as its territory, the BUF suffered considerably, but its decline was in process before the intervention of the state. Nevertheless the Public Order Act, which was seen to be primarily a response to the BUF, even if its implications were more widespread, had a negative effect on its political credibility. It has also been alleged that the state authorities acted in more subtle ways to undermine Mosley's movement by unofficially requesting broadcasting and print media outlets to not report the BUF's activities. Increasing numbers of local councils, possibly in response to covert police requests, refused to let their premises for BUF meetings. In 1937 the National Association of Wholesale Newsagents refused to stock *Action*, the BUF paper, which had previously enjoyed a national circulation. Whatever measures, official or unofficial, hampered the fascists, it was nevertheless the case that public abuse of Jewry remained strong and continued to be disseminated. Moreover, it continued to be revealed in quarters where the Jewish community's leaders least expected it to appear. This was especially the case with magistrates.

In 1939 when the "aliens scare" had both reflected and deepened popular antisemitism in several districts, several court cases were marked by the antisemitic insinuations of magistrates. Two Jews in an assault case were told: "It's a pity you are both not in Germany. Go away and try the German High Court." In the case of an antisemitic orator summonsed for insulting behaviour at a street meeting, the magistrate discounted the evidence of a Jewish witness, who was repeatedly asked by the former why he did not simply walk away from the meeting. He dismissed the charge. In a case involving two labourers, Israel Riscovitch, 32, and Stanley Philips, 26, charged with insulting words and behaviour, magistrate Metcalfe remarked before imposing fines: "I will not let a couple of young ruffians... especially with a name like Riscovitch, behave in a such a manner."

The state authorities took measures to maintain order, which served to undermine the political credibility and general effectiveness of the major organised antisemitic movement. It did so, though, at a cost to civil liberties which, among others, was deplored by the JPC, a movement centrally involved in the defence of the Jewish community. The JPC went as far as to claim that through the Public Order Act, one key fascist objective had actually been achieved: suppression of the freedom to demonstrate. Furthermore, it argued that, had the police acted in an impartial manner, concentrating on checking provocation, slander and incitement, the Public Order Act, which threatened to impact more widely on democrats than fascists, would have been unnecessary. A JPC leaflet entitled "We Protest!" explained:

> "Fascist meetings are a provocation to the people at all times, but they are an added provocation when held in areas which are mainly Jewish, and where Jew-baiting is indulged in even on the doorsteps of the Jewish people. The fascists come among the Jewish people not to convert them to their policy of Jew-baiting and racial incitement – but to provoke disorder. They could not do this were they not amply protected by the police."

The JPC did not assume that the state would act in a neutral or benevolent manner. Nor did it view the authorities as giving priority to the protection of the Jewish community from its defamers, particularly in their actions in response to the situation in London's East End. In practice the law was inconsistently applied and offered no guarantees to Jews that they would obtain justice through the courts. Often magistrates defined the victims of antisemitic defamation as a problem in equal proportion to that of their defamers. One magistrate told three Jews charged with insulting behaviour at a fascist meeting: "You people complain of provocation by the fascists and then you do this sort of thing. There is nothing to choose between you." The courts constantly advised Jews, just as their communal leaders had implored them, to "stay away" from fascist meetings. For the *JC*'s special correspondent, however, this merely indicated how distanced the courts were from the lived reality of those enduring the constant hostile attentions of organised antisemites. He commented: "When insults and abuse are practically hurled by loudspeakers through windows at Jews, it hardly meets the case."

Magistrates also showed themselves to be uncomprehending of non-Jews feeling affronted on behalf of fellow citizens who were Jews. In Leeds in 1936, John Hodgeson, a 19-year-old warehouse worker, was fined £2 for throwing a stone at Sir Oswald Mosley (which missed). When Magistrate Horace Marshall asked Hodgeson which words of Mosley's annoyed him, he said that Mosley "made a reference to the 'Yids' and referred to the crowd as 'socialist scum'," to which Marshall replied: "I do not in the least understand why these remarks offend you if you are none of these things."

The leaders of the Jewish community retained their strong, almost unshakeable faith in "British justice" throughout the period, although they recognised weaknesses in the law as it stood, which did not attend to community libel. They welcomed every partial statement of government commitment to the protection of Jewry as confirmation that the authorities in general would ensure fair treatment for the community. Essentially, the leaders of the Board of Deputies such as Laski and

246

Waley-Cohen, shared the state's dominant conception of the problem posed by Mosley's movement as one of public order, in which antisemitic incitement was an albeit conspicuous ingredient, and they directed much of their energy towards endeavouring to contain the oppositional activities of Jews within channels that would not bring into question the attitudes and behaviour of the authorities. To members of the community most directly threatened, however, the general question of order was intimately related to the level of deliberate antisemitic incitement.

Notes

[1] *The Fascist* No 69, February 1935
[2] *Jewish Chronicle*, 13.5.1932
[3] *Hansard*, 5.3.1936
[4] *Jewish Chronicle* 13.3.1936
[5] *Hansard* 5.3.1936
[6] *Hansard* 10.7.1936
[7] ibid
[8] ibid
[9] ibid
[10] ibid
[11] *Jewish Chronicle* 2.10.1936
[12] *Jewish Chronicle* 13.11.1936
[13] *Hansard* 4.11.1936
[14] *Jewish Chronicle* 28.5.1937

Conclusion

Jewish people living in 1930s Britain were forced to confront a many-sided threat, emerging from a set of overlapping ideological currents, which cast Jews as a malign, alien presence. Antisemitism was principally propagated through the British Union of Fascists – a mass political movement active most menacingly at a public level between 1934 and 1937. The BUF elevated the nation and state, opposed sectional interests, and fought against what it saw as the malevolent influence and activities of international financiers and communists. Initially it couched these battles in the conventional language of politics and economics but, for the majority of its life, the BUF came to express its creed through an increasingly integral and bombastic antisemitism that moved well beyond the parameters of mainstream political debate in Britain.

At first, it introduced political antisemitism cautiously, but from autumn 1934, it showed far less restraint. The BUF built upon and exploited an existing, though uncrystallised, antipathy towards Jews, evident in many areas, which was frequently manifested through a range of incidents and practices. Underpinning the BUF's activities was its central ideological tenet: that Jews constituted an alien and disruptive body engaging through corporate action in a set of machinations detrimental to the national interest. And furthermore, Mosley and his acolytes believed that the Jewish community had organised as a corporate body to destroy the very movement which they proclaimed could save the country – a country mired in economic crisis and suffering political paralysis in the hands of tired and discredited, "old gang" parliamentarians.

Though the BUF claimed that the first arrows it slung at Jews were in self-defence and in response to what Jews

had *done* rather than who they *were*, many BUF ideologues increasingly embraced and enhanced elements of a
deterministic racial ideology. Through a process of stereotyping, the original specific charges against individual
Jews or groups of Jews became more generally applied to
Jewry as a whole. And the elements in the ideology that
were consistent with a general anti-alien stance gave way
to a more particular attack on Jews, as Jews, which borrowed from historical and contemporary Continental
antisemitic mythology. After the BUF declined as a
potent political force, a deep imprint of antisemitism
remained, which resurfaced forcefully during the "aliens
scare" of 1938-39, propagated largely by sections of the
mainstream media.

Although Jews were attacked as a unified whole, the
responses of the Jewish community to antisemitism in
this period illustrated its profoundly heterogeneous
nature. They brought to the surface deep internal conflicts located in class, authority and representation,
identity, prospects and aspirations. At the very peak of
antisemitic activity in 1936, when the urgent debate on
defence measures dominated the pages of the *Jewish
Chronicle*, large sections of the community, rather than
standing behind the established leadership, the Board of
Deputies, chose instead to lend their support to the
Jewish People's Council, which had more closely articu-
lated their needs and demands. Between 1932 and 1935
Jews had been advised by their leaders to utilise accepted
arms-length channels of redress through the police, law
courts and the press; but from the summer of 1936, in
response to the deteriorating situation, the defence of the
community was more publicly based. In making demands
on state institutions in this period, to a large extent, the
community – both at grassroots and leadership levels –
engaged actively in its own self-defence, though in doing
so it sought and attracted allies beyond its own ranks.

The Board of Deputies, through the Co-ordinating
Committee it set up and through the energetic campaign

of the London Area Council, mounted a defence campaign which centred on anti-defamation. It provided indisputable facts, figures and general information about Jewry for non-Jews, whilst at the same time appealing to Jews to strive for impeccable and blameless behaviour, so as not to create or provide any justification for antisemitism. Any such "justification" would have been entirely superficial, since it depended upon a stereotyping process by those who defamed Jews, but the stress it placed on correcting Jewish behaviour typified a response directed at the surface rather than the underlying basis of the problem.

Fundamentally, the Board of Deputies viewed antisemitism as a Jewish issue, capable of redress largely through the actions of the Jewish community itself, supported by sympathetic actions by the authorities. In responding to antisemitism, the Board of Deputies participated alongside non-sectarian, non-political groups, whilst imploring Jews to abstain from overtly political campaigns and militant forms of oppositional activity, which it argued caused more harm than good. It firmly believed that the information provided through its anti-defamation work would undermine the threat the community faced, but it made representations to the authorities as well for more lasting safeguards.

The campaign organised by the Jewish People's Council, though it included anti-defamation, was far more concerned with tackling causes than merely responding to symptoms. It was convinced that the ideology of antisemitism could not be separated from its propagators – fascist organisations. The Jewish People's Council identified how and why the antisemitism of this period was different from previous episodes of hostility to Jews, precisely because it had become integral to the ideology and practice of a large and menacing fascist party striving for political power in order to establish dictatorial rule unencumbered by democratic opposition. It demonstrated why antisemitism – a doctrine of hate directed at all Jews but used also to strengthen support for fascism – was therefore an issue that was relevant equally to Jews and non-Jews. Its spokespersons argued in every forum that fascist ideology and the political party that was propagating antisemitism, were a threat to all democratically–minded people and the democratic institutions they had created in their communities and workplaces. This belief was reflected in the cooperative relationships the JPC established with like-minded bodies both within and beyond the Jewish community, including those with explicitly political anti-fascist approaches.

These different responses were based upon contrasting and divergent analyses of the nature and extent of the antisemitic threat. Initially the Board's view of antisemitism was characterised by denial and dismissal. It denied that antisemitism could flourish in Britain, and dismissed incidents as isolated events, until the patent reality of a vigorous antisemitic party demanded explanation. Antisemitism was then characterised as a foreign import promoted by British individuals, motivated by political ambition and an irrational hatred of Jews. The BUF, it believed, found support among individuals who were ignorant of Judaism, hence ignorant of Jews, and could be mobilised to oppose them. However, the heterogeneity of the fascist movement and its supporters, and the readiness with which its message was welcomed in particular areas, made it clear that this explanation was inadequate, and the Board of Deputies later combined these analyses with an intensely critical attitude towards the Jewish community itself. It saw the behaviour of Jews in different capacities as contributing significantly to the generation of antisemitism. In the late 1930s, those who admonished Jews for sharp practice in business, or as dishonest and vindictive landlords, or for ostentatious behaviour or violent confrontations with political opponents, were not just Mosley's British Union of Fascists but also the leaders of the Jewish community.

The Board of Deputies perceived the ideas at the core of antisemitism in Britain as an attack on Judaism and on Jews as a religious group. In contrast, the Jewish People's Council believed that antisemitism had its roots in the society in which it developed, that these roots were essentially economic, and that this permitted it to be exploited as a political instrument by a political movement in pursuit of both its economic and political goals. The JPC rejected the notion that Jews could be responsible for antisemitism, since this not only constituted victim-blaming but conceded the generalisations and stereotyping about "the Jews" that were inherent in the antisemites' arguments.

Underlying these contrasting responses were conflicting sets of ideas about the nature of the Jewish community and its actual and desired position in relation to the wider society, as expressed, respectively, through the organisations of the "old community" and the "new community". Jewish society in Britain was undergoing a process of change – socially, economically, culturally and politically. The "old community", which still clung to its dominant position in Anglo-Jewry's representative institutions in the 1930s, saw Jews essentially as a religious group, tolerated as guests in a host society which was distinguished from many other European nations by its benign attitude towards "its" religious minorities. This "old community" was happily completing its successful integration into the highest levels of that society when it was brought up short by the dramatic growth of domestic antisemitism. The existence of a powerful antisemitic movement in Britain contradicted and undermined every expectation the "old community" had built up about the nature of British society and it engendered considerable uncertainty regarding the requirements that it might need to fulfil to facilitate its process of integration. The confrontation with antisemitism also exposed the changed reality of Anglo-Jewry. It brought to the fore – and forced Jewish political leaders to fully acknowledge –

the existence of the "new community". It was, after all, this "new community", still concentrated in economically distressed areas, that was primarily bearing the brunt of fascist activities on a daily basis.

Rather than being an assault upon the Jewish religion or Jews as a religious group, British antisemitism of the 1930s was a many-sided assault upon Jews as a varied ethnic group who merely wished to play their part as equals in the society in which they lived. The communal leaders of Jewry derived their standing in the wider society from their authoritative and, they believed, unassailable position within the Jewish community. This position was endangered by the growth of an external threat. In confronting this threat, the leaders of the Jewish community did not wish to risk exposing the real political gaps that might exist within the Jewish body politic, so they satisfied themselves with attempting to develop a narrow, tightly controlled, communal response rather than a broader, more open and inclusive strategy.

The "old" community's narrow response to antisemitism, essentially limited to anti-defamation, was developed without haste, principally by those who were cushioned from its effects by wealth and status. It was the response of a generally optimistic and secure minority that located itself, by and large, as living a comfortable existence within a tolerant and fair-minded society. The more encompassing responses of the "new community" were consistent with an understanding that antisemitism was a threatening domestic product operating against an exposed minority. They rested on a much more equivocal evaluation of British society and a more vulnerable self-image, which more closely reflected reality for the bulk of British Jews in the 1930s.

The British Union of Fascists failed to achieve its goals. Its last political foray, however, just before the onset of the Second World War, illustrated just how deeply fascist and antisemitic ideology had penetrated the body politic. The largest indoor meeting that Britain had seen up to that point took place in London's Earls Court Exhibition Centre on 16th July 1939. It was filled to the brim with around 20,000 supporters of Mosley, largely representing "Middle England". By all accounts, the assembled crowd gave a tremendous ovation to their leader's one hundred minute speech, in which he promised his audience that:

"...if any country in the world attacks Britain then every member of British Union will fight for Britain. But just as straight this, too, we tell them. We say to the parties who clamour for war, a million Britons shall not die in your Jews' quarrel."

In May and June 1940, 1,769 individuals deemed to be a threat to British defence were detained under a piece of emergency legislation – Regulation 18B. Nearly half of them were BUF members. With its leaders and key functionaries locked up, including Mosley himself, the party was unable to continue organised activities in any meaningful sense, though individuals still managed to churn out antisemitic leaflets and posters clandestinely. Some members went underground and evaded recruitment for military service against a National Socialist cause they had come to firmly believe in. Most rank and file BUF members, though, served in the war, fighting alongside other Britons – including the Jews they had slandered – not just to defend Britain against Hitler's armies but ultimately to defend the country against Hitlerite fascism.

The war challenged and changed many attitudes, but not all, and even before the bloodshed ended, a small but growing number of released detainees were mounting soapboxes at Speakers' Corner in Hyde Park to make thinly-veiled pro-fascist and antisemitic speeches. Shortly after the war, those who remained unapologetically committed to the fascist cause began to reorganise themselves into clubs and societies, and a new wave of fascist periodicals appeared. But now there was no Jewish People's Council to fight back. It had been an inspiring and energetic grassroots response in a period of crisis that mobilised the time, enthusiasm and goodwill of community members who had very little to offer in terms of material resources. It, too, though, was a victim of the extraordinary situation of war. The political credibility of some of its most committed members who were also prominently associated with the Communist Party, was undermined at the beginning of the war by the Molotov-Ribentropp non-aggression pact, which put pressure on national Communist parties to mute their criticisms of the Nazis. Then, with many of its members called up rather than locked up, it simply lacked the human and financial resources to continue beyond 1940. But Jewish ex-servicemen and women returned from the gruelling fight against Nazism in 1945, ever more determined to resist those who would still persecute them, even as knowledge of the shocking scale of the crimes perpetrated by the Nazis on the Jewish people was starting to become more widespread, through cinema newsreels and news-paper reports.

If the sight of unreconstructed fascists organising in Britain *after* Hitler's war shocked them, they were also startled that, when this occurred, the leaders of the Jewish community still advocated the discredited softly, softly approach to countering antisemitism that they had exhib-ited in the face of rising anger from many sections of the community through the 1930s. Again there was an inde-pendent move from ordinary people in the more economically deprived areas of the Jewish community to fill the vacuum. This time the vehicle was called the "43 Group". Its courageous and ultimately successful battle over five years to beat back the sustained attempts at a post-war fascist revival in Britain, focused particularly on the Dalston area of Hackney, some two and a half miles north of the East End, has been graphically described by one of its surviving members, Morris Beckman.[1]

When Sir Oswald Mosley turned his back on conven-tional politics in 1931 and launched the New Party, which then transmogrified into the British Union of Fascists, he claimed that the watchwords of his movement would be "truth, courage, intelligence and vigour". These watchwords were a smokescreen. In place of truth there were wicked lies about the Jews, and there was nothing at all courageous about the acts of verbal and physical intimidation and violence his fascist movement perpetrated against its victims young and old. He used his own undoubted intelligence to persuade his adherents to abandon theirs, and instead follow their basest instincts, while he continued to portray his party's ideal as one of dynamic progress for society and social betterment for its most disadvantaged members. Whatever vigour he personified or sought to mobilise, was ultimately channelled mainly into self-aggrandisement.

Few of Mosley's activists from the 1930s survived to see the 21st century. But his constellation of ideas still resonate today through new outlets. His movement married self-love and nationalist pride with hatred towards others, through which he aroused the passion and commitment of followers. He satisfied their desire to feel they had contributed to their country's greatness and convinced those who felt abandoned and disenfranchised that they too could be empowered through a process of national renewal leading to social improvement for the many at the expense of the few. The National Front, the British National Party and, now, the English Defence League follow in his footsteps and have sometimes been able to touch the same emotions among those layers of society today who feel a similar sense of powerlessness. The resonances of Mosley's ideas are felt, too, in a more physical sense, by new victims of racist and fascist abuse and thuggery, and also through the harsh attitudes and oppressive practices of state institutions that continue to heap further indignities and hardship on the lives of migrants and refugees. Like other minorities before them, many migrants and refugees are confined to the margins of society and scapegoated for society's ills.

In an age of plenty, where each person felt valued and secure, and none experienced pangs of hunger and resentment, Mosley's malicious sentiments would have floated away with the wind. The beliefs of his movement could only touch and manipulate people's consciousness when there was profound and pernicious social and economic inequality, in a society beset by mass unemployment, low pay, poor housing, poor access to education, neglect by those with power and wealth, a widespread sense of hopelessness and a longing for personal and national salvation.

Such problems, unfortunately, have not been confined to the past. They have followed us into our new century. Those who are aware of how perniciously the politics of hate can gain a foothold and spread, will continue to be vigilant and seek to expose and combat both the underlying social and economic problems and the vultures who feed on them. And, perhaps in doing so, they will be able to draw inspiration and ideas from those ordinary people who, in the maelstrom of the 1930s, disregarded the complacent and hollow advice of those with more comfortable lives and more blinkered vision, and found collective ways to face these problems with such courage, imagination and determination.

Notes

[1] See *The 43 Group* by Morris Beckman (Centerprise) 1992.

Further reading

Alderman, G., *Modern British Jewry* (Clarendon) 1992

Beckman, M., *The 43 Group*, (Centerprise) 1992

Benewick, R., *The Fascist Movement in Britain* (Penguin) 1972

Billig, M., *Fascists, a Social Psychological View of the National Front* (Academic Press) 1978

Cesarani, D., *The Jewish Chronicle and Anglo-Jewry 1841-1991* (OUP) 1994

Dorril, S., *Blackshirt* (Penguin) 2007

Endelman, T., *The Jews of Britain 1656 to 2000* (University of California) 2002

Evans-Gordon, W., *The Alien Immigrant* (Heinemann) 1903

Fishman, W., *East End Jewish Radicals* (Duckworth) 1975

Gainer, B., *The Alien Invasion* (Heinemann)1972

Garrard, J., *The English and Immigration* (OUP) 1971

Gartner, L., *The Jewish Immigrant in London 1870-1914* (Simon) 1960

Gottlieb, J., *Feminine Fascism* (I. B. Tauris) 2003

Gould, J., and Esh, S., *Jewish Life in Modern Britain* (Routledge) 1964

Griffiths, R., *Fellow Travellers of the Right* (Constable) 1980

Holmes, C., *Antisemitism in British Society 1816-1939* (Hodder & Stoughton) 1979

Jacobs, J., *Out of the Ghetto* (self-published) 1978

Kushner, T., and Valman, N., (ed) *Remembering Cable Street* (Vallentine Mitchell) 1999

Laski, N., *Jewish Rights and Jewish Wrongs* (Soncino) 1939

Lebzelter, G., *Political Antisemitism in England 1918-1939* (Macmillan) 1978

Linehan, T., *East London for Mosley* (Cass)1996

Melville, C., *The Truth About the New Party* (Martin Lawrence) 1931

Morris, A., *Unfinished Journey* (Artery) 2006

Mosley, O., *The Greater Britain* (BUF Publications), 1932

Mosley, O., *Tomorrow We Live* (Greater Britain Publications), 1938

Pugh, M., *Hurrah for the Blackshirts!* (Pimlico) 2006

Piratin, P., *Our Flag Stays Red* (Thames) 1948

Reed, D., *Insanity Fair* (Cape) 1938

Reed, D., *Disgrace Abounding* (Cape) 1939

Srebrnik, H., *London Jews and British Communism* (Vallentine Mitchell) 1995

Zukerman, W., *The Jew in Revolt* (Secker) 1937

Five Leaves' books on the Battle of Cable Street

Battle for the East End: Jewish responses to fascism in the 1930s
by *David Rosenberg*
978 1 907869 18 1

October Day
a novel by *Frank Griffin*
978 1 907869 15 0

Everything Happens in Cable Street
oral history from *Roger Mills*
978 1 907869 19 8

The Battle of Cable Street
by *The Cable Street Group*
978 1 907869 17 4

Street of Tall People
a children's book by *Alan Gibbons*
978 1 907869 23 5

Available from bookshops or, post free, from Five Leaves, PO Box 8786, Nottingham NG1 9AW, www.fiveleaves.co.uk

Index

261